Dreams, Counselling and Healing

Brenda Mallon

Newleaf

Newleaf

an imprint of

Gill & Macmillan Ltd

Hume Avenue, Park West,

Dublin 12

with associated companies throughout the world

www.gillmacmillan.ie

© 2000 Brenda Mallon

0 7171 2998 5

Print origination by O'K Graphic Design, Dublin

Printed by ColourBooks Ltd, Dublin

A catalogue record is available for this book from the British Library.

1 3 5 4 2

CONTENTS

CHAPTER 1   THE HEALING PATH OF DREAM WORK:
             STARTING OUT   1

CHAPTER 2   USING DREAMS IN THE
             THERAPEUTIC SETTING   26

CHAPTER 3   DREAM DIAGNOSIS   58

CHAPTER 4   CLIENTS IN CRISIS   86

CHAPTER 5   A LIGHT IN THE DARKNESS OF MERE
             BEING: RECOVERING THE SELF   109

CHAPTER 6   RITES OF PASSAGE   135

CHAPTER 7   CREATIVE SOLUTIONS   159

CHAPTER 8   HEALING THE SOUL   185

CHAPTER 9   HEALING INTO LIFE,
             HEALING INTO DEATH   213

REFERENCES   242

CHAPTER 1

THE HEALING PATH OF DREAM WORK: STARTING OUT

'A light in the darkness of mere being' for me encompasses the process of counselling and the therapeutic relationship on which it depends. Initially both client and counsellor, patient and therapist, are metaphorically, in the dark. The healing process illuminates 'the darkness of mere being'.

The journey taken together includes the land of dreams, stories, myths and fantasies as well as recalled experiences of pain and psychological insecurity. The reality of day-to-day anxiety and suffering is the tip of the iceberg below which the world of dreams and the unconscious are submerged. In this sea, where unexpected collisions may occur, some of titanic proportion, the counsellor often needs to be the anchor that holds the steady line. By appreciating the vastness of the dream world, we can plumb the depths where danger lies, understand how it may be circumvented and even enjoy the magnificent beauty of the awesome territory in which we travel, because travel is what we do — counselling and therapy are a process, not an arrival point.

The unconscious, the metaphorical unseen part of the iceberg, has a particular capacity (Von Franz, 1987) to:

> . . . transform and guide the human being, who has been blocked in a situation, into a new one. Whenever human life gets stuck and arrives at a shore from which it cannot proceed, the transcendent function brings healing dreams and fantasies which construct on the symbolic level, a new way of life which suddenly takes shape and leads to a new situation.

However, first, as part of our preparations for this journey, we need to look at our shared understanding of dreams. What do we mean when we talk of dreaming and what have those who have gone before made of them?

DREAMS: ALTERED STATES OF CONSCIOUSNESS

Dreams are a different form of consciousness to our waking consciousness. Whilst sleeping we operate with images, characters, and time frames that do not follow our usual, waking pattern. People may 'shapeshift' or morph in front of our eyes, a dream 'friend' may transform into a wild cat. But why is this? What have we to gain from the altered state of consciousness (ASC) that dreaming brings about? Why do we need to dream?

The need for dreaming has been shown to exist independently of the need for ordinary sleep and is not an accidental by-product of sleep: 'one may sleep in order to dream.' On a psychological level, dream deprivation causes:

~ heightened levels of tension, anxiety, irritability
~ a marked difficulty in concentration
~ an increase in appetite
~ a decrease in motor co-ordination
~ disturbance of perception of time
~ memory intrusion — the waking person feels they are dreaming and dream images break through whilst they are awake
~ feelings of emptiness and depersonalisation, as shown by the crucial research of William Dement.

In addition, there is increasing evidence that being deprived of dreams leads to personality disorganisation. Thus, if dream deprivation causes personality disturbance then it would seem reasonable to assume that at least one of the functions of dreaming is to maintain personality organisation.

In dreams we travel through layers of connection that may be blocked by the rational, more constrained and censoring aspect of our waking being. Dreams come largely unsolicited, and frequently indicate the action or the path we need to take. That storehouse of memory, the unconscious, is revealed symbolically in dreams. Dreaming allows us to expand our state of awareness so that we can tune in to that part of ourselves which has many labels: the unconscious, our higher self or higher nature, the inner self or inner wisdom, the source of our original being or our divine self or God. Whatever label we choose to use, dreams 'translate' these deep inner experiences into symbols and images we recognise and sometimes only after lengthy work can understand. As in meditation, dreams touch the intuitive rather than the rational self.

Candace Pert's work described in *Molecules of Emotion* is highly relevant. She says that, when we dream, different parts of the body mind are exchanging information:

> the content of which reaches your awareness as a story. On a physiological level, the psychosomatic network is returning itself each night for the next day. Shifts are occurring in feedback loops as peptides spill out into the system ... and bind to receptors to cause activities necessary for homeostasis, or return to normalcy. Information about those readjustments enters your consciousness in the form of a dream, and since these are biochemicals of emotion, the dream has not only content but feeling as well.

THE HEALING NATURE OF DREAMS

Before looking at healing in any form, it is important to understand that health and well-being are not discrete entities divorced from the social fabric of our lives. They are woven into the warp and weft of the whole person and the whole process of therapy. Dreams draw from interwoven memories and felt experiences and the everyday dynamic that the dreamer is living. Based on the belief that each person holds the key to their own healing, part of the role of the counsellor or healer is to enable people to access that personal power, to connect to that deep wisdom. Dreams reveal the multi-layered tapestry of life in all its intricacies, which is why they are so valuable in the healing process. (One particularly important aspect is the way in which dreams offer intimations of physical or mental ill health before the dreamer has any conscious awareness of it; in subsequent chapters we will explore in more detail the potential that such dream diagnosis offers.)

So, how do we define healing in relation to dreams? Perhaps in its widest sense, healing looks at the whole person which includes mind, spirit, emotions and body and is concerned with the cause and meaning of ill health. Whilst we are not looking at ways of treating a client as a doctor would a patient, we are nonetheless concerned with the impact of attitudes on well-being.

Together, client and counsellor work in a healing space, a sacred space that is dedicated to the process of finding some relief and understanding of the distress that initiated counselling. In this space the purpose is to find a path forward, a healthier, more satisfying way of being in the world; indeed, many who seek therapy talk of having 'lost their way'. Those involved in the therapeutic process are thus companions on the journey to the wise heart and this journey takes place in the sacred space of the counselling room. It is sacred because this healing place honours the process of connection to the innermost aspect of humanity. It is a dedicated space, protected from interruption and intrusion as we work through anger and anguish. The client may experience a level of vulnerability that they have never before allowed another person to see or share and the space must honour and respect this experience. If the place in which counselling is taking place does not accommodate the client in this way, it can signal a lack of care or a devaluing of the person that may make it very difficult for the client to trust both the counsellor and the therapeutic process. Of course, in reality, counselling takes place in all sorts of venues which are less than ideal and in many instances hardly adequate. Where this happens it is all the more imperative that the counsellor recognises and guards the sacredness of the interaction by their complete presence and attention in the session.

One process lies at the heart of counselling: *listening*. As Lao-Tzu, the author of Tao-Te Ching, on which Taoism is based, said:

> Such listening as enfolds us in silence in which at last we begin to hear what we are meant to be.

Active listening — listening to the music behind the words, taking into account the body language of the client as well as the subtle inflections of words — is at the very core of counselling. Listening in an active, accurate way is essential. It encompasses other skills such as empathy, understanding, attentiveness and awareness. Listening is an underrated skill and possibly a dying art since it is more and more difficult to find an uninterrupted space in which to listen or be listened to. Yet, as Thomas Moore so lyrically describes in *The Re-Enchantment of Everyday Life*, our soul longs for quiet in which to reflect. Effective counselling can satisfy this longing.

> It is the disease of not listening, the malady of not marking that I am troubled withal.
>
> (Shakespeare, *Henry IV*, Part 2)

Active listening applies not only to what the client is saying but also to what they are listening and responding to — you, yourself, your reactions to the voice within as you attend the client and empathise. From the quiet, deep insights often emerge to illuminate the path you travel together but sometimes finding that silence within is difficult. However, as Fritz Capra tells us: 'When the rational mind is silenced, the intuitive mind produces extraordinary awareness.'

Dreams and healing spaces have played a part in human life since the dawn of time when our early cave-dwelling ancestors painted dream-like images on walls. Tribal societies as far apart as Africa and Australia, America and Ireland, have all believed that the 'Great Spirit' spoke to people in dreams and could heal the body and soul.

ANCIENT SUMERIA

Dating from at least 2000 BC, the world's oldest heroic tale, 'The Epic of Gilgamesh', tells the story of a quest for immortality and is full of dream accounts. It reveals how dreams were highly regarded in ancient Mesopotamia, both in their capacity as bearers of omens and portents of the future and as a way to penetrate other realities. In one dream, Enkidu, the travelling companion of Gilgamesh, sees what the afterlife is like and, in common with many others, from shamans to visionaries, thereafter his certainty of life after death influences his whole view of the world.

ANCIENT GREECE

The relationship between health and dreaming is not a new phenomenon. Healing temples were consecrated in the honour of the ancient Greek **Aesclepius**, a healer in the eleventh century BC. These were staffed by temple priests who were part physicians, part metaphysicians and part shamans. Skilled in medicine, incantations and with a knowledge of herbs, they not only interpreted the dreams of those who sought answers to problems and cures for illnesses, they also prescribed medicines according to the nature of the dreams. They knew that dreams had the power to heal.

Oneiros, the Greek god of dreams, gave his name to *The Oneirocritica* or *The Interpretation of Dreams* which was one of the first books ever written and only the second book to be printed on the Gothenburg Press. In five volumes and written by **Artemidorus** of Daldis, Asia Minor, in the second century AD, this first ever comprehensive book on the interpretation of dreams was the most important book on dreams right up to the nineteenth century when Freud used the same title for his own seminal work on dreams. *The Oneirocritica* is somewhat similar in style to modern dream dictionaries though it also contains broader advice on how to interpret dreams.

The healing path of dream work: starting out

Artemidorus's view is very close to the present outlook on dreams in that he postulated that they were unique to the dreamer and were affected by the person's occupation, social standing and health:

> If we wish to interpret a dream correctly, we need to take a note of whether the person dreaming it is male or female, healthy or sick, a free man or slave, rich or poor, young or old.

Throughout antiquity there was a belief that dreams had a divine origin and carried messages from the gods. The ancient Greeks believed that the great god, Zeus, god of gods, sent warnings, messages and prophecies in dreams with the help of Hypnos, the god of sleep, and Morpheus, the god of dreams. This is an area we will consider in later chapters.

Many Greek philosophers devoted time to the subject of dreams. **Plato** (428–348 BC), in his early works, for example, *Apologia* and *Symposium*, viewed dreams as channels of communication between man and his gods. Plato recognised that dreams could radically influence waking actions and gave as an example the fact that Socrates studied music and the arts because a dream had instructed him to do so.

Plato's biological theory of dreams argues that dreams originate in respective organs in the body, with the liver being the most important. He noted that dreams can be triggered by over-gratification or frustration of bodily organs — theories taken up and developed in more recent times by many psychologists, including Freud and Jung. They also developed his notion that when reason is suspended in sleep: 'the other two elements of the soul — desire and anger — and all the repressed aspects of personality break through with all their power, and the soul can accept incest, murder and sacrilege' (J.R. Lewis).

... in all of us, even in good men, there is a lawless wild-beast nature, which peers out in sleep.

(Plato, *The Republic*)

Other Greek philosophers, such as **Aristotle** (384–322 BC), attempted to study dreams in a rational way, though Petronius, Nero's counsellor, is the first person recorded who had a 'rational' approach to dreams:

> It is neither the gods nor divine commandments that send the dreams down from the heavens, but each one of us makes them for himself.

Aristotle argued that so-called 'prophetic' dreams were simply coincidences and he proposed that the most skilful interpreter of dreams is 'he who has the faculty for absorbing resemblances', that is, the person who can make connections between waking events, society at large and the life history of the dreamer. He also argued that dreams could reflect the physical state of the dreamer and could therefore be used as an aid to diagnosis — an idea later supported by **Hippocrates** (460–357 BC). The Greeks believed that each person carried within them the knowledge of their own cure, and that such inner wisdom needed to be expressed and used in healing. Access to this came via dreams.

At the peak of this dream incubation culture, there were some 420 temples to Aesclepius all over the ancient Greek world, the most famous being the temple at Epidaurus. Healing cures at Epidaurus were well known and recognition of the power of dreams was a given. However, the ancient knowledge of using dreams in the diagnosis and treatment of physical illness has been steadily undermined throughout history, as we shall see — doctors today do not routinely ask about their patients' dreams.

The incubation of healing dreams continued in the Roman Empire. The word 'incubation' is derived from the Latin word, *in* (on) *cubare* (to lie down). It refers to the practice of deliberately seeking help from dreams in healing temples. During the process, the seeker of healing would sleep in the company of sacred snakes. The snake was the symbol of the god of healing and symbolically represents renewal. The snake casts off it old skin and has a new one beneath. Modern medicine has inherited this link between healing and renewal in the form of the staff of Aesclepius — a staff wound around with two snakes, the emblem known as the *caduceus* which is used by physicians today. The *caduceus* is the symbol of the eternal science of transformation and integration.

From the marble *stelae* — stones inscribed with affirmations — around the Temple of Aesclepius at Epidaurus we have details of miraculous cures:

> Arata, a Roman of Lacademon was dropsical. Her mother left her in Lacademon and came to Epidaurus to beg god to cure her daughter. She slept in the Temple and had the following dream: it seemed to her that the god cut off her daughter's head and hung up her body in such a way that her throat was turned downward. Out of it came a huge quantity of fluid matter. Then, she took down the body and fitted the head back on the neck. After she had seen this dream, she went back to Lacademon where she found her daughter in good health; she had had the same dream.

Arata's experience is in no way restricted to ancient Greece. It happens now in the twentieth century (later, we will hear more of people who share the same healing dream on the same night).

> A woman from Athens called Ambrosia was blind in one eye. She came as a supplicant to the god. As she walked about in the Temple, she laughed at some of the cures as incredible and impossible, that the lame and the blind should be healed by merely having a dream. In her sleep she had a vision. It seemed to her that the god stood by her and said he would cure her, but that the payment he would ask of her was to dedicate to the Temple a Silver Pig as a memorial to her foolishness. After saying this, he cut out her diseased eyeball and poured in some drug. When day came, she walked out of the Abaton completely sound.

This is similar to the dream of Heather who discovered the cause of her 'dry eyes' in her dreams (Chapter 3).

Hippocrates, known as the father of modern medicine, believed that some dreams were divinely inspired whilst others were a direct result of physical activity within the body or stimuli from external sources. A poem written by Lucretius (80 CBE) expresses the essence of this physical influence on dreams:

... kids wet the bed
Soaking not only sheets, but also spreads,
Magnificent Babylonian counterpanes,
Because it seemed that in dreams he stood
Before a urinal or chamber pot.

A modern example of the inclusion of external stimuli is the classic 'alarm bell' dream. A bell ringing in a dream may be the incorporated sound of an alarm or telephone ringing next to the bed. The brain receives the signal and enmeshes it into the dream so that the dreamer can continue sleeping. However, if the noise continues it will finally force the dreamer awake to the true source of the sound. This function of dreams as the protector of sleep, as described by Freud, explains why some internal and external stimuli become the stuff of dreams.

Dreams can also incorporate physical events into the dream narrative in highly dramatic ways. Alfred Maury, a French doctor whose book on dreams was published in 1861, believed that they would occur almost simultaneously with the outer stimulus. He gave an example of his own dream which was set in the Reign of Terror in the French Revolution. In it he was condemned to death and led to the guillotine. As the blade of the guillotine fell, he woke to find the top of the bed had fallen and struck him at the exact point at the top of his spine where the guillotine would have cut.

DREAMS AND RELIGIOUS BELIEF

> In dreams begin responsibilities. (W.B. Yeats)

Early Christian worshippers sought dream-healing at pilgrimage sites, particularly at churches built over the remains of Aesclepius's temples. Just as the Christians built on earlier sacred sites, so they inherited ideas about the world, the universe and the purpose of dreams. Layers of history physically available on these archaeological sites provide evidence of continuity, in much the same way that metaphorical levels of awareness of the past are carried in dream work. Our connections with this distant world are still with us, not only in our dream investigations but in our language. Panacea and Hygea, the daughters of Aesclepius, gave us 'panacea' and 'hygiene' and the word 'clinic' is derived from the Greek *Kline*, which was the name for the bed on which the 'patient' lay. All are linked to health and healing and stem from temple practices of dream incubation.

Early Christian writers such as **Tertullian** (160–240) recognised the value of dreams, saying that God 'especially intended dreams to be of particular assistance in natural foresight', thus continuing the Greek and Roman view of dreams as omens and portents. Christians revived the idea that dreams could come from a supernatural source — though not from the gods; rather, God. There are more than twenty accounts of dreams in the bible which refer to divine guidance and some of these changed the course of history. In one of his own dreams, Moses was told of their powerful significance:

> 'Hear now my words,' he dreamt. 'If there be a prophet among you, I, the Lord, will make myself known to him in a vision and will speak to him in a dream.'

The early Christian belief that dreams came from God diminished after **St Jerome's** intervention. Plagued by sexually explicit

11

dreams, he denounced them as the work of the devil, so dreams fell from grace, and by the time of the Inquisition they were seen as the work of the devil. The Church was the interpreter of God's word and only priests had the power to interpret his word. Any revelation given to an individual in a dream was seen as satanic. Later, **Martin Luther** (1483–1546), the founder of Protestantism, endorsed this view. In his eyes, sin was 'the confederate and father of foul dreams'. Thus, dreams were relegated to the realm of evil and any interest in harvesting their power was dismissed if not punished. Today, this view is still held in some quarters, which explains the reservations some people have about working with dreams.

Dream interpretation played an important role in Jewish life. Around the time of Christ, the Talmud records that there were twenty-four dream interpreters in Jerusalem. Rabbi Chrisda said: 'The dream which is not interpreted is like a letter which has not been read.' All dreams were seen as meaningful.

Dreams are also significant in Islam. The prophet, **Mohammed** (*circa* 570–632), had his first revelation in a dream and received spiritual instruction that was profoundly important to the foundation of Islam. This invitation into the mysteries of the universe happened during a great dream known as 'The Night Journey'. He said that most of the teachings of the Koran were given to him in a dream. He interpreted his disciples' dreams and dreamt that on the way to heaven he met Moses, Abraham and Jesus.

The Muslim scholar, **Avicenna** (980–1037), was one of the most amazing men of his age. Born in Bukhara, Persia (now Iran), he was a polymath and his writings covered science and philosophy, but more importantly in our context, he wrote extensively on healing. Avicenna's two major works were *The Book of Healing* and *The Canon of Medicine*.

The Book of Healing, a large encyclopaedia covering the natural sciences, logic, mathematics, psychology, astronomy, music, and philosophy, is probably the largest work of its kind ever written by one man. *The Canon of Medicine* became and remained the definitive work in its field for centuries. In it was a systematic exposition of the achievements of Greek and Roman physicians. Much of Avicenna's work was subsequently translated into Latin and thereby became available throughout Europe. His contributions to medicine, theology and philosophy are invaluable in the Islamic tradition and beyond, though he is still largely unrecognised in the West.

DREAMS AS GIVERS OF WISDOM

In many cultures, dreams have a special importance to the tribe or community and there are many different approaches in which dreams are taken to provide structure, guidance and wisdom.

Australian Aborigines, in their five hundred distinct tribes, share the certainty that nature and human life are inextricably intertwined, as are the past and the future. The *dreamtime* is the mythical age of the past which is at the same time the present. The link with this heroic past is kept by rites of initiation in which participants act out their early myths. Waking and sleeping life have equal importance for the Aborigine. Many of the rituals which appear in dreams are later applied to waking life, as are ceremonies which are first witnessed in the dream state.

The native American Mohave tribe of the south-west United States also interpret their culture in terms of dreams rather than interpreting their dreams in terms of cultural influences. Omen dreams, for example, are seen as foretelling what *could* happen rather than what *would* happen and the dreams of their shamans are told to the tribe and are used as a basis for decision-making and problem-solving. The Mohave also believe in the power of dreams to cause illness. These pathogenic dreams come in two forms: the first, in which the dreamer falls ill because of harmful events encountered in a dream by the soul; the second, in which a dream is so upsetting that the dreamer reacts by becoming ill. Particularly dangerous are dreams in which the dreamer is fed by the ghosts of the dead or has sexual intercourse with a ghost.

The Jesuits in the 1600s thought that the Iroquois had only

one deity — the dream. They followed the dream literally and acted out the content of their dreams — for example, travelling over a hundred miles to get a dog in Quebec after they had met the dog in a dream.

These *visitation* dreams are similar to the ancient Aesclepian healing dreams of the Greeks (see particularly C.A. Meier, *Ancient Incubation and Modern Psychotherapy*). The Iroquois recognised the importance of the dream signal and the whole community would often become involved in visitation dreams. Supernatural figures would appear in dreams and usually spoke personally to the dreamer, bringing a message of importance to the individual and/or the community. Such figures that appear in dreams are likely to be archetypal ones or people who have special significance.

In a highly diversified and individualist society, each person becomes his or her own myth-maker. The Iroquois had their own specialists who would help tribal members to understand their dreams. The dreamer's relatives would be involved in working out what the dream meant and, as in family therapy, each member could contribute to the process of understanding and would help clarify for the group the significance of the dream for each and all of them.

Barbara Hannah has described how the Senoi: '... a group of Malay aboriginals who had succeeded in creating a culture of peace and harmony based upon working with dreams', regularly set aside a time each day for the community to discuss dreams and to act out their dreams through dance and communal reveries. Dreams were not seen as an end in themselves. The Senoi sought power in their dreams. In power dreams, dreamers can do things which they cannot do in reality — fly, breathe under water and so on (Tart):

> The Senoi [of Malaysia] believe that any human being, with the aid of his fellows, can outface, master and actually utilise all beings and forces in the dream universe. His experience

14

leads him to believe that, if you co-operate with your fellows or oppose them with goodwill in the daytime, their images will help you in your dreams and that every person should be the supreme ruler and master of his own dream or spiritual universe and can demand and receive the help and co-operation of all the forces there.

Senoi children were taught to be responsible for what happened in their dreams — to be of service to their friends if they were present, to face animals or monsters if they appeared and to match their strength to them and not run away — and were encouraged to be active and fully expressive in all dream encounters (Tart): 'The child's dream was taken as a vivid and non-symbolic representation of the child's needs and problems.'

This gradual process of learning from childhood to maturity, with dreams as a central part of the process, encompasses many cognitive and behavioural techniques:

~ exploring what it is that causes fear
~ rehearsal and problem-solving in the face of fear
~ desensitisation towards the feared object or event
~ using the power of the peer group for support
~ gaining rewards in the form of dream gifts or meeting the animal totem.

We can still use these techniques as a means of increasing self-confidence and personal esteem in the counselling setting, as we will see in Chapter 2.

Usually when we talk of reaping rewards from dreams, it is a psychological understanding or gain that we refer to. In Japanese myth, however, rewards can be tangible and stories show the link between dreams and the supernatural and physical worlds. In one story, two pedlars were resting on a beach. When one fell asleep, his companion saw a fly come from the sleeping man's nose. It flew towards an island called Sado and then returned to creep again into his nostril. At this point the man awoke and related a

15

dream he had had in which buried treasure was found on Sado. Following this, the dreamer took money for the relating of this dream; in effect, he sold his dream. The 'buyer' of the dream went to Sado, found the treasure and 'then went his way, not to become a pedlar again, but to enjoy the luxuries his dream investment had brought him'.

Though the idea of selling dreams is not usual to us, there are many reported cases of people dreaming, for example, of winning lottery numbers. We examine this precognitive element of dreams in Chapter 8.

THE NEW PSYCHOLOGY

In the eighteenth century, **Johann Fichte** (1762–1814) and his disciple **Friedrich Schelling** (1775–1854) suspected that dreams revealed unconscious fears and desires but it was not until the early twentieth century with Freud's publication of *The Interpretation of Dreams* in 1900 that this idea was fully developed and the new psychology of dreams was born.

Erich Fromm (1900–1980) was a psychotherapist who put forward the view that the human race had one universal language which was the symbolic language of dreams — the 'forgotten language' as he termed it. Fromm divided symbols into different categories: *conventional* symbols were regarded as those with only one meaning, such as a plus or minus sign; *accidental* symbols were personal to the individual in the dream or personal to a group of people, but not real to people in general; *universal* symbols were those found in common throughout the world, such as water representing emotion and intuition or fire representing power, energy, purification.

Sigmund Freud (1865–1939) was the founder of psychoanalysis. He came to believe that dreams represented the royal road to understanding the unconscious. Of his seminal work on dreams, *The Interpretation of Dreams*, he wrote: '[It] contains even according to my present day judgement the most valuable of all the discoveries it has been my good fortune to make. Insights such as this fall to one's lot but once in a lifetime.'

Regarded as the father of modern dream interpretation Freud in his introduction to *The Interpretation of Dreams* wrote:

> In the following pages I shall attempt to prove that a psychological technique exists which permits the interpretation of dreams and that, by the use of my procedure, every dream will show itself to be a meaningful psychological structure, capable of taking its place among the psychological drives of waking life.

His main theory was that the purpose of dreams is to allow repressed infantile fantasies, such as those of a sexual nature, to be expressed and satisfied. He stressed the sexual dimension of dreams which centred around sexual frustration. He identified five processes during dreaming:

~ displacement

~ condensation

~ symbolisation

~ projection

~ secondary revision, where all the aspects of the dream are brought together to give it a comprehensible surface meaning which Freud called the *manifest content*.

The process of psychoanalysis involved exploring and decoding the dream to access the hidden, or latent, content of the dream. He believed dreams always had serious meaning and reflected our earliest, deepest desires. Freud's theory purported that though dreams may be triggered by external events, they really represented wish-fulfilment. He acknowledged that anxiety, fears and sexual difficulties, for example, affected the body and resulted in psychosomatic states.

Dreams were cryptic, a puzzle to be unlocked and understood and, for Freud, the tools were in the symbolic language of the dream and in particular in the sexual symbolism — the root of it all. Freud encouraged patients to talk about their dreams, to freely associate to them, that is, to talk about whatever came into their minds as they reflected on the dream and the connections it made for them. He argued that by doing this they accessed repressed, emotions that were censored in daily thought.

Freud's personality theory of *ego*, *id* and *superego* provided a template to be used with dreams. Ego dreams reflected the conscious aspect of our selves; id dreams, the primitive side; and superego, our socially conditioned, culture bound self. The id, with all its savage, untrammelled urging towards reproduction and survival, came to the fore with the expression of the full force of the dreamer's latent sexual drives. To protect the ego and the superego, Freud argued, dreams were disguised so as not to shock the dreamer into wakefulness and, for this reason, he called dreams the 'guardians of sleep', though many have disagreed vehemently with this view.

Carl Gustav Jung (1875–1961), a prominent Swiss psychotherapist, broke away from his mentor Sigmund Freud to set up his own branch of psychoanalysis. In the unconscious, he argued, lay both our baser, instinctual drives as well as higher spiritual impulses and the purpose of dreams was to communicate to the conscious mind. Unlike Freud, Jung argued that, far from being deliberate disguises, dreams inform the dreamer directly and teach what he or she needs to know. Far from concealing desires, dreams reveal our deepest wishes and longings and help us to realise our unconscious ambitions and potentials. The dream gives voice to the unconscious which seeks to guide and assist the conscious self. For Jung, each person's symbols are idiosyncratic, unique to each individual and situation, yet they also connect to a universal, collective communication and understanding, often taking further symbolic form.

According to Jungian theory, dreams have two functions. The first is to compensate for personal imbalances, making up for that which might be missing in waking life or which was being neglected at the time — he believed dreams heal by bringing the psyche into balance. The second function is to assist in the individuation process by bringing about prospective dreams which indicate future potential or events.

Jung also introduced the concept of *archetypes*, that is, the storehouse of human experience which is contained in prototypes. Archetypal dreams are linked to core issues: death and rebirth; the Hero's journey; rites of passage; and creation. Some examples of these eternal motifs are to be found in the anima/animus, the wise woman or wise man, the shadow, the mandala and the persona.

The anima/animus for example, represents the inner qualities balancing aspects of gender: for a woman the animus is her male aspect; for the male dreamer the anima is his female aspect. The whole self is formed when we can integrate these complementary sides — the anima/animus is to the inner world as the persona is to the outer.

In Jungian work with dreams, the process is one which aims to help interpret messages coming from the unconscious. As he said in *Memories, Dreams and Reflections*: 'the dream is a little hidden door to the innermost recesses of the soul.' He said that we must first approach a dream at its simplest level. If an umbrella appears in a dream, then first take it as an umbrella instead of assuming it is a disguised phallus, for example. The sexual factor in dreams was not regarded by Jung as the determining aspect. He believed that dreams were not censored but were the revelations of the unconscious, a communication from one part of the dreamer to another. And he saw dreaming as a way to contact not only the inner wisdom of the individual unconscious mind but also that of the collective unconscious.

Jung's research took him further into the world of depth psychology which he divided into the personal unconscious and the collective unconscious. For Jung, the unconscious is nature and so it never lies. By this he meant that there is at work in the world a principle existing beyond individual experience and physical history and yet determining both.

Dream analysis had a prime place in Jung's approach to understanding the unconscious. He used dream amplification to expand the dream content and place it within the dreamer's life, to imagine a way deeper into the dream scene and then to move it further in relation to myth and symbol. As Kovel says in *A Complete Guide to Therapy*: 'In this way the dream itself was revealed to be a higher form of cognition, guiding the patient to a superordinate knowledge.' Jung believed healing could occur if contact with the deep unconscious could take place. It is akin to tapping into the foundation, the basic roots of existence which keep each one of us, each organism, stable.

Jung distinguished between two main types of dreams: ordinary, everyday dreams; and *numinous* dreams. 'Numinous' derives from the Latin *numen*, which means 'deity' or 'presiding spirit'. In such dreams there is the sense of the divine or sacred and for some people a numinous dream has led to major life changes. The other 'smaller' dreams are less immediately impressive and are more usually to do with everyday aspects of life. Although they are still very useful for dream work, they lack the vividness and urgency of numinous dreams.

His extensive travels, including journeys to Africa and the United States of America to visit black Africans and Native Americans, confirmed Jung's belief that there are two levels of consciousness, the personal unconscious and the collective unconscious. The latter comprises archetypal symbols that represented all the knowledge and wisdom of all humanity. He put forward the theory that each individual carries all the wisdom of previous generations, just as scientists have argued more recently that we each carry in our cellular structure knowledge of everything that has happened since time began.

These original images he called *ancestral memory* archetypes and we inherit them just as we inherit the colour of our eyes. Archetypal images are symbols that are not invented but contained in the subconscious of all people, no matter what their race or colour. He found that these archetypal symbols frequently occurred in dreams of people who were experiencing life-threatening conditions or were in life-transforming crises. This is a view supported by others such as Maria Louise Von Franz and

Elizabeth Kubler-Ross, whose work was with those nearing death.

Jung explored Eastern philosophies, the occult, alchemy and anthropology in order to understand what is at the core of what it means to be a human being. He regarded the spiritual journey of each person, which he termed *individuation*, to be central to the human condition. The individuation process, which counsellors may be familiar with in Maslow's concept of actualisation in his hierarchy of needs, is the force within each person to seek greater self-understanding, to become more self-aware and integrated and to seek personal fulfilment.

The monumental range of Jung's work led to a re-evaluation of the importance of mythology and influenced people like Joseph Campbell, who showed how mythology actively influences psychological make up. Campbell's later work carries this view into the market place of everyday life in the form of film, for example. He was crucially influential in the *Star Wars* series of films which depict the mythic journey of individuation and the quest for truth. The films, like enduring stories, touch the very essence of our own personal journeys whether we are familiar with the concepts or not.

Innumerable difficulties during Jung's life arose because he believed dreams to be prospective, that is, forward-looking, as well as retrospective. Mainstream scientists of the day viewed this idea as the mystical meanderings of an occultist. They saw him as a man who had lost his way by becoming involved with ideas such as synchronicity, which could not be proved by scientific methods nor repeated in laboratory conditions. There are many who share that same attitude today — if you can't measure it, tabulate it, then market it, it isn't 'scientific' and if it isn't scientific it isn't important.

This reductionist attitude is limiting. The vast wealth of dream experiences of 'ordinary' people who have had prospective or telepathic dreams is impressive in both volume and consistency, as we will discover in Chapter 8 when we explore insight from dreams that cannot be explained 'scientificically'. Common-sense knowledge, which was so often abused by early scientists and then vindicated by other scientists at a later stage, seems to have served us — women in particular — well for a long time.

A specific aim of Jungian therapy is to bring about contact with the transcendent, ineffable and mysterious. 'The spirit still reigns supreme in Jung,' as Kovel points out; he 'provides the most systematic and serious grounding for the transcendent approach to therapy.' We have a sense of the unique support system of the collective unconscious. In the healing process it helps to know there are powerful unseen aspects of existence which aid our survival and growth. Such contacts touch the transcendent, albeit fleetingly at first, like a butterfly's wing on a petal, but as with dream symbols, the more archetypes are appreciated, the richer the depth to be mined.

At one time closely associated with Freud, **Alfred Adler** (1870–1937), like Jung, broke away to develop his own form of psychotherapy and dream theories. His focus was on power and status and he believed that the most powerful human drive was for control. He introduced the terms *sibling rivalry* and *inferiority complex*. Dreams, for Adler, were part of this process — to master life. They were rehearsals for future events so that people can prepare for them, anticipating the future rather than discharging tensions from the past (see Chapter 7). However, he did acknowledge that some dreams are misleading and would lead to failure rather than success. Adler played down the unconscious and sexuality, preferring to focus on social influences as well as aspects such as assertiveness, self-esteem, goals — the *active striving* of the individual in the therapeutic setting.

Gestalt psychology is based on the idea that the mind seeks to make a whole out of various parts: *the sum of the whole is greater than the parts*. In relation to dreams this means that, when all the different aspects of a dream are explored and combined, we get a fuller picture than the fragmented pieces we initially see. **Fritz Perls** (1893–1970) saw dreams as the way to integration rather than to the unconscious, as in Freud's view, and he saw them as being the most spontaneous product that we have. And, as Jung before him, Perls recognised that we need to acknowledge the negative in ourselves if we are to become whole, integrated human beings. By doing this we re-own the hidden potential that is also present in our dreams.

A Jungian analyst, **Arnold Mindell** developed *process oriented psychology* and the term *dream body*. This he describes in his book *Dream Body* (1982) as: 'a multi-channelled information sender which is asking you to receive its message in many ways'. He noted how the dream body gives vital clues about disease, again and again in order to capture the dreamer's attention. Peter Fenwick comments: 'Because of the mercuric nature of the body's energy, it needs a flexible and adaptable attitude to be able to "read" body symptoms of illness or disease using whatever channel is being activated at the time whether it be tone of voice, body language, dream work or language itself.'

DREAMS AS INDIVIDUAL MYTHS

Dreams may delineate an individual's personal story, their life narrative or mythic journey. Myth, according to some, comes from the Greek word *muo* which means to close your eyes and shut your mouth and is associated with the word 'mute'. Myth also means story — it is possible that the two together mean being silent as the story flows over and into the listener. In dreaming, the dreamer's body is still and silent as the internal myth or the story of the dream flows on. The dream is the story told when the eyes are shut. Thomas Moore in *The Re-Enchantment of Everyday Life* says: 'Joseph Campbell taught that myth makes the cosmos meaningful, helps society to find an identity, guides the individual towards a life of value and establishes for all a sense of religion.'

Myths describe deep levels of experience or transcendence that lie beyond the dreamer's life; they depict the invisible and the eternal, a 'sacred story'.

Dream is a personal experience of that deep, dark ground that is the society's dream. The myth is the public dream and the dream is the private myth. If your private myth, your dream, happens to coincide with that of society, you are in good accord with your group. If it isn't, you've got an adventure in the dark forest ahead of you. (Campbell, 1993)

Calvin Hall, working in America in the 1960s, collected dreams from hundreds of 'ordinary' people, that is, people *not* undergoing therapy or psychoanalysis, and showed how dreams reflect everyday life and waking concerns. His book, *The Meaning of Dreams*, helped to show that our dreams are personal documents to ourselves.

SLEEP RESEARCH

Much of the research currently in progress is concerned with the mechanics of dreaming. The researchers attach recording devices to volunteers who then bed down in sleep laboratories and their sleeping and dreaming states are monitored. A great deal of useful information has been discovered in this way; for instance, in the 1950s Aserinsky and Kleitman found that during what is termed *dream sleep* or *paradoxical sleep*, the eyes moved about rapidly beneath the closed eyelids. They found that 80 per cent of dreams from these rapid eye movement (REM) periods were remembered and only 7 per cent from non-REM sleep. It became clear that dreaming must occupy at least a quarter of sleep time and that everyone, if woken at the appropriate time, will be able to describe dreams.

There are many books on the subject of dreaming as a physical activity and the bibliography to this book contains useful starting points. Here, however, such research will only be discussed to the extent that it is relevant to dreams, counselling and healing.

THE WORLD WIDE WEB OF DREAMING

Each year new developments in dream research are reported at the American annual conference of the Association for the Study of Dreams (ASD) to which hundreds of professional dream workers, therapists, and non-specialist dreamers are drawn. In addition, there are many sites on the Internet which chart dream progress.

As we experience the new millennium, the study of dreams is going through a rebirth as more and more modern research reveals the essential links between mind and body, *psyche* and *soma*. Dreams reveal these connections in all sorts of areas and it is the methods of uncovering these connections to which we turn our attention in Chapter 2.

CHAPTER 2

USING DREAMS IN THE THERAPEUTIC SETTING

> A dream is a theatre in which the dreamer is himself
> the scene, the player, the prompter, the producer, the
> author, the public and the critic ... [This] conceives all
> figures in the dream as personified features of the
> dreamer's own personality.
>
> (Jung, 1974)

Dreams are sensitive, multi-layered communications which, amongst so many other things, highlight personal difficulties. Rosalind Cartwright, one of the foremost researchers working in the field of dreams today, in explaining the role of dreams says that when we go to sleep the brain doesn't switch off; rather, it changes channels, and the dream channel is a special educational channel (1988): 'Dreams offer the Three Rs, and in times of stress, a fourth R. They allow us to review, revise and rehearse the program of ourselves. And when life is tough, as in depression, they also provide a mechanism for repair.'

Experiences when dreaming are as significant as waking experiences. They can be life changing, directive, revelatory and comforting at times of crisis. Whatever their content, their power as healing tools is often underrated and their 'vital therapeutic effect', as Freud put it, lies in the way in which memories from the unconscious can be brought to conscious attention. There are a number of ways to access this potential and, as we explore the methods, bear in mind that whenever we work with dreams, the fundamentals of active listening should be consistently applied.

A FLEXIBLE APPROACH TO DREAM WORKING

> There is probably no psychological product that is less
> fettered or more spontaneous than the dream.
>
> (Stolorow)

The original meaning of the word 'dream' is related to the Anglo-Saxon *dreem* which meant joy, music — and ghost. The ghostly, misty meaning can be as elusive as shadowy figures that appear at dusk, the liminal state between day and night and, to honour this quality, we need to cultivate a flexible attitude, a gentle approach. Try not to think of a dream as something to be hunted, captured or controlled; instead, try to cultivate an attitude of inviting and welcoming clients' dreams. Take time to look at dreams from different angles, don't be dogmatic or rigid in your thinking. Your clients need to feel comfortable and will gain far more from not feeling pressured to come up with an interpretation immediately. This requires a willingness to play and the patience to let the creative spark be kindled gently.

> I find that rather than extract meaning from dreams, I
> want to remain susceptible to their enchantment.
>
> (Moore)

Working with dreams is like looking at paintings: they must not be analysed so thoroughly that they no longer have mystery, nor should they be so over-inspected that they cannot offer something at future viewings as our knowledge deepens and circumstances change. They need to be appreciated, admired and enjoyed. Thomas Moore wrote: 'We could also treat our dreams as altars of initiation, where attitudes may be deepened and perspectives broadened.' Candace Pert explains her approach:

> One of the best ways I know to integrate awareness of emotions into lifestyle is to develop the daily habit of recording and transcribing your night time dreams. Dreams

are direct messages from your body mind giving you valuable information about what's going on physiologically as well as emotionally. Becoming aware of your dreams is a way of eavesdropping on a conversation that's going on between psyche and soma, body and mind, of accessing levels of consciousness that are normally beyond awareness.

KEEPING A HEALING DREAM JOURNAL

There are many ways to work with dreams which make interpretation easier and understanding of the healing process more accessible. However, underpinning them all is the need to keep an accurate record of dreams. When I begin to work with clients I ask them to keep a record of their dreams in a note book, with unlined pages which make it easier to include drawings and illustrations. On the right-hand page of the book I ask them to write the dream narrative and keep the left-hand page for illustrations, notes and connections to the dream, as well as symbol interpretation. A dream journal is still the best way to truly develop the gift of self-knowledge that dreams provide, though it shouldn't become a burden. Sometimes clients come and say, as if guilty of a crime, 'I haven't had a dream' or 'I don't remember any dreams.' I am always at pains to reassure them if they do not recall a dream: it's fine, we invite dreams, we don't compel them. Below I have outlined an approach that works very well, making interpretation easier and understanding more accessible.

A guide for clients

Plant a seed. Before going to sleep, tell yourself that you are going to dream. Keep a positive, inviting attitude. Think about and write down the important issues that were on your mind that day and then the kinds of things you would like to dream about. Read over what you have written. Keep that idea in the back of your mind as you fall asleep. Don't analyse or think too deeply about it, just hold it lightly in your mind.

Record the date and place before you go to sleep. At the top of each new entry, record the date and location. The place is important since it may influence the dream. For example, staying in a bland hotel room may trigger one sort of subject, whilst sleeping in the bedroom you occupied in childhood may spark something very different.

Catch the dream. When you wake up from a dream lie still for a moment and turn your mind inward towards the memory of the dream. Allow the various pieces of the dream to come back to you. Be patient. It may take time for the different parts of the dream to surface and come together. Even if only fragments of the dream return to your mind, that's OK. Don't strain trying to remember. Let your mind be light and easy. Gently repeating the dream over and over in your mind may allow new pieces to emerge.

Write the dream. Write down the dream as soon as you can after you had it. If you can only remember fragments of it, write those down without worrying about how to put them in order. In general, don't worry too much about the grammar, spelling or logical flow of what you write. Just get the dream down including any words that you hear or speak. These rough notes are very valuable so put in as much as you remember.

Dream title. Give the dream a title. Some titles seem inspired, and automatically suggest themselves, others reflect the basic content of the dream and seem more prosaic. It really doesn't matter. Giving titles to recorded dreams will help to recall them over long periods of time and will enable patterns to be seen more clearly. New dreams are understood more readily in the light of the old ones.

First or final dream. Where there is a very rich recall of dreams, record when the dream came in the sequence. The final dream just prior to awakening often provides practical problem-solving insights.

Reflect on the dream. Now look at your dream record and, on the left-hand side, make a note of any connections that occur to you and include illustrations to help you remember objects or parts that feel hard to describe in words. These notes in fact may be a kind of 'free association'.

Keeping an ongoing dream journal is a good way to stimulate your recall of your dreams. The more attention you pay to your dreams, the more your dream life will open up to you. Rough notes are useful for your immediate off-the-cuff recall and reactions to your dreams and working on these later can make the journal a place for detailed, in-depth, systematic thinking and exploration. Use the rough notes as fuel or as a springboard for ideas that you investigate further. You may also use the journal to try out the various techniques for working with dreams.

One client expressed her view:

> I have been having psychotherapy and have been told to write my dreams down and to try to work out what they mean. The dreams have been very helpful as they show what has been going on subconsciously. They reveal fears, anxieties, parts of one's personality, relationships to others and so much more, which consciously I was not aware of knowing. I can begin to make changes in my conscious attitudes to life. The dreams explain the unconscious motives behind my behaviour and sometimes show how unhealthy they were. If I had not studied my dreams I don't know how I would ever have been able to discover what was behind my anxiety and panic attacks.

Thomas Moore in *The Re-Enchantment of Everyday Life* writes of the value of keeping a dream journal:

> We can keep a record of our dreams, so that our dream journals or logs serve as a personal sacred text, a compilation, much like sacred literature, of mysteries that have special relevance to our own lives and fate ... Conversations about dreams, when carried out with respect for the imagery, can also bring people close to each other because of the inherent intimacy of a dream.

Using dreams in the therapeutic setting

Kathleen Jenks' *Journey of a Dream Animal*, graphically illustrates how keeping a dream journal can help in the journey through that dark night of the soul. Writing of the whole process of dream discovery, she says:

> There are times when it can be terrible. But there are also times of radiant beauty and times when one's battered spirit is given a balm that heals in ways no words can describe. Through dreams I learned to deal with reality.

DREAM INCUBATION

We no longer have the resources or opportunity, as a general rule, to engage in the lengthy purification rituals that the ancients engaged in during dream incubation, as described in the first chapter. However, there is a great deal to be gained from modified millennium incubation, so we can still take part in 'sacred' dream practices.

By clearly formulating the intention for a desired dream, as an answer to a problem, for instance, the dreamer sets in train a process. This form of self-suggestion — *auto-suggestion* — can be every bit as powerful as external suggestion. By practising dream incubation we give ourselves the message that dreams are important and we are rewarded by receiving and remembering valuable dreams that are highly relevant to our waking lives. We can induce healthy images, successful resolutions and gain important insights.

In *The Use of Pre-sleep Instructions and Dreams in Psychosomatic Disorders*, Dr Loma K. Flowers describes how dream incubation was successfully used to help people who suffer from post-surgical vomiting, tension headaches and hypertension and, more recently, she has described its use in helping people recovering from addiction. Whilst there is clearly scope for using dream incubation in medical settings, we can incubate them at home whenever we wish to.

THE GESTALT METHOD

Gestalt therapy arose out of the study of perception. The 'Gestalt' is the whole; it provides the complete picture. When we look at something where there is a part missing, our brains fill in the empty space to make up the whole picture. For instance, if part of a letter of the alphabet was missing our mind will attempt to supply what has been left out. In Gestalt therapy the aim is to help fill in the missing parts, the emotional 'holes', that make us feel less than complete, and dreams are one arena in which this can take place. As we saw in the first chapter, Fritz Perls believed that each part of the dream was an aspect of our own multi-faceted personality and in order to unify these fragments we have to re-own those 'lost' parts. To illustrate this, let's look at a dream in which a woman, let's call her Maria, is being followed through a dimly lit street by a dark shadow. If I was working on the dream in a Gestalt way, I would ask Maria to tell me the dream from the point of view of the woman, from the point of view of the dark shadow and from the point of view of the street. I would also ask her to 'become' that part of the dream, so that she re-experiences the emotional energy raised in the dream. So I might say: 'Tell me the dream as the street sees it. Begin by saying "I am the dimly lit street." Describe yourself and whatever else you see or feel. Really try to become the street.' In this way many important feelings come to light which are all parts of the dreamer but they are the parts which are usually hidden from public view. This approach also, by changing from 'it' to 'I', reclaims the dynamic energy of the dream and increases vitality, which in turn makes the process a much more active one that reaches the emotional dimensions that are so often obscured in the dreamer's waking life.

The Gestalt method had been adapted and re-adapted all around the world and has probably continued in the place of earlier traditions. In different guises the interview method has been used by many dream therapists, from Jung to Delaney, who is a leading dream worker in San Francisco.

Using dreams in the therapeutic setting

The dream interview method recaptures the energy of the dream rather than merely reporting the dream narrative. I ask the client to speak as if they were the object, place or character in the dream. For instance, they may introduce themselves as the wolf in the dream and describe their physical characteristics and their personality, depending on what is appropriate.

When using these methods learn to trust you own reactions: be prepared to ask unusual questions, to play with words, to joke and recognise puns, try to keep preconceived notions to a minimum. Clear your mind of previous ideas about dreams, for instance, a Freudian view that a pencil represents a penis, instead see what it 'says' to you.

Imagine I'm from Mars! The 'I'm from another planet' approach is an interview method I find very revealing. After my client has related a dream I ask them to consider me to be from another planet and, although I can speak English, the language we share, I am not familiar with what some words mean or what certain concepts are. So I ask for explanations: 'I don't know what a window is, can you define it for me?' or: 'What is a street?' The client then explains in their own unique style and their response shows underlying thoughts and feelings.

Let's look at this section of a dream: 'I am walking down a dimly lit street when a huge wolf appears and bites me.' Referring to the part of a dream in which the dreamer is bitten, we could begin: 'Pretend I am from another planet. I have just arrived and although I speak your language there are many things I do not understand. Tell me what "bites" means so that I will know.' Our dreamer might say: 'Biting is done with teeth that are in the mouth of an animal or a person. It enables the animal to take food and then to eat it so it won't starve. If the animal couldn't bite it might die because it couldn't get food.' Then I could ask, still as the alien from outer space: 'Is biting a good thing?' Our dreamer might then say: 'Sometimes, in the wild, yes, but I'm not food and it hurts me. It should be under control.' We could ask if there was any way in which the dreamer feels that they should be 'under

33

control', does anything come to mind? Or do they feel that anything is 'biting' them or feeding off them?

This non-intrusive, non-directive approach is highly effective. What you find is that people's descriptions are very idiosyncratic. Another person would describe 'biting' quite differently and it would reflect aspects of that person's life and view of the world. We have very similar experiences to others who share our culture and speak our language, but for all of that, each one of us is unique as are the dreams we dream. Respect the dreamer's need to relate their dream to their own personal sense of meaning and avoid the temptation to swamp them with your associations. How the client dreams, what images arise and how they feel about them and subsequently interpret them will reveal a lot about how he or she deals with the world.

Fritz Perls introduced **the empty chair method** which can be used when working with dreams. Place two chairs opposite each other. The dreamer sits in one and in the other is placed the dream, that is, the client imagines their dream is there, able to answer questions and assist in clarifying its meaning. The dreamer asks a question, for example: 'Why is the dream so difficult to understand?' and then they would swap seats and answer the question as if the client were the dream. They should be encouraged to say what immediately comes to mind without censoring their response, no matter how ludicrous it may seem at first. Many gems of wisdom come from these spontaneous responses. The process of swapping chairs, questioning and answering may take some time but eventually there is a much clearer idea of the dream message.

Dreams, of course, have always been linked to the state of our emotional well-being and at times it will be distressing dreams that spur a client into therapy, as it was for Lisa. She had a recurring nightmare over a six-month period, 'every night without fail'. She said: 'In it I am driving my car, alone, at high speed and fighting to gain control of the vehicle. Either it was too dark to see or I could not find the light switch and I could not reach the brake pedal or I could not reach the steering wheel.' She regularly woke up shaken and frightened with her bedside lamp, clock and books strewn everywhere. Even in her sleep she was trying to turn on the light. The emotional intensity of the nightly experience finally made her seek out a therapist and we worked on her dreams together.

In exploring the series of car dreams, I asked Lisa to use Gestalt techniques, to 'become' the car. I asked her to describe herself as the vehicle and to tell me the dream from the car's point of view:

> I'm a fast car, I've got strong body work but I've been dented. I was in a crash. I used to be really shiny, top of the range but now, since I was hit, I'm not working properly. My brakes are unreliable, sometimes I think I won't be able to stop in time. It's all a bit erratic, hit and miss. I'm just not sure what's going to happen, and the driver's not really doing anything to help either. She's just carrying on driving, putting her foot down and I have to respond even though we will have another crash if she doesn't do something. She just doesn't look after me properly, in fact, I think she wants to damage me.

Saying these words out loud visibly stunned Lisa. She understood at a gut level that she was talking about an aspect of herself. She identified the cause of the 'dent' straight away, a violent encounter with her partner, with whom she was still having a relationship and she recognised that some repair was in order. The 'dent' symbolised a breach of her own protective boundaries and the additional imagery of the reckless driver intensified the sense of self-destructiveness. These were the central issues that were at the heart of Lisa's difficulies.

Since beginning therapy the dreams have not recurred and Lisa now has a different perspective on them. She said: 'I'm really glad I had those dreams now though I hated them at the time. They alerted me to the danger I was in. If I'd not accepted that I was out of control, speeding towards disaster then I'm sure I would have completely cracked up. They clarified the danger I was in, the relationship I had was destroying me yet I refused to face that when I was awake. I was truly in danger of destroying myself, I was so out of control.'

Like many of us, Lisa didn't want to face painful truths and denied them in her waking life; yet they impelled her to seek support before it was too late. Now Lisa's dreams help in other ways: 'Some dreams urge me to try different ways of doing things, show me ways that I would not normally act. My unconscious demonstrates that there is a choice to be made and that I am not totally driven by past hurts. I feel so much more confident now.'

THE DREAM SERIES: SELF-REFLECTION

In *Dreams and the Growth of Personality*, Rossi describes dreams as a process of self-reflection in which the dreamer moves through a series of incrementally more involved stages. Dream series can represent movement from one level to another with all the attendant feelings that this may bring.

The first stage begins with no people or personal associations in the dream: 'A huge storm *threatened* the coast,' or 'Some sort of *fight* took place.' The threat and conflict are within the dreamer but she can't sense any relation between these inner dramas and affairs of her waking state. Usually the dreamer does not have meaningful associations to the dream. The client often needs an outside point of view to reflect back possible patterns and, as a counsellor, you can help the client make useful links:

> Dreams seem to show me how I feel about important people in my life, or issues or my own self in a very intense, symbolic fashion which can have a powerful effect on my conscious experience. For instance, I dreamt of my parents as cardboard cut-out type figures, they were totally silent or disinterested, just there. Eventually, as my dreams changed, I realised the 'message' coming from deep inside me about my feelings both early and recent, about their lack of real emotional support.

Using dreams in the therapeutic setting

In the second stage, people and personal associations are present but the dreamer is not. It seems as if the dreams spring out of nowhere, for instance, a dream might be 'My mother cleaned the room,' or 'My cat had four kittens.' With these dreams, by exploring the connections, new patterns of self-understanding can develop.

The third stage brings dreams in which the dreamer is completely caught up in the drama of the dream and they have no outside perspective on themselves in the dream state. The dream gives an accurate self-image of preoccupation which the dreamer recognises as being about his or her own life, their current concerns.

> I am with lots of people, usually friends, I have some big problem and am crying bitterly but no-one seems to notice and they speak to me as normal ... showed me I needed to be more open.

★

> ... being chased, also being attacked and raped. I always get knocked around but someone 'rescues' me just before intercourse takes place. I put this down to a natural fear of rape and trying to know how I would react.

At the fourth stage, the dreamer is present as an observer in the dream but takes no active part in its drama. These dreams represent the first stage of detachment, where an outside perspective or different level of awareness, necessary for self-reflection, takes place within the dream state itself.

Quite often at this stage, the dream 'observer' sees reflections through mirrors, studies photos or a series of pictures. Events may be witnessed with a detached attitude or from afar, as from a plane or the dreamer may be a visitor in a foreign country. Whatever imagery is involved, it is the sense of witnessing which is noteworthy. There is a distinct separation between the client's role as an observer and the essential drama of dream which reflects the inner workings of the psyche.

In the fifth stage there is soliloquy and dialogue in the dream. These may be spoken words or a printed statement; both are a classical form of self-reflection which show how things are being synthesised.

> . . . dreams about pregnancy — being afraid of being pregnant — refusing to deliver the baby ... one dream where I was pregnant and about to cross a river and I refused to cross the river until the baby was born. The whole dream was a stalemate because it was saying you won't deliver the baby unless you cross the river and me saying I won't cross until I've had it.

This dream shows not only two 'selves' but expands this further with the notion of the 'delivery' of a new baby — fresh potential, a new aspect of the dreamers' self. This person has been actively working with dreams for a number of years.

There may be two or more selves present in a dream. This can be an indication of a life crisis and represents multiple levels of awareness in pictorial form. The recognition of two or more levels of awareness in a dream is an indication of a psychologically 'talented' mentality. Individuals with this capacity for self-reflection generally have a good prognosis for in-depth psychotherapy.

At Rossi's sixth stage, multiple states of being happen within the dream. Each image of the dreamer represents a different state of being, and the interaction or dialogue between them are instances of self-reflection and change. This might involve physiognomic changes in the body, such as losing teeth or changing body shape, or different chronological states where different ages are represented within the dream, for example. Seeing ourselves at an earlier age may reflect the motivation for our current behaviour or show that earlier states of being are still active and need resolution or development.

Sometimes there are dreams of growing older, depicting developmental trends which can be continued or discarded. There may also be changes in feeling state, or role changes which may be symbolised by changes of dress, nudity dreams, or alterations in appearance generally.

In the 'room series' which follows, we see how development is shown in the change in position from frustration to awareness. It includes reflection and dialogue:

> ... recurring dreams about empty and unused rooms and blocked sensuality. There is always a man in the dream saying 'No' to me and the place which we are in, whether it be a flat or a house, has lots of unused space. The last dream I had in this series, or rather the last two ... first of the night ... the man was refusing me because his mother was around all the time ... so we stayed in the kitchen area as all the rest of the space was full of cobwebs and mostly empty of any furniture ... the next night his mother was French and understood such matters and I began to talk about taking over the empty rooms ... Basically these dreams are to do with creativity and the ways in which I have curtailed it because of other duties and responsibilities, like being a mother, and earning a living ... I have basically always said 'No' to what I want to do, other things are always more important ... I have a lot of guilt about spending time doing things which don't have an obvious financial or easily justifiable return. At the same time I begin to feel that I'm just spending my life ticking over and I become very frustrated because life seems to be about cleaning the house and working, that it has no point to it other than maintaining life.

THE SENOI APPROACH

The Senoi, a pre-literate tribe of people from Central Malaysia became famous for their dream work and their peaceful, co-operative and democratic culture where there was little crime and no mental illness. Though there has been some controversy about the authenticity of anthropological findings, the essence of the research points to a society in which dreams played a central role in both personal development and communal harmony. As we saw in Chapter 1, the Senoi sought power in their dreams and great emphasis was placed on children learning and growing through dreaming. If the dream of a Senoi child had not reached a satisfactory conclusion, they would be told to re-dream the dream the next night and would be taught to be aware of dreaming while doing so. Once the child was aware, in the dream, that they were dreaming — in effect, *lucid dreaming* — they were encouraged to confront and conquer any danger and even to demand a gift of the conquered enemy. (Within the confines of this book, lucid dreaming is covered more fully in Chapter Seven.)

Liz uses the Senoi technique of dream control: 'If I find myself falling, I say to myself, "you must not get hurt or wake up before you are safe." I find I control the outcome because if it is not favourable I will worry.'

In the Senoi dream approach, dreams of falling were seen as gifts from the gods and children were trained to let themselves fall and look for a gift or treasure which could be brought back to the community and used in waking life. They were further instructed in how to approach pleasure in dreams and find positive outcomes (intentional dreaming techniques are discussed fully in Chapter Five) and, though the dreams of Senoi children had largely the same emotional tone as children's dreams/nightmares anywhere, anthropologists found that by the time the Senoi reached adolescence there was a distinct absence of fear and anxiety in their dreams. For the Senoi, dreams were a great source of pleasure, creative inspiration and confidence, and through them they were able to exercise more control in their daily lives.

Gestalt psychodrama and guided imagery are an aid to rehearsing the dream changing process. When it is used, failure dreams are reduced and self-confidence enhanced:

> I have dreams in which tremendous fear is released as a safe
> context in which to be discharged. One thing chronicling
> my dreams has taught me is how kind they are, and how,
> even in the grips of innermost fear, I am not to run away but

to stay and learn its lesson. I know if I respect them they will not damage me and they will not put on more than I can bear.

PROJECTION

> I feel very good about my dreams. I try to analyse them since they seem to be telling me a lot. I find them fascinating, so simple, so imaginative. They tell me a lot about my inner conflicts, my state of mind, my fears and my projections onto other people.

Dreams are one method among many of communicating the unconscious fantasies, memories, projections, introjections and perceptions on which much psychological distress is founded. They help make emotional sense of our experiences and projection plays a central role in dreams, as it does in waking life. Frequently, emotions and attitudes are projected onto another person or object in much the same way as a film is projected onto a blank screen. However, unlike the screen, the object or person who acts as the 'holder' of the emotion also has meaning. In Gestalt work, all the people in the dream and all the features act as projections — that is, they are parts of the dreamer's own personality. As dreamers, we are the makers of the dream, and whatever we put into it must be what is inside us and therefore available for constructing the dream.

Dreams with 'projected dental aggression' are those which contain imagery of teeth which are dangerous or attacking. Introjectors, those people who hold back strong feelings when they are awake, are more likely to have dreams of dogs baring teeth, crocodiles or teeth in the vagina. Swedenborg had a series of dreams that preceded his conversion and images of anxiety and mistrust dogged him and fear of attack was everywhere. In one dream he was lying next to a woman and when he felt between her thighs he discovered that her vagina had a set of teeth.

Projection is also a defence mechanism. It is easier to project our own unacceptable feelings onto others rather than accept them as our own. By disowning them and putting them 'out there', we uphold the image of ourselves as 'good'.

FREE ASSOCIATION

Using this technique, the client takes each object, person and situation and freely associates to them, one at a time. To prompt them, you might ask what the element of the dream reminds you of or what comes to mind when you think of it. Encourage them to let their imagination go and their attention wander to come up with as many associations as possible. We should also encourage them to make uncensored responses; inevitably something will come up, perhaps a memory, an idea, a feeling. It may not tell you the 'meaning' of the dream but it will provide helpful pieces for the puzzle. Quite often the lightbulb 'Aha!' experience tells the client they have understood the message of the dream.

Free association allows a less habitualised, more fluent response to the dream and its meanings and helps to break the patterns of response so that the unplanned may come to the surface. The client is also encouraged to explore the unexpected aspects that come from the darkness and must be made a partner in the interpretations. This also helps to provide the tools for self-exploration so the 'expert' is not in the powerful position of doling out answers and acting as the authority in all matters.

FREE WRITING

Free writing is free associating on a piece of paper. The client writes down stream-of-consciousness reactions to their dream. They start anywhere and just keep writing whatever comes to mind. Advise the client not to censor or edit anything out but to record everything they are thinking and feeling. If they get stuck, they should simply write 'I'm stuck, I'm stuck' over and over again until a new association comes up and they can write freely again.

Each element of the dream can be written on a separate piece of paper and a stream of consciousness recorded for each one. Each element is then compared in terms of similarities and patterns, key images or emotional tone. It is useful to hold on to this writing so it can be referred back to at a later date. Days or weeks later something that was missed the first time around may come become visible in the light of new dream work.

DAY RESIDUE

People, things or events from the previous day that get incorporated into a dream are there for a reason. They spark off ideas, feelings and memories in the unconscious and if clients examine thoughts and feelings about these events it will help them understand their dream and why it is 'commenting' on these events.

> Dreams inspire me in my daily life; help me to overcome violence and pain from the past; sometimes when life has been particularly difficult a dream has raised my spirits so much so that I've been woken by the sound of myself laughing in my sleep.

DREAM INTANGIBLES

There is a tendency to focus just on objects, events and people in a dream, but there is more to the dream than that. Consider:

~ *feeling tone.* What is the primary feeling in the dream. What does it remind the client of? Does the feeling tone change at different points in the dream? Why?

~ *colours.* How are colours used in the dream? What feelings and meanings might be associated with them? What do the colours remind the client of?

~ *time and space.* How are time and space used in the dream? What feelings do these create? Is the dream communicating an idea by how it uses time and space?

~ *missing and vague parts.* What parts of the dream are vague or unclear? Is something missing that should be there? These might be the points where dream censorship by ego is at its strongest so it is useful to focus on these parts — there is something important going on there. Use free association and the other techniques described above to fill in the gaps. If there is a vague part to the dream, try to catch whatever details are available. For example, if the client can't remember a person in the dream, can they remember what they were wearing, the colour of their eyes, the colour of their hair? What does this remind them of?

CONNECTIONS BETWEEN DREAMS

Dreams are often connected to each other and there may be similar patterns or themes across them. Are the dreams progressing or changing somehow over time as we saw in the room series earlier? This might indicate something about the client that is changing over time. Pay particular attention to recurring dreams since these are repeated messages for the dreamer and they point to a persistent theme or issue in life. They may indicate some 'unfinished business'. How are the recurring dreams similar to each other? And how do they differ?

> Sometimes my dreams are symbolic of feelings that I am having, as in the following dream. I dreamt that I had a small pinprick in my finger that was bothering me. I located it and as I pulled it out, it turned into a huge thorn that wouldn't quite come out. Drops of blood were dripping very slowly from it. At the time I was depressed and under therapy.

It is interesting to note that Selene was beginning to pinpoint where some of her problems lay. The therapeutic, healing blood is dripping slowly and not gushing forth, showing steady progress.

Frequently important 'core' dreams come in pairs that complement and clarify each other. Their proximity can reveal a new direction, a new way of being and understanding. Recurring dreams are highly significant because in a repetitive dream the client reiterates, over and over, their symbolic statement of the core difficulty.

OPPOSITES

Remember that the unconscious thinking that affects a dream is unusual and illogical by conscious standards; things can mean exactly the opposite of what they seem to mean. Something the client fears in the dream may be something unconsciously wished for. There may be contradictions which suggest the dreamer has conflicting feelings about an issue.

Try *exaggerating* some important aspect of the dream. Help the client to amplify the feeling, action or situation in the dream. Take it to the limit and make it as intense as possible. Where does this take the client? In order to understand messages from the unconscious, Jung advocated the use of what he termed **amplification**. This involves taking each symbol, image or figure and expanding on it by thinking of any connection or associations that the dreamer has.

Try *reversing* the important elements in the dream. Turn them into the opposite feelings, behaviours, or characteristics. Does this ring any bells? Does it change the meaning of the dream?

IMPASSE

At some point in working on a dream the client will get stuck. This is an impasse, a barrier. It means that they may have to take a different perspective on the dream or reorganise their thinking. Another tack is to get the client to immerse him or herself into that stuckness. Keep with it and eventually the client will be able to break through to a new level of understanding. If they are *really* stuck and frustrated, it may be best to set the dream aside and come back to it later. Let it rest in the back of the mind. Look at other dreams instead for they may help make that breakthrough.

LETTING THE DREAM REST

Some processes, like dreams and creativity, need to be left to work on their own to some extent. It is possible to abort the whole dream work process by analysing too deeply, too soon. Leaving the dream to rest is a form of gestation which has its own inner logic and timing. One client who had had therapy using psychosynthesis felt that the dogmatic approach was too invasive: '... sometimes therapy felt like tearing the child out of the womb before it was fully matured and ready to be birthed. I found that while I was in therapy I became neurotic and guilt ridden, suspicious of any symbols or ideas or drawings which I produced, as if they all contained some dark and dire secret that was best kept hidden ... I guess that I'd ingested a very Freudian view of creativity as sublimation, and although I would have denied this at the time, psychosynthesis also holds this view ... that art is somehow a substitute for real life and conscious knowing.'

> I find that dreams bring me up against myself, my true feelings about myself and other people, and my ambivalence about my dreams at present is due very much to this, a not wanting to see.

ACTIVE IMAGINATION
In this process, the dreamer is encouraged to relax or go into a meditative state and let the imagination work on the dream: it is dreaming the dream in the waking state. Questions can act as prompts, for example: What happens next? or: If you continue along the path, who or what can you see? (This process is covered in more depth in Chapter 7.)

COMPENSATION
Pamela said that her dreams fit into this category because:

> I live vividly at night. Without my dreams life would be dull and lonely; the quieter my life is, the more vivid the dreams ...
>
> I often dream of an abundance of food. I never realised this until I started writing my dreams down. I took note from this and started feeding myself better and learning to cook better ...
>
> Very often I go out of my way to have a dream about something or someone I particularly like. I do this usually

when I am feeling a little depressed. I have lived alone for many years and find the company of people in my dreams to be beneficial. I do find dreams comforting.

Jung was the first to point out that as a person increases in psychological health, they will tend to take a more active role in their dreams:

Being an introvert I find my dreams about confronting people helpful, as in reality I would not approach them; the dream eases the frustration.

THE BENEFITS OF USING DREAMS IN COUNSELLING

Using dreams can shorten the length of time spent in working with a client because it facilitates the revelation of unconscious conflicts quite readily and can directly relieve the symptoms that brought the client to therapy in the first place. Because of the empowering nature of dream work, it reduces dependency and regression and redirects energy towards creativity.

Gill Harvant in *The Life Context of the Dreamer and the Setting of Dreaming* highlights the critical role played by the life context of the dreamer and the setting of dreaming in the formation and interpretation of dreams. She suggests that we dream not to express repressed childhood wishes but to experience the repressed aspects of currently active developmental conflicts that are the stuff of our life context. It is a view that was supported by Karen Horney who considered the dream as a truthful holistic expression of her patients' current conflicts and as evidence of the dreamer's way of coping with them, whether constructively or destructively. My own work with clients certainly supports this view, as we see from Zarah's comments:

They shed light on what my subconscious is up to which has recently become important to me because this is an area I've started exploring in psychotherapy. They allow me to look at different aspects of myself which I would either avoid or not consider in the same way. They also trigger off associations which are important to me ... My dreams are particularly long and vivid. I am now having psychoanalysis and am told that they are punitive dreams. I do wish I didn't dream so much as it impairs my sleep and leaves me very fatigued. On the other hand, now that I am working with the dreams I do find them rather fascinating and wonder what is coming next.

DREAMS OF THE THERAPIST

I feel very good about my dreams. I try to analyse them since they seem to be telling me a lot. I find them fascinating, so simple, so imaginative. They tell me a lot about my inner conflicts, my state of mind, my fears and my projections onto other people.

Not surprisingly, clients dream of the therapist and the therapeutic process. Sometimes this is disguised whilst at other it is quite plain to see. In this example, Eva had a series of recurring dreams about cars — driving them, cars that were being driven away, cars out of control and so on. She told me of one she had at the onset of therapy: 'I had a dream about a car that was stopped — it wasn't clear what was wrong with it, it was just still. I went to ask for help at this house, this woman came out, she was very well dressed, perfumed and very feminine. We found a hole under the back wheels of the car which was full of old rubbish, old clothes and odds and ends of different sorts. The car was over a great hole in the road — in a sense the foundations of the car, the road, was unsound, and needed to be cleared out before I could proceed on my journey, and to enable me to have a safe and smooth ride.'

What struck the dreamer so forcibly was that the woman who came out of the house was an apt description of her therapist. 'She looked like she couldn't or wouldn't get her hands dirty,' and part of Eva wondered if her therapist could handle all the 'garbage' that was being uncovered.

Using dreams in the therapeutic setting

I once found a nightmare helpful. Just after beginning therapy, I had a dream about being tricked and raped. This definitely related to my fear of my therapist as well as past relationships.

Sometimes clients hesitate to discuss dreams lest they upset their therapist. Dee's doubts about her therapist were confirmed when she had a dream in which she was driving or being driven in a car. Somehow her therapist was involved, and Dee realised that they had taken a wrong turning and she was 'being led up the garden path'. This reflected the lack of a therapeutic alliance between the two and shortly afterwards she changed therapists.

FAMILY THERAPY

Dreams can be used to increase communication within families and as an aid in diagnosis and treatment since they help to explain the unconscious elements of family life. The dreams brought to sessions are pictures of feelings and guides to the emotional dynamics operating on each individual in a family system and can be of special value with families who block communication or only appear to be co-operative. Dreams are sensitive instruments to use in uncovering the dreamer's approach to coping with conflicts, whether constructively or destructively, and deciphering the dream helps to open up new possibilities in communication.

I use them as a regular way of contacting myself, and receiving guidance. I work through each dream noting down any connections it makes with what I am thinking about or doing at that time. I find that just writing and noticing them helps them to work up from my unconscious into consciousness. They help to integrate ideas from books I read or any therapy and help me see what I might overlook. Dreams draw us towards the unconscious roots of the problem. They allow the right brain to speak to us, if we will listen to it, as an equally valid counterpoint to all the 'normal' left brain, intellectual, patriarchal stuff we otherwise would treat as being 'reality'.

EMPOWERMENT

Clients can be empowered if they can accept that they create their dreams and that this includes the plot, the setting, the cast of characters, the mood and everything else involved in it. They are in sole charge and so it seems reasonable that they will appreciate and be capable of understanding their dream better than anyone else. The counsellor or therapist who assists is really the lantern bearer to help illuminate the territory.

> My dreams often remind me of things I have to do. When a problem has been solved satisfactorily then the dreams about it cease. I did not take much notice of my dreams before I had psychotherapy. It would have been almost impossible on my own. My therapist said that the healing would continue and my anxiety dreams would gradually decrease.

One of the great pleasures in working with dreams in therapy is the way in which clients come to value the potential of dreams and become empowered to use their own skills of investigation and interpretation which they can use outside the therapy sessions and when therapy has ended. The comments from two clients express this:

> Since using my dreams in psychotherapy I now feel able to study them myself and see what is on my mind. My dreams point to my real feelings about a situation and can lead my thoughts on to a possible solution to a problem.

★

> Dreams are my balances. I've found that if ever I ask for a dream to help me to begin a new project or make a difficult decision, a dream full of useful imagery will come the following night.

Dreams also help clients look at problems which they find difficult to face head on. Their subtle nature helps clients to address difficulties more tangentially, allowing space for gentle approaches, the unveiling of emotions rather than the blunt 'in your face' presentation that can take place with other methods. As Dwayne said: 'Dreams have helped to move me on when talking around it hasn't helped ... All dreams are acts of love in that they are a uniting of energies. I am always full of gratitude to them.'

The dreamer as scriptwriter. Once the dreamer sees him or herself as the talent behind their dream scenarios, they can begin to ask themselves questions:

~ Why did I choose the cave?

~ Why is the weather so bleak?

~ What am I trying to say here?

~ What is the purpose of putting X here?

~ Why is there so little light?

By exploring the dream elements, we can find a greater awareness of the import of the dream.

The dreamer chooses the mood. Fear, joy, despair or bewilderment, the dreamer sets the emotional climate. What do these moods reflect of waking life? What memories do they evoke? When did the client feel like this before? What response does the emotional climate bring? Does fear bring reassurance? What is this mood communicating about waking feelings that are concealed from the glare of daylight? Encourage the dreamer to assume that there are no accidental aspects, no coincidences; rather, there is a purpose for every bit, each offers a clue to the meaning.

Each dream has a purpose and, as Delayney points out in *Living Your Dreams*: 'Almost all dreams offer to assist the dreamer in the business of living and ... dreams are anything but neutral to the dreamer's welfare.'

Draw the dream. By drawing or painting the dream, the dreamer may find a deeper level of understanding and discover that they have emphasised parts which they were minimising previously. This is a very fruitful way of working on dreams 'out there', that is, with their own external existence.

> I believe my therapy sessions are influencing my dreams, making them more vivid. I am noticing a closer connection between the dreaming phenomenon and the occurrence of symbols and images during waking hours.

PROBLEM-SOLVING

Though we will consider problem-solving dreams in greater depth in Chapter 7, it is useful to remind ourselves briefly here that the stuff of dreams is concerned with the resolution of difficulties, be they about mind, body, spirit or day–to–day life.

> I used to ask for a dream when I was in my early teens and pre-puberty. If I had a problem I used to sleep on it, and sleep walk. Often I would wake up either with the problem solved or at least with some peace of mind; my cousin, who is a year older than me, used to solve mathematical problems in her sleep. My aunt recounts how she would walk around muttering to herself, having gone to sleep with some problem in her maths homework unresolved and would wake in the morning with a resolution.

This concerns the problem-solving side of our minds and the self-healing potential of the organism which is us.

> I decided many years ago to invent myself. I had obviously been invented by someone else — by a whole society — and I didn't like their invention.
>
> (Maya Angelou)

SYMBOLISM IN DREAMS

Symbolism is important because so many dreams will carry information in symbolic form. Dream symbols are like metaphors and similes in speech; they are multi-dimensional and can express so much more than mere words. There is no universal dictionary of dream symbols because each person has a unique view of the world and so there can never be singular, agreed meanings. However, various symbols can be taken to represent the same thing, for instance, running away, getting lost, missing the bus, all prevent further progress so relate to frustration at some level.

There are certain aspects of symbolism in dream work that you should look out for. Firstly, where symbols are repeated, the client is reiterating a symbolic account of his or her core issue. We find this particularly where there has been trauma, as you will see in the next chapter; indeed, in Chapter 4, we examine post-traumatic stress disorder (PTSD) of which recurring nightmares are symptomatic.

Changing symbolism often indicates an alteration in the dreamer's outlook: houses in disrepair become weatherproof; neglected dream babies become bonny; gloomy skies change to sun-drenched dawns. Where this happens it can give a real boost to clients who have felt stuck, which is another reason why clients are encouraged to keep a dream journal. Also, each person gradually builds up a personal glossary of symbols which encompasses his or her own 'vocabulary' derived from personal experience.

> Now that I have been working on my dreams I have found that dirty water indicates a problem, if it is deep dirty water then it is a big problem.

> *

> When I'm off colour or ill I have my childhood dream of giant letters of the alphabet chasing me to a low brick wall. I never get to climb over. Often this is accompanied by a

53

feeling of sandpaper on my skin. I know walls represent obstacles in my life.

CONTINUING PERSONAL DEVELOPMENT

It is always helpful for therapists and counsellors to work on their own dreams. You may find the following list of questions helpful (adapted from *The Jungian–Senoi Dreamwork Manual* by Strephon Kaplan-Williams, where you will find a much more exhaustive list of such questions, and from my own book, *Women Dreaming*):

~ How am I, the dream ego, acting in this dream? (aggressive, assertive, passive, active, etc.)

~ What are the various feelings/emotions in the dream? (both 'mine' and those of other characters)

~ What is the context of the dream? (what is going on in my life right now that could link to the dream?)

~ In the dream, who are the main characters?

  ~ Who (or what) is the adversary?

  ~ Who (or what) is being attacked?

  ~ Who (or what) is being healed?

  ~ Who (or what) is my companion or helper?

  ~ Did I dream of actual or imaginary people?

  ~ Could the characters all be different aspects of myself?

~ What are the outstanding features or symbols in the dream? (for example, fire, animals, cars, and so on). And how might these relate to me, my emotions, or my life?

~ How does the dream as a whole relate to my personality?

~ What are the main actions in the dream?

~ What would I like to avoid in the dream?

~ What does the dream want from me? What actions might it be suggesting that I consider?

~ Does the dream trigger any memories? Do any of the elements of the dream relate to my past? Why might this part of my past be called to my attention now?

~ Why did I need this dream? What is its positive message for me?

THE ISAKOWER PHENOMENON

Finally, before we leave the methodology of dream work, a consideration of something which may crop up and which can cause clients distress.

There are a number of unusual phenomena which can startle the dreamer and, though they are mistakenly linked to dreams, the explanations lie elsewhere — in the physiological activity of our bodies. The junction between sleep and wakefulness, like some transitional station in a journey when we change one train for another, is often the zone where such strange activity occurs. For example, a distortion of body image; a blurring of distinctions between internal and external sensations or where we feel invaded by some inexplicable terror. Isakower, a research scientist, offered an explanation, but first listen to one description of the terror that this dream-like state can induce:

> I cannot remember when I developed an interest in dreams, but perhaps it goes back years to my childhood when I had some terrifying nightmares. One recurring nightmare I used to have was when I was about three or four years old and at the time I did not realise that it was a nightmare but thought it was actually happening. It used to occur every single night and I was absolutely terrified of going to bed because I knew it was going to happen. I would get into bed and be terrified of falling asleep. Anyway, this is what I dreamt, but I must stress that I did not believe it was a dream at the time. Everything was very dark in my bedroom and a terrible, evil and frightening force would come to visit me each night. At the time in my own mind as a child, although I never told anybody, I believed this force to be the Devil. I could actually feel a great weight always pressing down into my

stomach and as soon as this happened I wanted to scream 'Mummy!' I opened my mouth but no sound would come out. I felt as scared and trapped as if this force was preventing me from shouting. I cannot stress how terrified I was at the time — I thought I might die. However, after trying several times to start running, the words and the sounds came, I could cry and my mother would come. All I could tell her, or she could tell me, was that I had a bad dream.

Now, all these years later, I have noticed that I cannot sleep with a hot water bottle on, or near my stomach, as it brings on this childhood nightmare. The water bottle is like the force that was pressing down on my stomach and brings on the dream. So even now, if I ever have a water bottle it never gets near my stomach but always stays at my feet because I am scared of having the dream again. I wonder if there is anything you can make of this?

Thea was both puzzled and in fear of her 'dream'. First impressions might almost be of a description of sexual abuse but as there was no evidence that this could have happened and, because of the family arrangements during her childhood, she ruled it out. Instead it appears to be an example of the Isakower phenomenon.

This phenomenon involves hypnagogic sensations associated with falling asleep. Isakower compared the feeling of a 'doughy' mass approaching from outside the body or filling the mouth cavity to the aura of epilepsy and to *déjà vu*. Such night terrors, where the dreamer feels unable to move or shout yet feels a terrifying threat, are in part the result of sleep paralysis caused by a dysfunction of the reticular activating system of the brain. One in twelve people have experienced this, which explains why so many people have described it to me. In this case, this is not a dream diagnosis of impending physical or mental breakdown but a dysfunctional aspect of the individual's personal wiring system. Night terrors, such as these, are more to do with the physiology of sleep than dreams.

Rosemary was eight years old when she had her most frightening 'dream': 'There were trees and enormous plants grasping at me, trying to hold me, trying to kill me,' she told me. She was so distressed by the terror that, though she woke up, the dream carried on like an hallucination. She screamed but still the images continued until her mother arrived. Her mother, in turn, was terrified by her daughter, apparently wide awake yet staring wildly into space and screaming to be rescued from strangling plants!

Rosemary only had night terrors when she had a fever and the time of the 'strangling plants' was when she was incubating chickenpox. Like most children, she outgrew this immature physical response and has no trouble at all now. However, it can continue in adults, especially where there is heightened stress. If this is the case then relaxation techniques, meditation or counselling may help to reduce the stress level.

CHAPTER 3

DREAM DIAGNOSIS

The study of dreams is currently going through a rebirth as more and more research reveals the essential links between mind and body, *psyche* and *soma*. As the science of psycho-neuro-immunology (PNI) — the study of how the mind affects the neurological system which in turn influences the immune system — develops, dreams may take their rightful place in the therapeutic panoply. PNI shows how mind and body are inextricably linked.

Our minds can have an amazingly powerful effect in strengthening the immune system. We now know that if a person is upset, feeling down and so on, the efficiency of the immune system is reduced and vulnerability to disease increased. An article in the British medical journal, *The Lancet*, reported that people who had been treated for depression and who were followed up five years later were found to have suffered twice as many heart attacks as those who had not, demonstrating how low mood can compromise good health. On the other hand, as we know from the work of Candace Pert, feeling loved and loving others stimulates our immune system and helps us fight off disease. In the case of cancer, for example, white blood cells can be stimulated to mobilise against the invasive cancerous cells. Caroline Myss in *Why People Don't Heal and How They Can*, says: 'Our biography becomes our biology.' The way we live and how we manage our emotions influence mind, body and spirit.

THE YELLOW EMPEROR

In *The Yellow Emperor's Classic of Internal Medicine* (*circa* 2696 BC), believed to be the oldest medical book still in existence, there is a section devoted to dreams and their relationship to illness. Any consultation about illness at that time would certainly have included a description of the patient's dreams. Patricia Garfield in *The Healing Power of Dreams* explained the Chinese approach:

> In the Chinese system, health is regarded as harmony or balance between two forces: 'yin' and 'yang'; disharmony brings disease and possibly death ...Yang is the more active force — fiery, hot and dry; yin is the more passive force — watery, wet and cool. To be healthy, according to this tradition, one must have these two powers in balance.... Applying these ideas to dreams, the ancient Chinese said that dreams of 'wading through great waters which cause bad fears' indicate that 'yin is flourishing' ... dreams of excessive water indicate too much fluid is present in the body (too much yin) and there is a lack of vital energy (too little yang).

Translated into modern research we can see a link, for researchers have observed dreams of drowning in great waters among heart patients whose water retention is excessive — or, in Chinese medicine terms, where yin is flourishing. We will see more later in this chapter of the ways in which dreams inform us symbolically of physical illness.

In dreams we can be given signals about bodily changes in very subtle ways. As early as 1913, William Stekel talked of 'endopsychic awareness' meaning that the mind–body knows of events to come in our physical and mental life long before overt signs are apparent. He commented in the preface to Freud's *The Interpretation of Dreams* (1943): 'I have found the dream to be an infallible mirror of the sick mind,' and tells us that 'premonition' dreams are fairly common during the incubation period of severe infectious disorders.

PRODOMIC OR DIAGNOSTIC DREAMS

Great importance was attached to such diagnostic dreams in

earlier times. The Hippocratic texts on which Western medical traditions are based advise that 'accurate knowledge of the signs which occur in dreams will be very valuable for all purposes.' The example that follows shows just how valuable.

THE LIFE-SAVING X-RAY

Ten years ago, Sophia suffered a series of persistent, low-grade infections which left her fatigued and hardly able to cope:

> I instinctively knew that there was some underlying problem which was causing all these non-specific symptoms, but my doctor disagreed and treated each incidence of infection with antibiotics. He said that my other symptoms were psychosomatic and eventually prescribed valium, which I didn't want to take. I'd almost begun to believe that I might need a psychiatrist when I had a visualising dream of great vividness.
>
> I 'saw' my own skull as blue and translucent, almost like an X-ray but with greater living detail, down to the pulsing of the veins. I could see a glowing turquoise 'hole' in the middle of my head, down behind and below my eyes. I knew that I was being shown the cause or site of my illness.

The dream's intensity galvanised Sophia into action. She changed her doctor, insisted on a thorough investigation and was immediately referred to a consultant at King's College Hospital, London. He arranged for X-rays and a CAT scan which showed a benign tumour on the pituitary gland: 'on the base of the brain,' Sophia said. 'I didn't have any idea where the "base of the brain" was until I saw the X-rays. I could see the tumour clearly sited below and behind my eyes, exactly where it had been in my dream.'

After successful chemotherapy Sophia is healthier now than she ever was before the dream pinpointed the source of the problem which had eluded her doctor for years. Together, dreamer and physician solved the puzzle and treated the tumour successfully. Anyone working in a therapeutic setting needs to pay heed to this important dimension of their clients' dreams.

When clients like Sophia talk about their dreams it is important to be alert to their diagnostic and predictive potential. Some clients need reassurance that they are not 'going mad' when such dreams occur; they may link them to the occult, witchcraft or unfathomable magic powers and in their fear they may reject important communication from the body. Where this is the case, it is helpful to explain the concept of 'inner knowledge' and the power of the mind–body link. They may be reassured by the highly respected, and conservative, *British Medical Journal* in 1997, where it was reported that 'dreams may reflect the presence of organic disease ... even when the patient is unaware of it.'

When a person has a highly intense dream, it very often colours their mood for the whole of the next day if not longer. Such preoccupation is common and clients who bring this type of dream need to have enough time to work through its various elements and its emotional tone. In a way the dreamer is spellbound by the intensity of the dream and cannot be free until he or she finds the key that unlocks it.

There are many recorded cases of dream healing in chronic illness. Arthritis, which is linked to emotional tension and stress as well as organic causes, is manifested in joint inflammation. Theodore Tihansky discusses the case of a fifty-nine-year-old unmarried woman with a history of twenty-four years of gradually progressive arthritis which did not respond to traditional treatment. Through hypnoanalysis and dream interpretation the woman realised that she had assumed the identity of her placid mother. While her anger and tension remained pent up, her physical problems became more pronounced. This realisation of her own mis-identity enabled her to express her feelings and her physical symptoms disappeared.

Remedies may be illuminated in dreams which in waking reality have left consultants in the dark. A woman client, Heather, told how a recent dream offered her a solution to a problem that had defeated various ophthalmic experts. For months she had been having 'dry eyes' and no one had offered an explanation or cure. Then one night she dreamt that the cause was directly linked to breast-feeding her baby. Certain the dream had come up with the correct diagnosis, she went back to her doctor and told him about the dream. He at last made the connection between breast-feeding, dry eyes and dehydration which he, as well as the consultants, had overlooked previously. The dream revealed the cause and the remedy was quite clear.

George's dream involved his consultant. He had had an eye operation that had not been as successful as had been expected and remedial treament was underway. 'I had frequent appointments with the Consultant,' he told me, 'but nothing improved. One night I dreamed that I was walking home through the snow with the Consultant and when we still had a way to go he said something like: "I can't go any further with you now you will have to go the rest of the way on your own." When I woke I realised there was no hope of my eye improving and that I should have to get on with life as it was.'

Our bodies also incorporate physical changes into dream symbolism and the inner wisdom of dreams, so uniquely personal, illuminates all aspects of our psychological, physical and spiritual health. Others have warnings of impending illness:

> My dreams are more bizarre and sinister when I am unwell. When I had meningo–encephalitis at the age of forty they were so vivid that they haunted me for some time.

SUBLIMINAL CLUES

Penfield and others have demonstrated that the brain retains many memories not available to the conscious mind. Amongst these are subliminal experiences which have not been consciously thought about or registered in waking perception. In spite of this, they are still woven into dreams. This is sometimes known as the *Poetzl* phenomenon.

Elizabeth has been married for forty years and has believed in listening to her dream messages, though sometimes she feels confused as to who she is dreaming for:

> I continually dreamt that someone was telling me to take life easier, that I was overdoing things, but it was my husband who suddenly burst an artery, which was undoubtedly precipitated by a period of great stress at work. He lived for five weeks and at one time, when he was unconscious in hospital, I dreamt that we were sunbathing. An odd dream as neither of us was in the habit of sunbathing. It was a lovely dream, warm and peaceful. My husband asked me to put some sun cream on his back. As I did so, he suddenly flinched. I looked and saw a red angry patch on his shoulder blade and said, 'You're burnt.' The next day I went to hospital and managed to look at the shoulder blade. He had a nasty bed sore there which the staff had not spotted.

Subliminally, she had picked up non-verbal clues from her husband and the dream had translated them for her.

EARLY-WARNING SYSTEM: CANCER

Finding a lump in your breast is a waking nightmare. Having a dream about finding a lump in your breast can also be a nightmare, with the saving grace that it can give the dreamer information long before there is any waking evidence of a tumour. This was so for Judi who woke up convinced she had a lump in her breast because of a disturbing dream. Initially she was relieved when, on self-examination, she couldn't find anything abnormal, though the dream had been quite specific regarding the position of the lump. Throughout the day, however, she couldn't get the dream out of her mind. She decided to have a bath. 'Whilst I was drying myself,' she said, 'I felt the lump where I dreamed it was but when I felt again I couldn't find it, but because of the dream I knew something wasn't right.'

Judi made an appointment to see her GP that evening. He finally confirmed her suspicions. Two days later she had a lumpectomy. 'The surgeon congratulated me on finding the lump so early,' she said. 'I told him that if it hadn't been for the dream I wouldn't have had any idea about it.'

This dream certainly alerted Judi and pushed her to seek the help her body needed — but why the dream? How do we get information from dreams that we are not aware of in waking life? The answers are quite simple yet complex at the same time. Basically the mind–body connection is so inextricably melded that our sleeping mind recognises the physical and mental distress which we may be blind to when awake. Not that such denial is deliberate of course, sometimes we are completely unaware of signs or symptoms of disease, as Judi was, whilst at other times we have an inkling, a vague awareness that something is amiss but we do not really want to accept the implications, we don't want to face the fear that the subtle symptoms present. Yet dreams confront us with such knowledge precisely because it can enhance our well-being at so many different levels. Dreams are part of our survival repertoire.

REPEATED DREAM WARNINGS

Marie had a series of dreams about people dying from cancer and recently discovered that there are pre-cancerous cells in her cervix. She is about to have a minor operation and told me that her dreams forced her to recognise her high level of anxiety which she actively avoided facing when awake. Marie's dreams focused her attention on the whole issue of cancer and persuaded her to have the smear test she had previously cancelled. When there is a linked series of dreams with a recurring theme as Marie had, it is important to consider the significance of the dream message. Repetition is a way of continually bringing the dreamer back to the central message of the dream until the core issue is addressed.

When clients present with recurring dreams it is important to ask when the dreams began and try to discern any pattern in their occurrence. Do they happen at only one time of the year, for instance, or whenever the client is experiencing emotional difficulties? If such a pattern is not immediately apparent, ask the client to keep a record, as described in Chapter 2, and note both the dream and any significant waking events that happened around the time of the dream. In my experience, such links are readily apparent after a short time and this gives enormous comfort to clients. Once they recognise that dreams are linked to physiological changes they no longer feel hounded by inexplicable fear and ignorance. In fact, they can then use their dreams as a barometer of physical and emotional health.

For two years now Harriet has not been able to work full-time. Following a viral infection she developed ME which severely restricted her ability to work as a full-time college lecturer. Now, whenever her energy levels are especially low her dreams repeat the same motif:

> I dream that I am back at work full-time — this might be in a bar, a restaurant, in an office, anywhere in fact that I have ever worked — and I simply cannot cope. For example, I arrive at 4 p.m. instead of 9 a.m. I wonder where I am or what I am supposed to do; occasionally, like the other night, I dream I am roaming the streets totally confused and upset as if I am prematurely senile.

What Harriet has learned by recording her dreams and paying attention to them is that ones which are fraught with anxiety precede a period of nervous exhaustion in which she needs very deep sleep for a long period, fourteen hours following that last dream. Gradually her energy levels climb and the anxious dreams fade. There may be even earlier warning dreams and if Harriet can track them, they could notify her that she needs to rest earlier and so avoid the total exhaustion that dogs her at present.

If clients keep a record of their dreams, eventually patterns emerge either in the dream themes or the timing of certain types of dreams. Once linked to the waking state clients can see how dreams can help to prepare for, or avoid, times of stress and illness. Focus on recurring dreams to enable the client to resolve the issues that cause them.

During the first few weeks of her pregnancy, Jane had a

recurring dream which disturbed all sense of well-being. In it there was a man with a knife and there was a big white towel which was soaked in blood. The rest of the details were vague but nevertheless, Jane was filled with an awful dread. Unsure whether the dream was triggered by her anxiety about her first pregnancy or had a more ominous meaning, she told no one of her fears. When she had a spontaneous abortion eleven weeks later she was not surprised. She was upset and miserable but not shocked. Part of her had known that something was wrong, her distressing dreams permeated her waking thoughts and, in a way, prepared her for the loss. The purity of the white towel was destroyed in her dream by the raw blood, whilst assault was threatened by the knife. Such a dream could be prompted by something other than a threatened miscarriage, but Jane's inner awareness of the meaning of the dream stayed with her.

How much more bearable that time might have been if Jane could have talked to someone about her dream. All too often, dreams are kept secret because others don't listen or say that dreams don't mean anything, let alone reveal what might happen. Yet, I have found over years of working with people that their dreams hold the key to what is important to them. When we share the dream we often touch the essence of life itself which is why using dreams in therapy is so important. Sometimes too, we must listen for the warnings. As Susan Bach, a doctor who specialised in holistic approaches to treating life-threatening illnesses, writes: 'Dreams ... reflect the total situation of the human person. I have come to see in decades of clinical work, that through the [drawing of] spontaneous pictures and of dreams something shines through, which I have called "inner knowingness".' You may well come across this 'inner knowingness' in your own work with clients.

DIAGNOSTIC DOUBTS

The pressure on hospital staff, combined with their own desire to make patients well as quickly as possible sometimes leads to mis-diagnosis or to an overenthusiastic rush to surgery. This happened to Carla. However, a pair of dreams caused her to doubt whether

her body needed what the consultant prescribed and she rebelled. She described her dreams:

> The first dream I had was of my Grandmother. I was frantically searching for a special 'Get Well' card for her because she was ill, I don't know what kind of card I was searching for but I could not find it and it caused me great concern. A few nights later I had a second dream where I was ill in hospital. I had to have an anaesthetic and died during the operation due to incompetence on the part of the anaesthetist.

These two dreams were extremely vivid though Carla did not put too much emphasis on them until a few days later when she was taken into hospital as an emergency admission with abdominal pain. She had been feeling perfectly well prior to her admission. The doctor queried an ectopic pregnancy or pelvic inflammation and after a series of tests wanted to take her to theatre to operate. However, Carla, because of the dream, would not consent and, as she told me: 'became so emotional about the whole thing, I'm sure they thought they had a real crackpot on their hands.' Withstanding the pressure of the medical staff was a feat in itself, but because she would not sign the consent form, they grudgingly started her on antibiotics and put her on bed rest for five days. Her symptoms disappeared, the swabs were all clear and she was fully recovered on her return home in less than a week.

Though she found the dream frightening Carla is grateful that she listened to the 'warning' of the dream. And while she still can't explain it, she is willing to believe that some inner awareness 'knew' that she did not need an operation, even before she had any overt symptoms and at a time when she had no conscious inkling that she that she was going to be rushed into hospital only days later. The mind–body connection, the *psyche–soma* bond, sensed at a deeper level that something was amiss.

In working with clients it is important to respect the validity of their experience. Carrie felt her dreams were not really listened to by any of her family and she was never asked about them by any physician she saw. She said: 'When I was in my early teens I had a dream about cancer. Basically, I was on a train and was for some reason trying desperately to get off the train but I couldn't. The reason for this was because I was attached to a huge thing that filled nearly all the carriage I was in; it was a yellow, pus-filled, onion shaped thing, and it was cancer.' About five or six years later, she had to go to have an MRI scan on her head and neck and was diagnosed with tumours in her skull base and a lymph gland in her neck. Carrie's treatment involved radiotherapy along with counselling: 'I'm still here six years later.'

Carrie is in no doubt about the inner wisdom of her dreams. 'I have often thought that maybe our subconscious is much more aware of our body than our conscious, on a "deeper" level.' In revisiting her dream records and diaries of her teens, she found the shapes and symbolism in her spontaneous art were very specifically related to her cancers. 'The fact that in my younger years I always felt my right was better than my left, and all three cancers I had were on the left-hand side of my body. Up until the last few years — I am twenty-six now — from the age of nine or ten, I always hated the shape of hips, that is, the natural shape of my bone structure. My third cancer turned up in my left hip-bone.'

Hartmann (1998) confirms that the emotional impact of physical illness may become apparent in dreams before the waking patient is aware of illness. He quotes the story of a man who was waiting for vascular surgery on his leg. He was afraid of losing the leg and had dream images of defective tools or other defective objects in eleven of fourteen recorded pre-operative dreams.

SICKENING STRESS

Scientific research has shown that intense stress following bereavement or trauma weakens the immune system and can lead to many illnesses, including cancer. Not everyone who has been faced with major stress will develop a serious illness, of course; we all have different thresholds and susceptibilities. However, as we have already seen, there is compelling scientific data to show that how we feel can influence our body's ability to ward off illness. In one sense, this is not new because people have always known of the body–mind link. We talk of people who have died of a broken heart. We say: 'She was never the same after it happened,' recognising the power of emotion to make or break health. But now science is proving that link as never before, as Paul Martin graphically describes in *The Sickening Mind*.

Dreams signal these stress points in our lives. However, we often fail to notice them even though they could save our lives. As counsellors, we can help clients by enabling them to explore their ability to heal themselves by studying dreams and recognising the information they send to the waking brain.

Exam stress. Tania, a twenty-year-old final-year university student, was concerned about her dreams:

> My recent dreams were about a deformed person staring into my eyes. The other night I dreamt a friend I had not seen for a long time came to see me. I went to kiss this person and could actually smell them, but as the person turned to face me it wasn't my friend at all but someone who I didn't know whose eyes were so piercing that I awoke. I always feel that these dream characters are going to hurt me.

Stress as she approaches her finals is aptly captured in the 'piercing eyes' which scrutinise, the eyes which focus on the performance of a nervous student. Part of Tania's nervousness is the fear of not being able to stand up successfully to that glare of judgement. These examiners, these 'lookers on' have the power to harm, after all, in waking reality, they could fail her, reject her and ruin her hopes of a career.

Deformity or evil presence in dreams sometimes refers to negative feelings that the dreamer has, indicating fear or sense of threat. It may be that the dreamer is projecting his or her feelings of being '*de*-formed' onto others. In working on the dream, what came to light was that Tania herself felt deformed by the rejections that she received and was not nearly as confident, as solid as she thought herself previously. 'What's wrong with me? Aren't I acceptable? Am I a freak or something?' When we experience or fear rejection it is easy to fall into the pit of low self-esteem. But recognising these underlying feelings of anxiety can be helpful to clients and dreams force that recognition to take place.

Stress at work. Work can be repetitive, soul-destroying, demoralising. If it is, then dreams can be the litmus test of just how stressed the dreamer is. As May told me:

> I work in the despatch section of a biscuit making factory which is boring, among petty-minded, unintelligent people. That is the reality. In my dreams, my days were spent in St Joseph's Mental Hospital which is the local hospital, though I have never been there. The dream interior resembled the biscuit factory with the beds arranged in the same pattern as the packing tables at work. The inmates resembled my colleagues. I was completely hysterical, screaming things along the lines of 'For God's sake, will someone get me out of this fucking loony bin'. But no one listened or took any notice. They just stared blankly as though I was making an unnecessary fuss which in no way concerned them.

So what difference did this dream make to May? 'The dream showed me my despair and helplessness in a more intense light than I could admit to myself in the daytime. It is difficult for me to tell people about my problems because I fear their rejection; that kind of "You're only drawing attention to yourself" response. So, I tend to keep quiet and bottle things up.'

The following dreams contain typical stress themes:

> I have anxiety dreams about work such as over-sleeping and finding myself with a whole day's work to do in the hour

between four and five. Others are more general and involve travel difficulties but these dreams help me confront the anxiety consciously.

★

My recurring theme occurs after particular periods of stress and involves being lost or not being able to find my way round places I know like the back of my hand.

If we ignore bodily early warning signals, minor aches and discomforts, stress builds up until we become incapacitated in some way whether it be emotionally or physically.

MIGRAINE

The view that dreams are a system of communication of inner conflict was confirmed by Heather-Greener *et al.* in a study into the role of dreams and the onset of nocturnal migraine. The study supports the use of dreams as a diagnostic and therapeutic tool.

The research found that migraine attacks were regularly preceded by dreams of terror, misfortune, anger and aggressive encounters. The clinical observations showed that physical and psychological factors associated with stress interreacted prior to the onset of a migraine and that identifiable patterns of dreams emerged which could be used to predict an attack. This means that sufferers of migraines, *migraineurs*, could benefit from plotting the pattern of their dreams because of this predictive value. As soon as they had one of their typical pre-migraine dreams, they could immediately take medication to prevent a full-blown attack.

Nina suffers from migraine:

When it was really bad I would always dream a frightening dream of water two days or so before the attack. I would be walking along a narrow path and water would be coming up to me from either side and I was hurrying to get to dry land. Now that the headaches are less severe but still troublesome, I dream I am either out in the rain and stepping into puddles or watching ducks on a pond — not very frightening dreams. But they are still about water and still two days before the headache arrives.

Dreamscapes provide maps of pathways and directions that can be transformational. In some instances, there is a direct bodily correlation, in others, the mapping relates to emotional or spiritual dimensions. This will be discussed later in this chapter but for now let us concentrate on the physical/emotional dimension and look at the role of dreams in asthma.

I met Catherine when I was making a documentary for BBC television about children's dreams. She described a vivid, recurring dream that is prompted by the onset of an asthma attack:

> These gloves appeared from nowhere and they kept coming in funny magician-type moves. At first I thought it was fun watching them but then they would come close and start choking me. Then they would float back in the air again, repeat it and start choking me again. And then I'd start screaming and shouting for my mum and dad to come in. When my dad came in I'd say 'Look, Dad! Look at the gloves floating about.' I could still see them even when Dad was there and I had my eyes open.

Catherine was about five years old when this dream first appeared — simultaneously she suffered her first asthma episode. Much later, she realised that the choking sensation she experienced was symbolised by being choked by the throat-grabbing gloves. When her asthma stopped so did the dreams. Such physical triggers for the attacks are translated into dream imagery and can be used as indicators to warn the dreamer. Once the illness is in remission or the person is symptom-free then the linked dreams usually stop, as they did for Catherine.

Mica also suffered from asthma but her linked symbol is quite different to Catherine's. In her recurring dreams she finds a huge fish thrashing about on the lawn of her garden. She has to struggle to get it back in the water otherwise she knows it will die. It is gasping for air just as she is when an attack is particularly severe. The fish symbolises her struggle and only appears in her dreams when she is about to have an attack. In both Catherine's and Mica's dreams, however, there is a desperate need for air and a sensation of acute anxiety. Once the dreamers understand the significance of the symbols as dramatic representations of inner physical disturbance they feel less anxious about their dreams.

FOREWARNINGS

Galen, the second-century Greek physician, believed dreams could forewarn of impending illness. In his *Prophecy in Dreams*, he told of the man who dreamt his leg was turned to stone. In a matter of days he developed paralysis of the leg. More recently in *Awakenings* Oliver Sachs described the prescient dream of a woman prior to the onset of sleeping-sickness:

> The acute phase announced itself (as sometimes happened ...) by nightmares of a grotesque and terrifying and premonitory nature. Miss R. had a series of dreams about one central theme: she dreamed she was imprisoned in an inaccessible castle, but the castle had the form and shape of herself; she dreamed of enchantments, bewitchments, entrancements; she dreamed that she had become a living, sentient statue of stone; she dreamed that the world had come to a stop; she dreamed that she had fallen into a sleep so deep that nothing could wake her; she dreamed of death ... Her family had difficulty waking her the next morning, and when she awoke there was intense consternation. 'Rose,' they cried, 'wake up! What's the matter? Your expression, your position ... You're so still and so strange.' Miss R. could not answer, but turned her eyes to the wardrobe mirror, and there she saw that her dreams had come true. The local doctor was brisk and unhelpful: 'Catatonia,' he said, 'flexibilitas cerea. Keep her quiet and feed her — she'll be fine in a week.'

For forty three years this patient, Miss R., was trapped in stone-like stillness, until the drug L–Dopa 'woke' her once more.

Susie, a religious minister, spoke of her dream:

> One dream I had of being on the edge of a dark wood and afraid to enter it, prefigured an acute anxiety disorder which happened five months later. Before the illness, when my spiritual director prayed with me about the frightening dream, I 'saw' sunlight come into the wood to illuminate the path. This subsequently had a sustaining effect, giving hope, although the illness was still very unpleasant and bewildering.

Peter and Elizabeth Fenwick in their book *The Hidden Door* give examples of prodomic dreams. They relate the dream of a journalist who dreamt that torturers were placing hot coals beneath his chin. This was followed by another dream in which hypodermic needles were being stuck into his neck. He became certain that his dreams were telling him he was developing cancer of the throat and persuaded a doctor to examine him. He was diagnosed as having cancer of the thyroid.

I myself had a dream which warned of impending change. This is the record I made later for *The Therapeutic Potential of Creative Writing*:

> The saliva glistening in their crimson, gaping mouths was the last thing I saw before the dogs leapt. I had never dreamt of being attacked by dogs before and it disturbed me, threw me off guard and confused me. I restrained them in the insecure kennel that was the back of my mind as soon as I woke up.
>
> Of course, working with dreams as a therapist and writer, I should have known better, considered more, avoided less ... however, I was preoccupied and of course, I wanted to deny the dream violation. Staying with such painful feelings is hard and it was as much as I could do to write the dream

down and tell myself that I'd work on it later.

In the dream I was standing in the back garden. It was a dark night and a man, a silent companion, was by my side. The dogs sprang out of nowhere, and I knew with that cold certainty that you often get in dreams that I was to be their victim. In the brief second before they jumped, I said, 'But I'm good with dogs. They're my friends. I never have trouble with dogs.' Incredulous words lost in the darkness as vicious mouths ripped me and blood spurted.

I began bleeding later that morning. The snarling dogs slipped their restraints and the baby I was carrying went with them. I had taken my body for granted, assumed it would not turn on me, because that is what if felt like, and I was shocked. The suddenness, the pain, the blood, it seemed as incomprehensible as the dream yet every bit as real. Nature, red in tooth and claw, was there in all her power and it hurt.

Dreams tell us more than we know. As I dreamt, my body was already engaged in the process that would lead to the early miscarriage. At the time I had no waking indications or symptoms that anything was amiss. On the contrary, I was deemed to be in perfect health. However, there was another truth, another story being enacted within my inner world that the dream narrates. In a way, the impact of the dream prepared me for the shock of loss and the feelings of vulnerability that followed. Nothing would ever be certain again.

As therapists, we too can deny the import of our dreams.

DREAMS AND MENTAL ILLNESS

Diagnostic dreams which are dreamt a few days before the manifest beginning of a disease are not difficult to understand. Freed as it is from the distractions of waking life, the brain via the dream is much more concentrated and there is increased awareness. The experience of some sufferers of schizophrenia are more puzzling though, since, as Bossard reports in *Psychologie des Traumbewusstseins*, in some cases ten or twenty years before the onset of their illness: 'some of them have had recurrent dreams of this catastrophic end to their human existence. These childhood dreams are distinguished by the fact that they end absolutely hopelessly in catastrophe and inevitable despair. However, in those ominous childhood dreams ... it is never the dreamer alone who dies. The dreamer himself often does not die at all. His whole dream world is annihilated.'

There are other examples. One woman aged twenty-six years had a twice yearly dream where she fused with a death's head. 'The patient told me', Bossard said, 'that she had known from the very start, that these dreams foretold her madness.' Does this mean that, at some level, we know not only the past and present, but the future that awaits us? This is a theme we will return to in Chapter 9.

There are numerous examples of a change in dream content and emotional tone prior to the onset of mental illness, particularly psychosis. Francesca, an Italian artist and therapist, told me that her mother had dreamt of a black insect eating her brain two years before she died. Bossard describes a young woman's dream of being engulfed by fire prior to her breakdown. Medard Boss, in his book *The Analysis of Dreams*, gave an account of a woman in her late twenties who, still completely well, dreamt that she was a fire in the stables — notice she is not *in* a fire but she herself is the fire. Boss wrote:

> Around her, the fire, an ever-larger crust of lava was forming. Suddenly she was entirely outside this fire and, as if possessed, she beat the fire with a club to break the crust and to let some air in. But the dreamer soon got tired and slowly she (the fire) became extinguished. Four days after this dream she began to suffer from acute schizophrenia. In the details of the dream the dreamer had exactly predicted the special course of her psychosis. She became rigid at first, and, in effect, encysted. Six weeks afterwards she defended

herself once more with all her might against the choking of her life's fire, until finally, she became completely extinguished both spiritually and mentally. Now, for some years, she has been like a burnt-out crater.

★

> The more frequently we find the details of events predicted in dreams the more certain becomes the impression of the existence of precognition.
>
> (Jung)

More recently, Caren found that the dreams which preceded her psychotic episodes, the boundary between waking and dreaming reality, became more and more blurred:

> I get my waking and sleeping self mixed up, confused. This happened before I had my breakdown and was diagnosed schizophrenic.

PHYSICAL INFLUENCES

All manner of external and internal factors can influence dreams. Recent transplant surgery has brought about an unexpected post-operative phenomenon. It appears that along with the new heart, for example, come the dreams of the donor. In *A Change of Heart*, Clare Sylvia describes how her whole dreamlife altered radically after her heart transplant, not only did she dream a 'young man's dreams', she at one point dreamt of the man who had donated the organ. This information was in fact confidential and she had not been told any details about him. As we saw at the beginning of this chapter, the molecules of emotion pass information to each cell of our body so perhaps it is not a surprise to discover dreams are stored too.

Drugs

There are different types of sleep disturbance that affect dreams:

insomnia, where we get too little sleep; *hypersomnia,* where we have too much; and *dyssomnia,* which includes such things as sleep-walking, sleep-talking, night terrors. In response to these symptoms doctors sometimes prescribe medication such as tranquillisers or sleeping pills — however, these may well exacerbate the problem rather than cure it. Many anti-anxiety drugs and anti-depressants inhibit or erase dream sleep, though patients may not be informed of this; indeed, the doctors themselves may actually be unaware of just how disturbing dream deprivation can be.

'Prothiadon stopped me dreaming for at least six months,' Jan told me. It led her to 'brood' rather than dream which was difficult for her since dreams had always been an outlet for her anxieties. Similarly, Hanna was completely dependent on nobrium for a 'good night's sleep' and she couldn't recall her dreams at all. Even mild, over-the-counter antihistamines affect REM sleep profoundly as do amphetamines and alcohol. Martine found that drugs for anxiety or sleeplessness affected her ability to dream and told me: 'The medical profession would seem to be controlling our dreams now as well as our waking hours.'

So, with all these interferences in our dream life, it is not surprising that we lose touch with our own inner healing potential. When Hanna decided to stop taking her medication, there were a whole host of unexpected reactions that her doctor did not prepare her for. 'The first night was horrible,' she said, 'virtually all anxiety dreams and nightmares. I kept waking up to escape all the awful things that were happening. I was exhausted.'

Deena used amphetamines and found, once she stopped taking them, that her dreams were very vivid. She said, 'I felt I was catching up on my dreaming more than my sleeping! They just did not stop from the moment I fell asleep to waking up.' Research backs up her view. We have to dream if we are to remain psychologically healthy and in this 'dream rebound', it is as if we are making up for all the dream deprivation suffered whilst taking drugs. This zealous compensation for lost dreams can cause real distress. Withdrawal from the chronic use of sleep medications, as

Dr Hauri of the Dartmouth Sleep Laboratory in America advises, must always be done very gradually, under the supervision of the prescribing doctor where possible. Additionally, anyone working with clients needs to take into account the effects of drugs on dreams. Of course, not all drugs are taken on a regular basis but, as in Sue's experience, even anaesthetics can affect dreams:

> My most intense dreaming periods have been after operations, one to remove the ovaries, the second to remove part of the thyroid, both traumatic glandular changes.

Alcohol too can influence dreams and dream recall. 'When I've been out to parties and had too much to drink I don't remember my dreams,' commented Tom. Alcohol suppresses dreams and there is a burst of dream activity which inundates the person when the suppresser, alcohol, is removed.

Fragmentation

Trauma in dreams may well be linked to a specific event in waking life. In *The Dream in Clinical Practice*, Harold Levitan MD describes one such dream:

> Mrs M., a thirty-five-year-old woman, had the following dream while hospitalised on the medical ward for a flare up of chronic dermatomyositis: President Nixon is going to have me shot from a cannon because this is the only way he can get rid of me. I am placed in a cannon and I am shot out. I explode into a thousand pieces like the atomic bomb ... She awakened in the morning after the dream in an acute catatonic state which lasted one month. She was unable to give any associations to the dream. However, on reviewing her hospital chart, I noticed that on the preceding day she had had a grand mal seizure which she did not remember.

Levitan quotes another woman suffering from epilepsy who after a grand mal seizure dreamt that she was thrown from the top of the Empire State Building and splattered into pieces at the bottom. She was dead and saw herself looking at the pieces. This shattering to pieces Levitan sees as a memory of the convulsion.

Mrs R., a twenty-year-old married woman, reported the following dream during a period of intense marital conflict:

> I am climbing the side of a mountain in the company of my husband and mother. I call out, 'Be careful because the rocks are slippery!' Then I lose my footing and fall into space. I am horrified and screaming all the way down, I see the bottom and hit with a thud, and my body splatters in several directions. I feel foggy and light-headed as if walking on air but I do not awaken.

Levitan said she had many other feelings associated with depersonalisation syndrome and being 'out of it' and that her husband's threat to leave had triggered this dream which symbolised her disintegration.

Menstrual influences

I discovered, when I concluded the research for my first book, *Women Dreaming*, that many women have dreams which incorporate changes during the menstrual cycle. Dreams in which there are woundings, knife attacks and violent accidents or where blood is spilled commonly occur just before the onset of bleeding. The body knows the bleeding is imminent before it gives outward signs and communicates this either directly or symbolically in the dreams. As the science of genetics has shown in other areas of study, the body knows its future long before we do.

FACING FEAR

When working with dreams in a therapeutic setting we have to face our own fears as well as those of the client. Is the dream the client presents us with an indication of paranoia? Does it reveal organic changes or express fears of illness? Is the level of anxiety in the client's dreams intense, relentless and significantly adversely affecting his waking life? Whatever the 'truth' of the dream, the essential element for the counsellor is that we respect and respond to that which the client brings. Place the dream in context with the client's waking behaviour; if the client is acting in ways which give you concern for their safety you clearly must respond appropriately and ethically and arrange a safety net if they are so mentally unstable as to be beyond their own control.

When fear is found in a client's dream it is vital you value its potential. Sonia's dream is helpful here. Frightening dreams or 'warning' dreams were not usual for her but, after a period of endometriosis which was not responding to treatment, she had what she called a 'prophetic' dream: 'I had a dream where my gut was being pulled outside on to my belly.' It disturbed and upset her but she could not make sense of it at the time. Within days she was admitted to hospital for further investigation and two days later owing to a critical development of the disease, she had a colostomy in which, as part of the procedure, a section of the bowel was brought to the surface of her abdomen.

In the therapeutic setting if a client brought such a dream, an unconfident counsellor might be tempted to express the view that this, the gut being pulled out, could not or would not happen. In a distaste for the gory details or in an attempt to quell anxiety the counsellor might seek to reassure the client. However, in this instance, it was essential to explore Sonia's dream operation and her feeling about it. Had she been told that such an operation might take place? How did she feel about that? What did she feel in the dream? Fear? Acceptance? Relief? What about the dream setting? Was she in a sterile environment or was it dirty ? Did it inspire confidence? Responses to these exploratory questions, sensitively asked, would enable the client to face deep fears and understand the basis of the dream and the reason she had had it — such knowledge empowers the client. The fact that a similar event took place shortly after the dream reveals the strength of the body–mind communication that is available to Sonia and others who appreciate them.

Sonia found the dream helpful because it served to lessen the shock of the operation when she had it. This preparatory aspect of dreaming, *dream rehearsal* as it is sometimes called, is another dimension of dream healing which we look at in more detail in Chapter Seven. These dreams frequently begin a train of recognition of disease or distress followed by a process of acceptance and healing but they must be valued if this healing potential can function fully.

Dream material is a valuable adjunct to medical treatment. Dreams before and after hospital treatment often give insight into the expression of fears and hopes and can be used to allay fears and increase personal hope, thus strengthening the psychoneurological network. They may indicate diagnosis as well as the prognosis of a disease and can reveal fears and ideas that the patient holds about their treatment outcome. Had the medical staff given Sonia the opportunity to talk about her dream, they could have explained whether such an eventuality was possible in cases of severe endometriosis and adequately prepared her for it. As it was, her dream prepared her, confirming that the body speaks to us through dreams.

In *Creating Health*, Deepak Chopra MD, an expert on the mind–body connection, describes an incident which took place early in his career, one which radically affected his view on the impact of dreams. He was working on a Sunday in a hospital covering routine work when he received a telephone call from a patient requesting that his operation for the following day be cancelled because he had had a disturbing dream in which he had died on the operating table. A more senior member of staff spoke with the distressed man and persuaded him it was merely pre-operative nerves.

Early on the Monday morning Chopra recounted the story to the man's physician, who had returned from his holiday, and was shocked to see the highly experienced doctor's response: he immediately set about trying to cancel the surgery. He was too late, the operation had already begun. The surgeon explained to a quizzical Chopra that when patients express such fear the body may be compromised and subsequently be unable to withstand the shock of surgery. The mind is needed as much for recovery as the body. Shortly after this discussion they were informed that the patient had died of a rare complication just as the operation was completed.

Whatever the reasons for his tragic death, we know that the man's dream was so intensely disturbing that it affected his outlook and his behaviour. He actively sought to halt the operation he had been waiting for without any previous signs of undue worry. The dream expresses acute anxiety and fear of death which remained with him when he woke up the day before the operation. It probably intensified as he telephoned the hospital locums, desperately trying to contact his own physician, who he believed would understand.

Some inner awareness may have enabled the patient to recognise that his body was below par or too stressed to actually cope with the operation and it spurred his attempt to stop surgery. What we can learn from it, as his own doctor knew, is that patients' dreams express truths which may dramatically affect their ability to respond to treatment. Only by giving dreams a place and honouring them when the patient brings them, can we harness the deeper level of knowledge they bring to waking life.

DREAMING OF THE BODY: SYMBOLIC LINKS

Dream symbols arise out of the specific life history of each person, in conjunction with his or her social and cultural experiences. As we will see throughout this book, dreams speak to us in the language of symbols and, in relation to health, the body in dreams may be specifically related to this. The following suggestions are merely starting points.

Skeleton: the bare bones, the essence of the matter; the spine can symbolise strength, support, signs of courage or the opposite when someone is 'spineless' and has 'no backbone'.

Legs: legs and feet connect to the earth, they 'ground' and carry the rest of the body. If legs have 'given way' does it mean that the dreamer doesn't feel able to carry the burden or has no support?

If the foundation goes, as at a time of crisis or radical change, the dreamer may have 'no leg to stand on'.

Breasts: connected to mother's milk, life-giving sustenance, the earliest form of pure nourishment.

Eyes: observing, looking, scrutinising, eyes are the mirror of the soul; also, the play on words 'eye' for 'I'.

Head: that which is at the top, often associated with the reasoning aspect of the dreamer; we may 'get ahead of ourselves'; and when things 'come to a head', there is some resolution.

> I walk into a room where there is a cupboard. When I open it and there are shelves with people's heads lined up. I recognise some of them but can't put names to all of them. I see a space and it is marked for my head. When I see this I wake up. I call it my 'Cupboard Full of Heads Dream'.

To his wife and colleagues, John appears very happy and contented but the severed heads indicate detachment, keeping something hidden away, out of sight and maybe out of mind.

Face: what we present to the world, our mask, our persona; we 'face up to' things; we 'put on a brave face'.

Hair: an important sexual symbol for both sexes; baldness can represent losing potency, being exposed and vulnerable, being 'bare' with no natural protection from the elements, no covering.

Blood: loss of blood, loss of strength — vital life force seeping away, being 'drained' of vitality; can symbolise sacrifice; also, there is a proverb which says 'When blood is spilt, battle is over.'

> I felt that a dream I had about many mice foretold a death. It was a dark room, lagged pipes and stacks of dirty clothes. There was a figure in the corner which was shrouded in white cloth. The mice in the room did not go near the figure though they were seething everywhere. I was horrified, though in waking life I am not afraid of mice. I saw the

dream as a death. My brother was ill with cancer at the time. The pipes seemed to be blood vessels. The dream prepared me a little bit.

Dreams of mice and rats often indicate that something in the dreamer's life is worn out by the gnawing 'tooth of time' and is about to disappear. Sometimes, we dream of those we love who are terminally ill as Dawn did.

Heart: the central issue, the 'heart of the matter', linked to love and devotion.

I was in a fight and was almost being strangled. I was scared, frightened of being dead, of being no more. Not being able to hear my own heart beat.

Liver: the Greek, Timaios, who influenced Plato, described the liver as the organ of the body which receives messages and acts as a mirror. As Plato said: 'the gods created in the belly an organ like a mirror, whose surface was sensitive to or sufficiently attuned to the mind to receive its messages and then had the power to project these rational messages as irrational messages into dreams.' This involves the indicative, predictive nature of dreams.

Teeth: teeth in the dream world are most often an archetypal image of the dreamer's sense of confidence and competence in the waking world. Dreaming that there is something amiss with teeth usually points to insecurities reflected in the phrases 'get my teeth into it' or 'bitten off more than I can chew'.

CHAPTER 4

CLIENTS IN CRISIS

Dreams give access to a whole variety of insights, including all manner of physical, emotional and spiritual ills that beset a client. Using the therapeutic potential of dream work, clients may be enabled to confront their deepest fears on their path to healing. We start with one of the most ubiquitous scourges of our age — abuse — the legacy of which blights adult life and haunts those who have experienced it.

ABUSE

> My home was broken. My sisters were battered. There were constant rows, very little money. We had to stay upstairs out of the way. I do not think I knew I was unhappy.

The Memory Birds (Malone *et al.*) is a profoundly moving collection of the memories of men and women who have suffered abuse. Throughout their testimonies weave the threads of dreams and nightmares. Ros Barber, writes in an open letter to her mother:

> The nightmares have stopped now. Those terrifying re-enactments of trying to escape by running through mud which gets thicker and thicker until it overwhelms me with the screams in my throat unable to surface. They have been replaced with a recurring dream where I tell you Uncle Daniel has abused me ... you promise it will never happen again.

For four years Ros told no one of the abuse and she lived with the waking fear that she might be sexually assaulted by her uncle whenever he visited her home and had the opportunity to be alone with her.

Runa's repeated nightmares about rape came at a time when she had no waking awareness of abuse in childhood. Her first nightmares contained men who were trying to break into her home, while she desperately attempted to bolt the doors, then, she said: 'Increasingly, in this repeating scenario, there was a sickening sense that the man was someone I knew, and there would be a child in the house — my child — who I was terrified I would not be able to protect.' Her dream re-plays the inability to prevent the abuse and to protect herself and the dream child which symbolises her early self.

She continued:

> ... in a particularly harrowing one, I was an amnesiac, fighting off the realisation that I had committed an unforgivable crime, one for which I would be boiled in oil. Then running, in nightclothes, through the streets, looking for my father to protect me, my father drawing me into his house for safety, my father sitting on my bed, my father ... *the man I was trying to escape from.*

The nightmares reached such a pitch that for days afterwards Runa would feel devastated. She began to look more closely at the experiences of her childhood, her fear and the physical revulsion she felt towards her father. The problems of her difficult life and incidents from her past began to slot into place and for Runa, these indicated that she had been sexually abused as a child. Research shows that dreams and nightmares can be significant indicators of sexual abuse in childhood.

Many clients, once they begin to explore dreams, recall dreams from childhood; in fact, I often ask in the first or second session whether there is a particular dream that they remember from that time since it provides a valuable means of exploring early formative experiences. Pattie recalled a particularly vivid nightmare from puberty. It was, she said:

> A nightmare in the fullest sense of the word. Over me was a
> male figure (an incubus?). He did not touch me flesh-on-
> flesh, yet seemed to be trying to possess some essence of me,
> suck the very marrow from my bones. I fought this figure
> that rocked me as though on a boat in a rough sea; not
> physical struggle but mental. It went on all night. The overall
> feeling was animal terror, not mere fear. I won the 'battle'
> and fell into a short light sleep and dawn broke.

The nightmare seemed to be a waking/sleeping state from which
I could neither emerge into full consciousness of the 'real'
environment, nor enter the comfort of oblivion. At the time I was
having the nightmare, I remember thinking 'When I am twenty-
one, I will think that this was just a bad dream.'

Since then Pattie said she had rationalised the dream as being
an aspect of her emergent sexuality but it did not stop the terror
of the dream, nor the daytime remembrance of it. Pattie had been
abused incestuously by her uncle, and, on one level, was totally
convinced that the nightmare was reality. The 'winning of the
battle' though was crucial in her successful struggle to build self
belief and avoid continuing feelings of powerlessness.

Pattie's dreams as an adult are often to do with lesbian
relationships, which reflect her sexual orientation. However,
others reflect her early abuse:

> Occasionally I have sexual dreams. They can vary from
> 'feelings' to specific sexual situations. They vary from incest,
> to sex with people I normally dislike, to paedophilia. They
> are pleasurable at the time. They surprise me, I only feel
> ashamed about exploitation of children.

They carry shades of her own abuse and she believes that the
abused child in her dreams is herself, though the dream 'children'
may bear no physical similarity. This echoes Suzy's experience:

My nightmares are not like a child's where you wake up with a start or in a sweat, I couldn't really therefore call them nightmares. They are just dreams of which the contents are so icily horrific, that I wouldn't know what else to call them ... one involved a general, some young man, and I was told he was quite reasonable. He had a harem of little girls of about eight years old. They were all little sisters of his.

Guilt and anger are characteristically emotions aroused by abuse, as Runa indicated in her comment 'I have committed an unforgivable crime' for which she felt she would be punished. Many abused clients carry this personal stigma — that they are sullied, damaged goods. When we respond to the emotional tone of the nightmare and work on that, the healing process can begin.

NIGHTMARES

Nightmares are anxiety laden dreams, like the one above, whose vivid and frightening imagery characteristically forces the dreamer to wake up. The emotional reactions to nightmares ranges from mild fear to absolute terror, much depends on the degree of anxiety about the trigger for the nightmare.

A fairly common nightmare that Aileen has involves a feeling of being crushed, usually by someone familiar to her. 'In the recent past it has been my stepfather who weighs about 18–20 stone. We would be fooling around and he would fall on me; I would be pressed to the ground and struggling to free myself. I couldn't make him or any onlooker understand that he was suffocating me. My mother watches smiling, oblivious to my struggle. I would become more and more terrified until eventually I wake, groaning, or my husband wakes me,' she recalled.

Aileen never cared much for her stepfather and would not be playful with him under normal circumstances. In fact, she finds it difficult to be in his presence for too long, the nightmare reflects her sense of suffocation and feeling of isolation:

I was in a huge building, maybe a cathedral, and was

surrounded by a group of about eight people in a close circle. I felt intensely claustrophobic and woke up screaming, 'Let me out.' I remember feeling tremendously anxious and as if I was drowning. This dream was after a session of trust games where we had been doing something similar which I found rather uncomfortable. My dream made me realise how disturbed I had been by the game.

Nightmares sometimes interweave multiple traumas into the whole dream though the events involved may have been years apart. Layers of feelings, anxieties, experiences all meshed together; they may even 'hijack' ordinary dreams causing a pleasant dream to take a sinister turn down a frightening alley that can terrify the dreamer. Usually some kind of conflictual issue is at the core of a nightmare. They bring into focus aggression, denial, projection and the shadow side of us that we would prefer not to notice. The most common nightmare theme is being chased and in it, the dreamer is powerless and has a sense of all-pervading threat. Nightmares contain information about unresolved issues, they are related to the re-experiencing of a stressful event from the past and therapy can bring about relief by resolving the issue, coming to terms with it.

Janov, author of *The Primal Scream* tells us:

> Many neurotics suffer from frequent nightmares. It has occurred to me that in a sense they go to sleep at night and, with their defensive guard lowered, border on insanity time after time. It is no wonder they are afraid to go to sleep. These nightmares, however, seem to drain off enough tension so as to prevent them being insane during the day.

Ernest Hartmann, American psychiatrist, made a particular study (1998) of nightmares and the people who have them. He found that those who are 'nightmare prone' are usually sensitive individuals who have experienced nightmares throughout childhood and are generally more anxious and have more fear of death than those who are not subject to nightmares. 'There also seems to be a relationship between personality and the type of nightmare you have,' say Peter and Elizabeth Fenwick in *The Hidden Door*: 'Type A people — ambitious, driving achievers, are more likely to report fantastic dreams and post-traumatic nightmares.'

Avoiding nightmares

If a client is prone to nightmares, clearly it is helpful if they avoid unpleasant stimuli, such as horror videos and so on. It is also useful for a client to know how drugs can affect body chemistry, for instance, beta-blockers prescribed for some heart patients increase the frequency of nightmares. L dopa, taken by people with Parkinson's disease, also tends to increase the vividness of dreams and the frequency of nightmares. However, anxiety, stress and major life changes are by far the most important factor in triggering nightmares. Nightmares do not always reduce feelings of anxiety, as the catharsis model would have it. Instead they may be a re-running of terrifying ordeals as sufferers of post-traumatic stress disorder know only too well. In sleep, the repressed experience cannot be held back, it will surface once more and recreate the horror.

Halliday identified four anxiety producing features of nightmares:

~ their uncontrollability
~ the sense of reality that pervades them
~ the terrifying nature of the dream story or narrative
~ the awesome sense of importance of the nightmare

and four main treatment groups:

~ analytic and cathartic techniques
~ storyline alteration procedures
~ 'face and conquer' approaches
~ behavioural techniques, including desensitisation.

Relaxation techniques and meditation may help reduce both the intensity and the frequency of nightmares. Facing the fear in waking life and going through the nightmare as a form of rehearsal has encouraging results. Instead of running away from an attacker, for instance, a client could try the Senoi technique of confrontation as described in Chapters 1 and 2. Encourage the client to rehearse what might happen and look for support in the dream. One reason that this repeated waking rehearsal of the nightmare helps is that, by continual exposure to the stimuli, it reduces the power of the nightmare because the dreamer becomes accustomed to it; it demonstrates the adage 'familiarity breeds contempt'. By keeping a diary of nightmares, then spending an hour a day rereading or reliving them, there is frequently a dramatic improvement.

When working with a client, the first step is to discuss the nightmare to better understand it and its contents. Next, any of the interventions discussed in Chapter 2 can be tried either in isolation or in combination. Later in this chapter additional techniques are described which will increase your repertoire of intervention strategies.

'Devastating trauma', says Ann Orbach in *Life, Psychotherapy and Death*, 'impairs imagination, emotion is denied and dreaming avoided.' Such experiences are surely shared by those who have worked with abused children, survivors of disasters and victims of torture. At some point, though, horrific nightmares may be all too present, which brings us to an exploration of post-traumatic stress disorder, first properly recognised in victims of shellshock in World War I.

WHEN THE WORLD BREAKS APART: THE IMPACT OF WAR

Dr W.H.R. Rivers at Craiglockhart War Hospital in Scotland, worked with soldiers suffering from 'war neurosis' during World War I. Although a follower of Freud, he found that his patients' dreams were not concerned with wish-fulfilment; rather, nightmares and dreams persisted because the soldiers did not want to remember the horror of their time at the front whilst awake and deliberately avoided any recall of their experiences. However, they could not control what happened when they slept.

John Stuart Ross eloquently captures the mood in his biography of the poet, Siegfried Sassoon:

> Sleep did not come easily at Craiglockhart. Many were assailed by nightmares. Screams made their anguish audible. Suppressed and denied by day, the memories took their revenge in the night. Accepting rather than denying the reality of their experience was the keystone in the bridge that connected past and present. Fleeing their past they could find neither present nor future, only no-man's-land.

Ferenczi, a close associate of Freud's, was the first to expressly suggest that dreams after a trauma gave a means for the traumatic experience to gain a kind of psychological representation. Rivers adopted the Freudian tenet: what we forget is more significant than what and why we remember. He found that it was only when the dreamer learnt to stop trying to repress the memories whilst awake that their frequency diminished. As an example, Sassoon was never freed from his overwhelming dreams and nightmares but he found an outlet in his poetry, making notes and drawing outlines for yet more poetry. Eventually, he became well enough to return to fight and die in the horrendous war that decimated a generation of young men and changed the lives of all who loved them.

War, external and internal, creates crises. In 1914, Jung began to experience a series of dreams that rocked him to the very essence of his being. As war in Europe raged around him, his internal war, a personal crisis that was almost psychotic, revealed itself in apocalyptic dreams and waking visions. Asked what he thought would be the outcome of the war, he replied that he had no thoughts on the matter, but dreamt of it repeatedly as Laurens van der Post recalls in *Jung and the Story of Our Time*.

We know that death can be psychic as well as physical and part of the process of owning the psychic dimension is to recognise the shadow and our own projection. In terms of war, whether it is the decimation of World War I or the barbarity of Kosova or East Timor, we need to mourn the victims of our foes as well as those of our friends, for we are all victims, just as we are all rescuers. Nightmares are likely to be recurrent and related to real, experienced events. By facing the 'horror' in dreams, embracing what one fears, it makes it possible for the psyche to cope.

> The first memory I have of extremely vivid and distressing dreams was of seeing and hearing about the treatment and extermination of Jews. My mind was probably trying to reject the reality in my conscious mind but at night awful images would occur. After I voiced my opinion on not wanting to see or hear anything about concentration camps etc., my nightmares became more infrequent and eventually stopped. But still now if I watched a harrowing account of Jews' wartime experiences, I fear that my nightmares could return. I avoid all media coverage of concentration camps as I realise that such appalling atrocities leave me with such a feeling of inadequacy for events I could have no control over. Born in 1941, I knew little of the Jews' suffering until in my late teens when the reality of man's inhumanity to man first struck me.

POST-TRAUMATIC STRESS DISORDER

Trauma has a profound impact on dreams. PTSD is a diagnostic term associated with response to events outside the normal experience range in which the person is a witness, participant or victim. Such events include serious emotional or physical threat, destruction of one's home or community or exposure to civil unrest or war. Other characteristics of PTSD include re-experiencing the traumatic event in nightmares or flashbacks, avoidance of stimuli associated with the event, numbing of emotional responsiveness and a heightened sense or arousal and alertness.

Recurrent traumatic nightmares are a 'hallmark symptom' of PTSD. Freud described such nightmares as part of the 'repetition compulsion' response following trauma. Reliving a traumatic event as a nightmare, according to Krakow and Neidtardt, reproduces the anxiety of the event and this is in itself an attempt to integrate it. By repeating it over and over the traumatised person unconsciously tries to come to terms with the experience, to let it sit within the other experiences he or she has had.

As Hartmann's research (1998) has shown that, though dreams following trauma may rerun the event, a dreamer is more frequently reliving the emotion of the event through dreaming. Alan Seigel, a clinical psychologist, reported similar findings in his research with victims of a firestorm in Berkeley, California. 'Several people ... who escaped from fires dreamed first about fires but then reported dreams of tidal waves or being chased by gangs of criminals.' The fear is the key aspect, though the source of threat may change. 'A great big wave suddenly appearing and rushing over me' is a brief description by a client of a recalled dream following trauma; the suddenness of the event and the inherent fear is all too apparent but the original incident in this case had nothing to do with water.

Horowitz developed his ideas on PTSD from working with people suffering 'stress response syndromes' — Vietnam war veterans and police who had experienced shooting incidents, for example. He showed that it was quite common for the victim to be plagued by recurrent anxiety dreams, which Horowitz saw as attempts to complete unfinished information processing that had been halted by the unexpected incident; there was a need in each person to try to complete an interrupted event. Horowitz described trauma as 'information overload'. To deal with this, the coping mechanism is to regress (cognitively) and return to a developmentally earlier mode of information processing, such as imagining or enacting. So, the person imagines how it could be different, wonders 'what if ... ', re-enacts the trauma in their sleep as if seeking a different outcome, enacting another conclusion. Interestingly, this is right–brain activity, plugging into the imagining and enacting mode rather than the logical, analytical left-brain activity. Having experienced a traumatic, possibly life-threatening situation, a person may discover that old modes of information processing are inadequate to deal effectively with experiences which are so new, so it is not surprising that dream content following stress reflects the dreamer's efforts to deal with it within the structure of old and tried solutions. What is so distressing and demoralising for the PTSD sufferer is that the dreams repeat their feelings of inadequacy.

Keep in mind the fact that dreams are information processing events; they integrate 'effectively arousing material', the shocks and scares we experience when awake. Witkin and Lewis studied the effects of certain films on subsequent dream reports. Two stressful films were shown; one about aboriginal initiation rites in which a crude incision, called Geza Rohem's 'subincision', is performed on the penises of the boys involved; and second, a gory film about childbirth using the Maelstrom vacuum method of delivery. They found that dreams following such films were much more likely to include evidence of stress. 'On the whole', they concluded, 'the film images that were highly stressful for the dreamer were exactly the images that most frequently appeared to be woven into the fabric of the dream' and that, 'the dream is formed by memory images of experience prior to sleep which are emotionally charged for the dreamer.'

In addition, they found stressful films, unlike neutral films, tended to arouse many more memories of childhood which, of course, has implications for the type of material we watch on television, videos and at the cinema. The trigger for stressful dreams are often daytime activities so it is always useful to check with a client what he has been watching.

THE EMOTIONAL SIGNATURE OF PTSD DREAMS

The dominant emotions in PTSD dreams are terror, fear or vulnerability as can be seen in the following examples from people who have experienced trauma:

The content is secondary to the feeling of fear and dread, which envelops me.

★

The one I have often is of the sea closing round me. I know I'm going to drown. Sometimes the tide is coming in in large waves, other times it is closing in but the water is completely calm. Sometimes I'm in a cave with other people but the water still drowns me.

In this repeated dream the dreamer cannot escape the inevitable consequences of being overwhelmed by the invasive water. Her death in the dream encompasses her terrifying fear at the time of the disaster which nearly killed her, indeed part of her still feels a sense of disbelief that she is still alive.

When she was eight years old, Ailsa was chased by a man who was trying to abduct her. Since that time she dreams a grey-haired man is chasing her and getting hold of her. It recurs when she is going through periods of stress. In a contrasting dream, Becky finds that the source of threat is everywhere and she is always powerless, which reflects her sense of complete vulnerability:

I have dreams about being attacked, dogs or animals snapping at me, being shut in, trapped in a building which is in danger. A recurring dream is being on a very fast moving London-type bus which is screeching and screaming round corners and I am terrified of the bus actually overturning, with me being flung into the road.

Later, dreams may progress to shame or guilt, also known as survivor guilt which we saw in dreams of survivors of sexual abuse.

ROAD TRAFFIC ACCIDENTS

Road traffic accidents, though not routinely classified as 'disasters', are a major cause of death and injury. Like victims of disasters, individuals involved are a randomly selected group and bereavement after a road accident has many of the same complicating factors of a sudden, violent death by murder or disaster.

Eight-year-old Callum was in a car accident in which his mother was driving. Both were injured, though not seriously. However, the motorcyclist who misjudged a bend and ran into the side of the car was almost killed by the impact. Ignoring instructions not to look, Callum saw his mother, a nurse, put the mangled biker in the recovery position. Shortly after this, Callum began to have terrifying dream re-enactments of the accident and repeatedly screamed out 'Blood! blood!' in his sleep. He was afraid to sleep at night and, when awake, had a heightened sense of danger concerning travel for himself and his mother in particular and became fearful of car journeys. He became hysterical if he was asked to travel in the back of a car, his position when he had the accident. This was followed by deterioration in schoolwork, lack of concentration, increased clinginess, irritability and daydreaming, all classic signs of PTSD.

Survivors often feel anxious, irritable, have flashbacks as well as intrusive thoughts and disturbed sleep patterns and some dreams only add to the distress. Peter Hodgkinson and Michael Stewart, Joint Directors of the Centre for Crisis Psychology in Yorkshire, England, report the case of a young, pregnant woman who was knocked down by an escaping criminal's car. Within four days she began having bad dreams, first about her own accident, then about car accidents in general. She too, was frightened to sleep in case she had a bad dream.

In Hungerford, England, 1987, Michael Ryans shot his mother, set fire to her house and went on to shoot at random a further fifteen people. One woman, unaware that the shootings had taken place, drove past a car which she recognised as her husband's and saw his body in a black bag. She 'knew' he was dead though she had not been informed by the police that he had died. Soon after she was widowed she began to dream about different aspects of the events (Hodgkinson and Stewart):

When I go to bed at night I sometimes cry. It's then that I see the car, all covered up, and just his hand — that's all I can see of him. When they show a picture of Hungerford on the news I have to look away in case they show a picture of the car. I sometimes wake up with it in my mind when I've dreamt about it — I think it will always be there.

The distressing dreams gradually became much more sparse, but at points of renewed interest in this tragedy, when the media returns to the story, the dreams once again increase in frequency. 'Even those who saw none of the shooting', reported Hodgkinson and Stewart, 'said there was no escape from feelings about the massacre: the smell of cordite was everywhere ... everyone was frightened.'

Following a disaster, a mass shooting, for instance, the common reactions are shock, disbelief, guilt, anger, the need to make sense of the event and the loss of a sense of safety in the world. After disastrous events such as air crashes or fires, some rescue workers report dreams in which they experience role reversal with the corpses. 'People were coming in smelling of burnt flesh' reported a doctor on BBC Radio 4 after the Paddington rail crash on 5 October 1999. The trauma of such events lingers not just with the victims, but their relatives, the emergency staff who attend the scene and even those who normally use that route. In follow-ups, after a year or two, PTSD sufferers who seemed to do best were those who had had sensitive counselling, a supportive social network and had changed their priorities in life.

DREAM THERAPY AND PTSD

Dream therapy is an integral part of client trauma treatment in a number of organisations that follow up crisis situations. Bob 'Sandman' Coalson, staff member at PTS Treatment Programme, a Veterans Administration Medical Centre, Washington, USA, has extensive experience of treating nightmares in a war veteran population, mainly those who experienced the conflict in Vietnam. A large segment of the three-month programme is devoted to rigorous trauma work and dream therapy is an integral part of each client's trauma treatment goals: 'In treatment, some Vietnam veterans have presented recurring nightmares that were continuing to be re-experienced twenty to twenty-five years after onset.'

> I am in, or go into, a place where everyone has their back to me. When I speak they turn to face me but their faces are either skulls or bloody masses.

There are no hard and fast rules about the onset and frequency of nightmares following trauma. In some cases they will start immediately after the event, in other cases years may elapse before a nightmare suddenly taps into it. The latter may be caused by some waking trigger that stirs up latent emotional fears associated with the past trauma. This may be a television programme or a news incident which has some relation or similarity to the original trauma.

ANNIVERSARIES

There may be a marked increase in nightmares around the time of the anniversary of the original traumatic event. In some cases, this may almost be date-specific whilst with others it may be more vaguely associated with the season. This is especially the case where there are unresolved issues from the past, such as guilt at survival. Also, periods of stress that create emotional tension and significant life changes or transition periods may well influence a renewal of earlier nightmares and feelings of anxiety. Understanding how these nightmares come and go is important in working with clients who are suffering from PTSD.

SHAPESHIFTING

A shapeshifter, according to Coalson, in a dream or nightmare is when people, objects or settings transform in some way. Coalson gives an example and I follow with another from a client:

I'm carrying the body of my recon team member, Tex, up the hillside on a trail. I lay him down. I look at him to find that Tex changes into my son. I hold him tight and begin to cry. I wake up.

★

I have many upsetting nightmares where my husband's personality changes completely from a happy but serious-minded, kind man into a womaniser who taunts me with other women while I look on. My husband and I are very close and he would try very hard never to hurt me in reality.

Coalson's experience with war veterans treated for chronic nightmares indicates that shapeshifts are fairly common experiences and that they serve a valuable function: 'The shapeshifter tends to mark thresholds of possibility for the healing and transformation of whole complexes in the course of therapy.' We will return to the significance of shapeshifting when we explore the potent shadow imagery.

A THERAPEUTIC APPROACH TO *PTSD*

The following techniques are helpful in working with clients who have PTSD. They may be used singly or in combination. These approaches not only offer a way of decreasing the disturbing nature of post-trauma nightmares, they allow creativity and innovation to aid recovery and healing.

~   Initial discussion to explore the narrative and feelings evoked and to place the dream in the setting so the dreamer can express his or her feelings and thoughts about the dream or nightmare. This should provide some ease of distress and identify relevant issues of concern. Link it to other events, previous nightmares and try to discover what connections your client makes.

~   Intermediate interventions, drawing, 'face and conquer', storyline alteration and so on to enable further reduction in nightmare distress.

Storyline alteration

This is designed to change the nightmare by rehearsing a new beginning, changing the help and support on offer in a dream, or introducing a more positive ending with modification of unpleasant detail. The idea is to create a different mood so that the client feels more in control. To aid the process the client draws or paints the dream, then cuts out the pieces they want to get rid of, substituting preferred objects or people. Psychodrama, sandplay, visualisation and other creative techniques can be used to alter the nightmare and so gain more active control over it. By doing this when awake, the power is frequently internalised and the nightmare becomes less threatening, or the content changes or the nightmare stops and disappears completely.

The confrontation of adversaries, introduction of support into the narrative and finding new strengths to enhance survival bring new insights into the major issues that lie at the heart of the client's concerns.

Change the title

This is a simple cognitively based procedure which allows the client to incorporate, or encode, new ways of viewing their disturbing dreams. Coalson describes how PTSD sufferers give titles to dreams; he calls them 'ghost titles', a subtle and hidden phenomenon among nightmare sufferers. Titles like 'My Death Dream', 'The Torture Nightmare', 'The Drowning' or 'Burning To Death', vividly portray the original horror of the trauma but they are self-defeating, continuing the negativity in waking life, and they reinforce the nightmare's awful anxiety-provoking storyline. Frequently, such titles are known only to the dreamer so it is always useful to ask clients if they have a title for the nightmare and, if not, what title they would give it. After the dreamer has worked on the dream they might then alter the title.

Affirmations

The ritual-like repetition, similar to the 'scratched record' technique in assertiveness training, can be used pre- or post-dream. For example, before the dream: 'This is my dream and it doesn't have to frighten me'; in the dream: 'This is my dream and I choose to be brave and end it happily'; post-dream: 'I kept control over my fear and the dream ended positively'. In this technique, we have preparation, action and celebration.

Follow-up work with PTSD clients may involve attempts to resolve issues which were identified but were not not necessarily the stuff of the nightmare. For instance, a client may discover that passivity characterises their action in nightmares. In this case, positive strategies to improve self-esteem, assertiveness and communication skills may lead to empowerment and a change in the quality of dreams.

Dee has been involved in many traumatic experiences and relationships and, when she is stressed or anxious, she has very strange recurring dreams with extensive brutal imagery where she is attacked by dogs who tear at her flesh. She also has dreams where her home is on fire and the emergency service telephone line is not available — it may be engaged or the line is dead. 'Sometimes, regarding the death of my sister (in a fire with her boyfriend), I see her (not him, only her), smiling and happy, pretty, healthy, waving at me in the sunshine, and it blocks out the fact she would have been choking — or burning in pain.' There is another recurrent dream, 'My mum, who committed suicide, sitting beside me in my room.'

She realises that her dreams highlight difficulties that she has not faced in 'real life'. Yet, in spite of the recurrent themes of attack and the anxious tone of her dreams, Dee chooses to view them positively in the sense that she thinks that waking life is better than her dream life. 'My dreams always help me to see what I have in my life. I am *not* being attacked. I am *not* ill. I am *not* lonely.' Yet, in her dreams, she says: 'I have dreadful pining, such a longing in my dreams when I feel so *lonely* and very black. When I wake up I realise it's a dream — and I'm glad my waking life is OK.' As a final point, Dee says that she has orgasms in dreams yet she never has an orgasm when having intercourse with her partner, and she wonders why. In her dreams, her partner is unfaithful. Her dreams reflect her fear of people who do not support her, but who leave her either accidentally (sister) or deliberately (mother's suicide). The loneliness and pining of some dreams, as well the blackness, indicate depression and isolation.

MENTAL CRISIS

At times of extreme mental distress dreams may indicate how incapacitated the dreamer has become. In *Psychoanalytic Phenomenology of the Dream*, Stolorow and Atwood discuss the case of a young woman whose sense of self had become fragmented. Violence and trauma marked her early life and this misfortune was compounded when she developed a brain tumour at the age of seven. A period of scapegoating culminated in a dream in which she is standing alone in a train station as flames sprayed up around her.

> Soon the whole building was engulfed in fire. After the station had burned to the ground, two eyeballs lay quietly in the smoking ashes and then began to quiver and roll about, conversing with each other by means of movements and glances.

Only two fragments are left after the inferno which has caused her disintegration, persecuted from both the world outside and her own destructive thoughts, all that remains are the very things that can watch but cannot act in any protective way.

Eyes or eyeballs were this young woman's principal way of relating to others. She was ever watchful, hypervigilant, a spectator who, in this dream, became a disembodied spectator, in the literal sense, for her body disappeared. In waking life she was perpetually scanning her environment for desirable qualities in others which she hoped to take on and assimilate into herself, a rebuilt self. What remained of her vanishing self in her recurring dreams is captured in the imagery of the eyes. She desperately wanted to maintain a sense of herself, yet these dreams show how fragmented she had become. Dement, a key figure in dream research in the twentieth century, found that chronic schizophrenics have dreams which are remarkable for their emptiness and sterility of content.

Anxiety

Anxiety dreams come in all varieties from being chased, teeth falling out or being rejected to dreams of one's own death and attending one's own funeral. Jo has recurring dreams:

> Always I am asleep in my own bedroom and alone. I awake (in my dream), it is very dark and there is a burglar in the house downstairs. I can hear the intruder rummaging amongst our belongings, sometimes there are two of them because I am aware they are communicating, but I hear no speech. I am so very frightened I cannot scream or even move from the bed, my legs are like lead and I cannot warn my family. I usually wake up when I am most frightened and I'm in a cold sweat and glad and relieved I was only dreaming. On two occasions, the dream has been so real, I have made my husband go downstairs to check and not to put the light on and be careful in case someone is there. (He gets mad at me!). He is sympathetic to my fear, but he cannot understand why I should be so frightened.

She dreams mostly about conflicts and how to cope so that she can survive. Her family think her views are radical and out of step with the norm. Jo questions the 'norms' strongly and wants to be heard and understood, something she feels does not happen. Conflict has to be expressed in some way and sometimes dreaming might be the only way to release the tension. She said: 'There is a message in the dream I'm sure — it's at the root of one or two of my conflicts. Maybe the answer is that I need to build up more self-confidence, be self-supportive and independent.' After working on her dreams, Jo decided to make some changes in the way she relates to people. 'Since attending the Assertiveness Training Course I have not had my nightmare dream.'

Jade, who has been suffering from depression had many disturbing dreams about her partner being unsupportive, then she had other dreams where she felt she was being attacked. These dreams symbolise her feelings of utter loneliness and vulnerability:

More recently, i.e. months, I began to have a recurrent nightmare about dogs. My job is health visiting and I would walk up someone's drive or path only to be greeted by a large Alsation. I would reach out to stroke the dog which would greet me in a friendly manner before suddenly attacking my hand, biting into the flesh, sometimes severing a finger, blood would be everywhere and the pain would be agonising. I would struggle to get back to my car, dragging the animal still snarling and holding onto my hand, eventually my husband would wake me. The pain would linger in my hand for almost a minute after waking.

I am a dog lover and these dreams with the Alsation happened prior to the sudden illness and eventual death of my own Sheltie. Since then that particular dream has not reoccurred.

After my dog died, a particularly painful dream occurred. My husband and I went out in the car to look for a child that had been reported missing. We were up on the Moors somewhere when we saw this child sitting by the side of the road. She was dressed in rather old-fashioned clothes, like a child from the early 50s. We pulled the child into the car and her clothes were soaked. She sat silently on my knee while I removed each layer of wet clothing. Suddenly the child turned into my dog and I was so pleased to see him and he me. He stretched out on my lap and began to chew gently at my fingers like he used to. The chewing became stronger until suddenly I could not bear the pain, his eyes became wild and his teeth bared, he gripped my fingers and wouldn't let go. The pain was agonising and I was so hurt by his action, hurt inside I mean. Once again my husband woke me mainly because I kept trying to attract his attention. In the dream he was laughing, not realising that the child had become a dog or that I was in pain or trouble.

Jade did not recover from that dream until morning and said that she cried most of the night. This dream was easily understood since she felt that the dog was almost a child to her and she felt his loss dreadfully. It took her weeks to grieve over him and her doctor said that her grief led to depression, which also arises from distress about infertility.

ABORTION AND DREAMS

Elizabeth worked through her experience of abortion in the counselling setting. At twenty-one weeks she had a termination which she found extremely disturbing. She felt loss guilt, loneliness, pain, anxiety and regret. Part of her desperately wanted someone to give love to, to influence, to care for, someone who would return love in 'a pure way'. She brought two dreams on which we worked. Here is the first:

> I'm riding a horse which I've won. I rode through the streets back to Clapham where I lived from ten years old until I was sixteen. We went to the playing fields, some parts were fenced off and some were cultivated — eventually found space for the horse. I left it there and went to my parents who were plastic people. Someone youngish came to tell me that the horse had been killed.

As the dream continued she felt distraught but her parents were uninterested and Elizabeth felt bewildered, especially by her parents' insensitivity. In working on this dream, it was apparent that Elizabeth held the hope that at some point her parents would come through and she hoped that, if the situation was desperate enough, they would finally show love and give her the support she had always felt had been lacking in her life.

The following week she had a dream which was once again set in her childhood neighbourhood. It had recurred twice.

I have a baby on my hip and I'm running across a demolition site, trying to get to the right station to take a train to my mother's but I can't seem to get it right, I can't get to where I want to go.

She felt that the dream was telling her that she wasn't 'on the right track', that trying to get back to the past would not change her relationship with her family. This led to work on her experience of abortion, finishing off, saying goodbye — tearful and upset. When Elizabeth described the dream as if she were the baby, she described the dream mother who is carrying the baby as being: 'indifferent, flustered, rushing and unaware how frightening it was to be hurled here and there in such a panic.'

Elizabeth's relationship with her father had been particularly destructive though Elizabeth blamed her mother for not protecting her from his criticism. The demolition site symbolised the sense of destruction she associated with both her early upbringing and the abortion in which she had 'demolished/abolished' the foetus. Frustration at not getting to where she wanted to go is also apparent, reflecting her waking feelings. In the next chapter we look at how dreams help clients like Elizabeth to recover their sense of self.

CHAPTER 5

A LIGHT IN THE DARKNESS OF MERE BEING: RECOVERING THE SELF

> The greatest discovery of my generation is that human beings, by changing the inner attitudes of their minds, can change the outer aspects of their lives.
>
> (William James)

Anxiety, depression and the loss of 'self' cause grave distress. Feeling at a loss or at the mercy of some ill-defined sense of hopelessness drives many clients to seek counselling, initially to alleviate their symptoms, then to delve much deeper into what lies at the heart of their 'self'. Using dreams in therapy brings insight and the inner strength to carry them through this period when they feel bereft of hope.

The first dream brought by the client is often highly significant. Jung believed it charted, symbolically, the course of the therapeutic encounter. Anne Coghill, writing about depression in 'Self and Society' had such a dream:

> I have had one great advantage. From early on in my first analysis, I had a dream. I was in a valley full of grass and trees. The earth on which I stood was shaken by a distant cement factory which covered the rich foliage with grey dust. I decided to climb out of the valley and pulled myself up the steep bank, hanging onto the moist blades of grass. At the top of the hill, I saw stretching away for miles and miles, dun-coloured tops of hills, like ripples in the sand. Only in the far distance was there a brilliantly coloured scene of blue

sky, golden sands and a blue-green sea, flecked with white. I realised for the first time that a journey lay ahead of me and that it was going to be a long one. That dream has been a beacon to me during the most arduous parts of the journey when despair threatened to take all meaning from my life.

From grey despair to a brilliant coloured destination on the horizon, this dream encapsulates the healing journey Anne undertook.

ANXIETY DREAMS

Typical anxiety themes are being trapped or chased, being naked or partially clothed in a public place, missing trains, not being on the right platform, not getting off at the correct station or being stranded on a platform where no trains come. Others are of being isolated, ignored or unrecognised by friends and family:

> My friend and my home and all points of reference have disappeared and I'm wandering around trying to find someone I know so that I will be safe; I'm panicking but trying to appear calm so that nobody will know how distressed I am.

★

> I have a recurring dream of climbing a high cliff and have nothing to hang on to. It is dark and I have difficulty seeing very well. Sometimes my mother is there but she does not help me. I always wake up before I get to the top.

Foreboding and helplessness frequently pervade anxiety dreams:

> I have to get the children — all the children — to a place of safety before the world blows up; I know this is going to happen but nobody believes me.

This sense of imminent catastrophe is overlaid with the feeling of being responsible for 'saving' others, and of course, the blame that will automatically follow if the dreamer cannot achieve his or her dream task. Anxiety dreams highlight and exaggerate the emotional aspects the dreamer is experiencing at the time and force them to really consider again 'what's going on?'

Fear of failure and rejection cripples us emotionally, creatively and physically and these are acted out in our dream scenarios:

> I'm little again and in the control of my father; he was vicious. I know he's going to get me or make me suffer in some dreadful way for things I absolutely can't help being or doing and I'm helpless.

Many people who experience anxiety dreams of being pursued; symbolically they are under threat and must be vigilant to escape whoever or whatever would assail them. This need not necessarily be a person:

> ... fleeing from water which threatened to engulf me. This theme recurred often at times of emotional crisis. These helped me to keep my bearings, to realise when there was turbulence around.

★

> I dream about me, my mum and sister walking through the country at night and a madman is chasing us. I see my mum and sister go to horrible deaths but I always survive or start crying and wake myself up.

★

> ... looking for people I cannot find or running away from someone, but they get closer and closer. In one nightmare a very fat lady was chasing me. I was calling for help but no one came. Then I started stabbing her and lumps of flesh hung off her body. Then I woke up.

The kind of 'fight' that the client puts up in the dream, whether they are passive or attempt to protect themselves, gives an indication of psychological strength and level of self-esteem.

Another common anxiety theme is of being lost or losing objects. Where these are symbols of the person's identity, objects such as a wallet with identifying credit cards or driving licences, the therapist is alerted to concerns about identity and self. Ella had a number of 'losing camera' dreams. 'On one occasion,' she said, 'it has been taken by the tide.' The need to take or have photographs is symbolic of holding on to the status quo which can indicate a need for security. Also, in this dream, the tide washes the camera away, this reflects the 'tide of events' in Ella's life at the time, when she had little, if any, control over her circumstances.

WORK-RELATED ANXIETY DREAMS
Sometimes anxieties about work and school feature in dreams. Sally dreamt that she was desperate to use the toilet but wherever she went they were either filthy, overflowing, there was no lock or there was no privacy. The worst one regularly happened the night before the start of a new term. In it she dreamt of going into the classroom with no clothes on and has to go to the toilet in front of her students. She is completely vulnerable, totally exposed without a shred of protection. Having to 'perform' in front of a class can be nerve-wracking, especially after a break. A sneaking fear creeps in 'Will I still be able to do it?' This happens to many people when they have had a period away from work, whatever their role, for absence, lack of practice, often undermines self-confidence.

The themes of 'no privacy', 'being exposed', 'elimination', ' no lock', 'overflowing toilet bowls' and 'public convenience' are worth noting. Toilets are to do with hidden functions and hidden parts of self being exposed — the concealed part of us which could be unclean or cause offence. Symbolically, we are getting rid of the 'waste' part of our selves, cleaning the inner, lower levels. Being 'watched', being observed, indicates a testing time — our performance is being watched and we may fear that what is revealed may be unacceptable.

In attempting to escape the gravity — in a way, in its literal sense — of waking anxieties, the dreamer may metaphorically 'take flight'.

> I dream a lot about flying. These are usually nightmares where I am trying to escape. Someone evil is trying to get me so I run and flap my arms. Sometimes I get just a couple of inches off the ground, other times I get about six feet high but I can never stay up in the air. I struggle to fly the most whenever the frightening thing is really close. I have never been caught.

Sometimes these dreams offer an overview so that the dreamer can experience the bigger picture:

> I once had a dream where I was way up in the universe/sky and the whole of Australia was edged with bright lights, the continent was lit up. It both made me realise how big the world is and also how important it can be to take a helicopter/plane view.

ANXIETY DREAMS AS TRACERS

Anxiety dreams can be said to act as tracers in that they often trace a path back to earlier, formative experiences in the dreamer's life. These often hold the key to understanding the origins of distressing dreams and once the causative event is dealt with, the client feels better.

Kay, thirty years old, has suffered from anxiety on and off for about seven years. Her various symptoms include giddiness, nervous headaches, churning stomach, hot flushes and strange feelings of detachment but the worst feeling, she finds, is panic and mounting tension that reaches an almost unbearable pitch. 'I wouldn't describe the fit and well me as a nervous person at all but I can't stand the feeling of anxiety and fear — the tension and anxiety circle is difficult to break.' In her teenage years she had a recurring nightmare in which she would be walking along a pavement and: 'a ball of grey stone, getting bigger and bigger would come at me. It was like a rolling snowball going down a hill gathering momentum and growing in size — but still going along the pavement.' Kay could see that this symbolised the responsibilities towards her family, which were mounting and threatening to engulf her. 'This ball, like grey stone, grew to such a size in front of me,' she said, 'that I would wake up in a terrible hot sweat and panic of being unable to cope.' Initially, this nightmare only came when Kay was ill in the sick room at school, usually once a term, but then appeared whenever she felt stressed. Now she believes that the experience has programmed her subconscious to react in this way whenever she is under stress. It can be set off by physical changes too, for instance, her acute anxiety phases have always been sparked off by a change in hormone levels after stopping the pill on one occasion and after giving birth to her children.

Some dreams come as personal survival packs; they tell the dreamer that they will get through and beyond their present painful existence, as we saw with Anne's dream at the beginning of this chapter. Clare's recurrent dream is a perfect example:

> There's a grey stone city with no mirrors, no sound, no colours and no joy, just despair, and I'm living there. A carnival/circus/procession comes from afar. I can hear it coming and everyone turns their faces against the wall; this prevents them noticing it. I'm very excited and look out of my high window and see the people dressed up in bright silly costumes, and the colours and the lights, and they're holding mirrors up to the stone walls, they flash in the sunlight. I can hear the music and I want to go down there and dance away, and then someone holds a mirror up for me and I finally see myself — and I look just like these joyful people — for some reason I'm not surprised. I feel release and recognition; then I'm down with them, dancing and laughing and we wind off down the street. We're going off to more grey stone cities to help more people escape.

Sometimes I think that dream was all that got me through my childhood.

Endogenous depression, that is, depression rising from within, often starts in childhood and continues in adult life. This was the case for Clare; and we can see that she was clearly glad of the glimpses of salvation her dream provided when she says: 'I feel release and recognition,' and, 'Sometimes I think that dream was all that got me through childhood.' Dreams from childhood contain not infrequently potential healing motifs.

Where the growth of self-esteem has been inhibited in childhood, from experiences of not being recognised or appreciated at critical junctures, then social and emotional development is frequently impeded. Feelings of inferiority abound where self-worth within the family has not been nurtured.

DEPRESSION

The majority of people seeking counselling are likely to be experiencing some form of depression. The World Health Organisation announced in 1999 that it is set to become the world's second most debilitating disease. It has been around for as long as mankind. Listen to Job's aching despair:

> Why is light given to those in misery, and life to the bitter of soul, to those who long for death that does not come, who search for it more than for hidden treasure, who are filled with gladness and rejoice when they reach the grave.
>
> (*Job* 3:20–22)

Depression, melancholia and longing for death are not the product of twentieth-century angst, they have dogged us wearily throughout our existence, though explanations have varied through the centuries. In Ancient Greece and in early Christian times, depression was seen as a mental illness inflicted by a supernatural force as a punishment for some wrongdoing. Hippocrates in the fourth century BC catalogued the symptoms. Melancholia was associated with loss of appetite, despondency, irritability, fear and restlessness. Later in the same century the Christian church was using 'melancholia' to describe 'a weariness or distress of the heart'.

An Arabic medical writer in the late tenth century saw it as: 'a certain feeling of dejection and isolation which forms in the soul because of something that the patient thinks is real, but which is in fact unreal'. We might disagree with this statement, however, because some causes which may be at the root of reactive depression are very real, far *too* real, in fact, such as the death of a loved parent or child. But we would surely not argue with the symptoms which characterise the stricken patient: 'sunk in an irrational constant sadness and dejection, in anxiety and brooding', as Lewis Wolpert described in his powerful book *A Malignant Sadness*.

Dreams in depression can often drive a client towards healing insight, in spite of — or we could say, through — their often horrifying content:

> Recently during the onset of my depression my dreams have become changed. Large spiders falling from the ceiling onto my face; eating faeces in newspaper or faeces everywhere which I couldn't clean away. Another where a plate of worms is pushed into my face.

Grief led to depression for this client. At the time she felt her life was 'shit' and was concerned that therapy might be opening up 'a new can of worms'. Worms are also associated with death, the eating away of the buried corpse and this seemed to indicate something was 'eating away' at her. The dream was forcing her to 'face' it. Her dream imagery mirrored her preoccupations; cleaning was a metaphor for removing the dirt that was depressing her. Another common nightmare she had was one in which she was being crushed by someone familiar to her — again, symbolic of the crushing, oppressive weight of her depression and the damaging relationships which were a feature of her life.

UNDER THREAT

Ali has had bouts of depression since puberty, which she put down to growing problems. She is now nineteen years old, working as a nanny, and has recently begun treatment for depression; however, she was frightened of becoming addicted to the medication prescribed by her doctor. Her dreams reveal typical features of alienation that can occur in dreams of those who suffer from depression.

Alien Attack. There seems to be a recurring theme in my dreams. I am always under threat from an alien. They are not the same in each dream but they are always small. In my first dream I can remember having to find a key to fit in a small hexagonal box, before this alien actually got up the stairs into the room. The house was unfamiliar, and I do not know what was in the box. I felt very panicky. There were many keys on a big ring. In the next dream, I was with a group of humans, children and adults, and we were running. We seemed to be in a house but it had trees growing in it. We were being chased by different aliens, and we had to climb a tree and get through a trap door in the loft, again before the aliens caught up with us.

★

Bloody Stumps. I am in a big, empty room like a warehouse. It is very high up and there are big archways cut down the right-hand side. Light glares through them. There is no glass and I have a terrible fear of falling even though I am well away from them. I seem to know we're so high up it's like looking down from an aeroplane. As well as the fear of falling I seem to feel that I might jump. I am at the back of the room, and there are many people in front of me, they are sitting on mats at regular intervals. They all sit cross-legged and seem to be meditating. The only way down is the lift (I am scared of lifts). Instead of opening normally they open horizontally and you have to crawl in. I begin to crawl, but I know that I won't get all the way in! The doors close just above my knees, and you can't imagine my terror as the lift jolts downwards. Immediately, the scene changes. I catch a quick glimpse of myself propped up in a wheelchair, with bloody stumps for legs. At this point I feel calm and relieved.

In these two dreams the imagery reveals a great deal. Who do these threatening 'aliens' in the first dream represent? What is the 'key' to her safety? The house is unfamiliar and she doesn't know what is in the box, as if she is caught in an unknown world of confusion. We will explore the significance of the 'house' dream later, but suffice to say that, for Ali, escape is at the top of the house which indicates that using her brain, her ability to reason, will be helpful.

In Ali's second dream, we find fear of falling as well as the fear that she might jump from the great height; she is grappling with her own self-control. Can she 'hold on'? Her terror of lifts, of going 'up', is fully justified in the dream by her losing her legs. She is left 'without a leg to stand on' yet feels relief. Masochism aside, there is a sense of comfort once the worst has been faced, we can face the truth, however awful, better than the uncertainty that debilitates so utterly.

People who suffer from depression have an unusually high incidence of masochistic dreams. In these dreams the dreamer suffers, is attacked, demeaned and generally hurt. In the dreams of depressives, unpleasant emotions and aggression against the dreamer are common.

I dream that my husband insists we return to the house we bought three years after we married. I hated it there and was so unhappy, in fact it was there my depression started. We actually move back into the house but in the end everything turns out alright and I always succeed in returning to where we are now, and I am safe. I always wake up with a great sense of relief.

Kathleen had been taking anti-depressants for twenty years and finally managed to wean herself off them but the REM rebound effect was terrifying for her. At times she felt she was going insane. The holistic approach she has been pursuing has helped and her sleeping pattern is steadily improving. Her fear of a return to previous unhappiness is revealed in her dream.

Depression is also present in Kathleen's earlier dreams of being lost, being sent in a different direction to the one indicated by her dream, or in which she is searching for her husband and family who disappear and reappear: 'Sometimes they go off without me and I am upset,' she said. Kathleen found her dreams therapeutic because they expressed her feelings and anger which she repressed in her waking hours.

Self-criticism and low self-esteem are major underlying factors in the development of depression. Like masochism, these are self-punishing. Where there is a high level of dependency on the opinion of others and reliance on others for the definition of self, there is often an inhibition of anger that is directed towards ourselves rather than others. Depression is generally seen as anger that has been directed inwards. As depression lifts; masochistic dreams decrease.

'MY OWN VOICE WEEPING …'

Very often I hear my own voice weeping above the noises or voices in my dream.

Candace Pert has shown that strong emotions which are not processed thoroughly are stored at the cellular level. At night, some of this stored information is released and allowed to bubble up into consciousness as a dream. 'Capturing that dream', she says, 'and re-experiencing the emotions can be very healing, as you either integrate the information for growth or decide to take actions towards forgiveness and letting go.'

Note the strength of the emotional tone of clients' dreams. Some people with depression have an overwhelming colour of dark grey or dull tones in their dreams. Michelle, a student suffering from depression, has claustrophobia dreams:

> In one I am in a manhole and somebody puts the cover on. In another I am trapped under the bed. When I was younger I used to dream I was trapped in a narrow tunnel and would wake up screaming.

Insight into our inner world is necessary for psychic change to take place. It is only through deep self-knowledge that the client is freed to make choices about his or her life without blaming others for whatever failures are perceived. It is the counsellor's role to facilitate the exploration of the muddles, the lack of understanding, to listen to the story that may never have been told before. This experience of being truly listened to, of being attended to, is itself deeply healing and for some clients that will be enough.

Guilt is a characteristic emotion in dreams of those who suffer from depression. Sam said: 'At one stage I kept dreaming that I had committed an awful crime, robbery or even murder, and I couldn't live with the fear of being found out.' Fiona similarly: 'I used to dream that I had been condemned by everyone for something I can't remember doing. In one I got as far as the electric chair.'

When continuity is threatened within a lifetime, for instance, when there is a break in a relationship, divorce, death or serious illness, when someone loses the thread of sense or meaning, there might be a dream of a broken circle or broken thread. Nor Hall describes how a woman who was quite 'broken in spirit' told her she dreamed that blue thread was falling off her spool in bits and pieces. This thread/circle symbolism is seen in the wider world, for instance, at Greenham Common when the women symbolically encircled the area that contained threat. We speak of losing the thread when we lose connection.

INTENTIONAL DREAMING AND DEPRESSION

Intentional dreaming is a process which emphasises the role of the dreamer in seeking gratification. In *The Effect of Intentional Dreaming on Depression*, Francis Manley describes intentional dreaming as an ideal therapy for depression because under stress the person regresses to a more primitive mode of information processing, and intentional dreaming 'plugs into' this mode. Guided imagery is used to get in touch with that part which produces dreams, and depressives can learn to use dreams to release feelings and gain greater control of their emotional life.

Manley found that significant results were obtained when depressives were taught consciously to influence their dreams using the Senoi principles of confronting and conquering danger, approaching pleasure and achieving positive outcomes. Thirty-five per cent of the experimental subjects in his study were able successfully to change their dreams at least once, and dramatic changes in mood were noted in some of the successful subjects. If, as Seligman states, depression is a form of learned helplessness, then this is a form of learning in which power is accessed and developed.

However, in terms of using intentional dreaming with those suffering with depression, it is useful to bear in mind that men generally find it more difficult to harness this approach. Wallin's research found that 'no male subjects were successful in changing their dreams ... People with intellectual defences may have difficulty relating to dreams because cognitive functions are primarily left-brain activities and dream work has a large right-brain component.' Women have more success with intentional dreaming because, as this study showed, men are 'more intellectually oriented and reality bound'. They have a certain intellectual curiosity about dreams but could not get emotionally involved and so could not truly benefit from the healing potential of dreams, whereas women were more flexible and willing to try this approach, which is a powerful tool in the therapeutic process.

> There is a struggle of will with some awful being. Sticks are pushed through my body to my eyes. It tried to control my eyes and therefore my thoughts. I had an almighty struggle to get free and managed to move a limb, which broke the spell. I felt a great deal of fear.

A woman who had successfully worked on dreams in therapy said: 'I think we should use dreams to sort out our priorities and problems. We may be worrying unconsciously about things which we could change but we tend to bury the feelings so that we can cope or appear to cope. Dreaming is a kind of self-help therapy which is free and we do not have to set aside periods of time for it, we can dream while we rest.'

SHADOW

It is essential that we become conscious of our darker side, if we are to develop self-knowledge. Failure to recognise our shadow, or the projection onto others that can ensue, leads to difficulties in relationships.

> ... if people can be educated to see the shadow-side of their nature clearly, it may be hoped that they will also learn to understand and love their fellow men better.
>
> (Jung, 1966)

Shadow literally means 'that which is not in the light'. In counselling terms we might say it is that part of the personality that has not been recognised. In order to become our complete 'self', to redress feelings of alienation, we need to find the shadow side, just as Peter Pan did. He cannot see himself until Wendy sews his shadow back on. Paradoxically, the shadow is always the guide to the light.

FACING THE SHADOW

> The growth of the human mind is still high adventure,
> in many ways the highest adventure on earth.
>
> (Cousins)

Clients in counselling are no different from the rest of the population; like it or not, they come face to face with their 'shadow'. We all have a shadow, just as surely as light casts a shadow so we each have a darkness of nature, a side we consciously or unconsciously seek to conceal. Exact definitions of the shadow are difficult. Jung at one point, frustrated by this difficulty, irritably explained (von Franz, 1987): 'This is all nonsense, the shadow is simply the whole unconscious'.

Ann Orbach says that the shadow is, 'what we disown, repress, dream about and project onto other people.' It is also archetypal and pertains to the collective unconscious: 'It causes difficulty because it contains the best and worst of humankind, all our creative potential and destructive force. The very contrary nature of the shadow is what philosophers, psychoanalysts and religious leaders have sought to explain; it's the symbolic yin yang of the psyche — it contains all.'

It is quite a shock to unexpectedly come across that shadow part of ourselves which we manage to avoid in the cold light of day. Most of us deny our murderous instincts, our 'abnormal' sexual desires and judgementally condemn those whose acted-out shadow appears in the press, for example (Jung, 1967): 'With what pleasure we read newspaper reports of crime. A true criminal becomes a popular figure because he unburdens in no small degree the consciences of his fellow man for now they know once more where evil is to be found.' As in early cultures, sins are laid on the scapegoat, the stranger, 'them over there, not us over here'. In counselling, part of the therapeutic process is coming to know the shadow side, and to know that it need not destroy us. Jung, who wrestled with his own 'shadow', almost to the death in the latter part of his life, acknowledged the benefit of embracing the shadow, saying that ninety per cent of the shadow is pure gold.

This potent archetype often appears in dreams as a threatening figure, usually the same sex as the dreamer, and may be faceless because the dreamer has not yet recognised that aspect of him or herself.

On three occasions I have dreamt of a sort of 'bogey-man'. The first time I had it, it was just a horribly physically terrifying nightmare that made no sense, but since then I've decided it's my confidence and sense of identity that is involved.

I had it for the first time two years ago, a few months before I went to college. I was walking down the street when this 'grey man' came up behind me putting his arms around my waist and lifted my feet off the ground. I was feeling half-fascinated, half-repulsed, and telling myself that I ought to fight him off as I felt myself to be in real danger in an obscure way, but not having the will to do so because he had some kind of hypnotic effect on me. It was like being sucked into a vacuum. The man himself seemed somewhat passive and lifeless, not particularly aggressive. My mum was in the background yelling for me to run.

In these dreams I feel as frightened as if I am going to be raped but the man is really more like a vampire, draining me of energy.

The second time I had it a year later, the grey man stepped out of a doorway, trying to take me by surprise but didn't manage to get hold of me because I fought him off so violently. At this time I was feeling very happy and much more assertive. At another less confident time, I've escaped from him by going into my room, locking the door and phoning the police; then, he was trying to persuade me to get in a car. The first time I had it the dream seemed like a warning, but having never been depressed before I didn't understand. Looking back it seems obvious it was a warning not to passively give in to my negative feelings out of self-pity and lethargy.

To become conscious of our darker side is an essential condition for any kind of self-knowledge. Failure to recognise our shadow, or the projection onto others that may result, leads to all sorts of difficulties in relationships. The tendency to avoid the dark, shadow side results in its growth to more extremism and decreased awareness. As Elizabeth Wilde McCormick points out in *Living on the Edge*: 'The whiter we make Christ in Christian cultures, the blacker becomes the devil.'

We are forced to accept the shadow side as part of each of us as we see again and again scenes of ethnic cleansing and recall the brutality of massacres in wars, world wide sexual abuse of children and so on. The recalled horror of the holocaust can no longer be viewed as an aberrant event when placed in the context of the ongoing atrocities that mar our world today. What may be harder to stomach is the ubiquitous nature of such acts. We can no longer avoid the fact that individually and collectively we need to face the shadow.

The shadow comes back to keep us aware of all the hostility and brutality that humans are capable of and which are perpetrated throughout the world in each generation. We need to recognise how we marginalise those at the edge of wherever we happen to be, these 'misfits' who express themselves in incidents such as the Dunblane massacre and the numerous school shootings in America. Eventually those at the edge may demonstrate the shadow to bring the visibility to which others prefer to remain blind. At an unconscious level each of us have a deeply held knowledge of the cruelty we are capable of and the shadow in our dreams does not let us forget this.

In working with clients to acknowledge and integrate the shadow and all its potential, exploring its nature, both positive *and* negative, frees energy for healing and healthy emotional growth. The shadow acts as a great melting pot of rich ingredients and it stops any arrogant ideas that we've got everything under control.

The most frightening dream I ever had was where I was turning into a werewolf. I could feel my face grow and my hands claw. I was starting to snarl. When I woke I was too frightened to look in the mirror in case it was true. I had this dream twice.

Robert Louis Stevenson's dream-inspired story of *Dr Jekyll and Mr Hyde* is about the man's duality. In Jungian terms, it is about what happens when the shadow is not acknowledged or integrated. The 'Mr Hyde' in each of us may stalk our dreams until we recognise him, if we don't, he may erupt in waking life and ultimately destroy us.

THE SHAPESHIFTING SHADOW

Shapeshifting happens in general anxiety dreams, as well as in PTSD, which we saw in Chapter 4. Gill says: 'I rarely have anxiety dreams but when I do they invariably involve facial changes, for instance, someone I think is trustworthy will suddenly appear menacing.' It is this lack of trust or sense of betrayal underlying the waking emotions that produce shapeshifting in dreams:

> ... long, involved dream in which I was captured by a 'monster' which was capable of metamorphosing to different and odd forms and appearing in front of me in various guises when I thought I'd got free. It was an amorphous dark blob, very evil and crafty, and with a personality. I tried everything to get away but it always appeared again. I got on a bus and got on the wrong one, and had to get off again, and I'd lost precious time and it was coming. No one would help me, the bus conductor remained aloof and inhuman.

In dream terms, where people are never who they seem to be, the doubt causes anxiety. These changes are akin to the donning of different masks that represent different aspects of the client's personality and life. The *persona* is a term to describe a mask which covers the essential nature of the person. It may become a handicap when the mask replaces the self and the person no longer knows who they really are, only the numerous roles they play. As Kate said: 'I had a recurring nightmare in which a group of distorted, gruesome tramps physically and sexually threatened and abused me.' Such nightmares usually occurred when Kate's life was in crisis but through counselling she has been able to confront these terrifying figures. They had become so distorted because she had so deeply repressed what they represented; her shadow side had been banished in waking hours but returned repeatedly to menace her in her dreams.

THE CREATIVE SHADOW

> We do not become enlightened by imaging figures of light but by making the darkness conscious.
>
> (Jung, 1974)

There is an archetypal creative impulse woven into the fabric of every dream, though it is hidden by a strong emotional tone. It may require an unusual effort of imagination to bring the dream's message more fully into the light of conscious self-awareness. The story of Elias Howe's invention of the sewing machine in 1845 is a case in point. Howe had been struggling to invent a machine that would sew with the same speed and efficiency as Hargreaves' and Cartwright's new machines could spin and weave, but with no success. As the tale goes, exhausted by frustration, Howe fell asleep at his workbench one night and had a dream in which he was in Africa, fleeing from cannibals through the jungle. Despite his frantic efforts to escape, he was captured, tied up and carried back to the village slung from a pole. There they dumped him into a huge iron pot full of water, lit a fire under the pot and started to boil him alive. As the water bubbled and boiled around him, he discovered that the ropes have loosened enough for him to work his hands free. He tried repeatedly to take hold of the edge of the pot and haul himself out of the hot water, but every time he managed to heave himself up over the edge of the pot, his captors reached across over the flames and forcibly poked him back down into the pot again with their sharp spears which had a hole close to the point.

As Howe came fully awake, he realised that the answer to making his sewing machine work was to place the thread hole in the point of the needle as opposed to the place in a customary handheld needle where the hole is in the base. He then designed the rest of the machine and, with the invention of the sewing machine, the last obstacle to the mechanical production of clothing was broken.

The dream is an extraordinary example of the Jungian archetype of the 'shadow' and its creative and gift-giving aspect. In Howe's dream, the creative solution to the technical problem is literally in the hands of the darkest, scariest, and most disturbing figures — cannibals. This imagery manifests one of the deepest truths about the archetypal energy of the shadow: the conventional waking consciousness views all that is not yet clearly manifested and understood in the world of the ego as nasty, ugly, frightening, dark, and dangerous. Yet once the dark and frightening mask of the shadow is stripped away the things the waking unconscious desires and longs for most, the energies of love, creativity and communion with the divine are revealed.

In nightmares there is this challenge to look into 'the magic mirror that never lies' to see the reflections of the least understood and most problematic shadow aspects of the self, and consciously acknowledge: 'I am that, too.' When we have the courage and imagination to do this, we are invariably rewarded with the gift of greater awareness of the creative impulse that is part of every dream.

BELOW THE SURFACE

Dreams let us see beyond the grime that coats surface detail. They lead us to what has, for whatever reason, been obscured and this in turn allows the therapeutic process of enlightenment to take place. Jung was the first to draw attention to the 'psychogenetic development' of dream phenomena; to serial dreams which take place during intense periods of maturing in the life of the dreamer. A re-connection is initiated as we see in this next dream of a woman who had for many years felt estranged from her 'self'.

> Bricks are being removed from a wall, and behind is a concealed room. It has in some strange way, as in dreams, previously been a small partitioned-off compartment in a dolls' house, but is now a normal-sized room. A small window near the ceiling is where I looked through as a child. Now I am on the other side of it, and inside the room. It is dusty and neglected, and small pieces of dolls' house furniture are scattered on the floor. They seem useless, but a woman, perhaps my mother, rubs the dust off one piece, and we see that beneath is an exquisite piece of craftsmanship, polished wood inlaid with mother-of-pearl. The value of these erstwhile toys has not been recognised before.

Part of the consciousness that has been unrecognised, hidden, which was perhaps glimpsed as a child, then neglected, has a value after all. In the process of working on this dream Tania remembered that her father carved wood as a hobby, something she had not thought about for years and she felt that mother-of-pearl related to her mother. She can appreciate the beauty of what she has once the symbolic dust has been removed.

> On holiday with friends, I go for a walk alone. I am followed by a seedy-looking man. Another man, the Sir Galahad type, approaches. I go with him. I come to a room — great expectations. Open the door and the room is completely cluttered. A complete shock, I am with the seedy-looking man. The shock awakens me.

This dreamer was concerned about the kind of man she wanted to have a relationship with. The good and pure or the earthy realistic type? Another interpretation was: 'It is my mind which is the room. I need a mental spring clean, meditation etc. When I get myself straightened out, then I will be able to know which man I want.' She needs to know herself better, to look inwards before she can have a positive relationship in the external world and to consider that the 'seedy' man and the rescuing 'Sir Galahad' are parts of herself that approach to deepen her self-awareness.

The aspects we ignore or miss in our conscious waking world are revealed in dreams to give balance and wholeness. Awareness of this unconscious element often leads to healing and reintegration of aspects usually too painful or difficult to incorporate into consciousness. As Lena said: 'Dreams help me get in touch with the marvellous richness and creative power of my *whole* self'.

RETURN TO ROOTS

Dreams often take us back to an earlier point in our lives, as we saw in the section on anxiety dreams as tracers. This may be a return — a turn again — to an experience, a place, an old friend, something or someone who has information that is pertinent to our present situation. The past and present are linked in the interests of the dreamer's well-being.

> For about twelve years I have been dreaming about a large house. The rooms all seem to interlink, instead of passages, one room leads into another. There is a large sitting-room with one wall of windows opening on to a balcony. The house is always near the seaside but not always in the same place and never anywhere I have been before. I have only recently mentioned the dream to my mother and she says it is like her aunt's house which she used to visit as a child but I do not remember having heard of it before.

The roots of fractured relationships are often found in childhood and sometimes dreams tell us the age at which distrust was first experienced:

A light in the darkness of mere being: recovering the self

I am upstairs in my bedroom aged about six or seven, and suddenly the house is full of dwarves. I rush downstairs to tell my mother and, when I do, I realise she is in league with them.

★

I regularly had dreams of trying to get to my childhood home. Night after night I failed. I was close in one dream when I was actually floating in a big boat up the road where I used to live. But the boat sailed past my home. I was powerless to get off or to stop the boat. I tackled these dreams by driving myself to my old house, parked up and sat there crying for almost an hour. I thought of what sort of person I was when I lived there. I felt the spark of my determination to be happy in life, to make my mind up what I really wanted out of life and to go for it, though never deliberately hurting anyone. I realised that some positive philosophy was still within me.

During periods of conflict, war imagery is common. It is a metaphor for destruction, for the fear that chaos will bring a time of intense change. People who have experienced trauma, as we saw in Chapter 4, do return to the site of their traumatic experience, as Toni does, who said: 'I was a war baby and my earliest memories are of skies filled with aircraft, barrage balloons or searchlights. These appear in my dreams either as straightforward memories, allegories or surrealistic nightmares; always in colour, and always accompanied by a powerful atmosphere.' She describes one particular dream:

> ... in a small, terraced house looking out of the window and seeing what looked like a huge silver bomb falling close to us in the garden of the block of flats opposite. I felt utter panic and knew I had got to get out with the children. All very confused, running from room to room calling my children, saw my son but not my daughter. There was a man

banging on the door to examine us for radiation. Closing up all the rooms and telling the children to get into the car. Suddenly realising my husband would not know what had happened and I had no way of contacting him. Next image of hundreds of people crowded together with all types of traffic on the road. I miraculously made my way through the crowds. My son was still there and I felt desperate to save him.

Next image of a huge place like an abattoir; full of blood, smelly and messy. I realised people were chasing me and that I had lost the children down a huge bloody hole in the floor. Ghastly feeling of utter panic and desolation.

DISCOVERING THE PATH

> There have been times when I have fallen asleep in tears, but in my dreams the most charming forms have come to cheer me, and I have risen fresh and joyful.
>
> (Goethe)

Unhappiness, like illness, is a universal experience and there is no magic formula that can make us impervious to its touch. Virginia Woolf said there are 'wastes and deserts of the soul' that appear when the lights of health 'go down'. I believe they appear when the lights of happiness go down too, when we feel isolated and untended. It is then that our clients struggle in the wasteland, longing for a sign to point them in the right direction.

Finding the path is a symbolic representation of discovering direction and recovering the self in the light of new insights. In dreams, new paths appear as clients move to a more positive frame of mind, where depression has loosened its grip.

I have a recurring dream of a house. I am walking through the countryside when I find a path. I follow it and it leads me to a beautiful mansion house. I slowly go through all the rooms.

Dream work leads to self-knowledge and knowledge of strengths and weaknesses previously hidden. It is a mechanism for integration, as one client wrote: 'I feel I'm on an exciting journey, a thrilling adventure finding out about me. There have been bad times, but my dreams have always been the light at the end of the tunnel and represent the possibility of acceptance, change and greater self-awareness.'

TEND THE DREAM AND YOU TEND THE WORLD

> We shall require a substantially new manner of thinking if mankind is to survive.
>
> (Einstein)

We are still confronted with the fundamental question of being. Natural science can only take us so far and although scientific knowledge may have changed the world, we still have the problem of understanding the world and our place within and, maybe, beyond it. Pinkola Estes, in her work as a Jungian analyst, has seen an increase over the last ten years in dreams of injured animals which she links to increased devastation of and assault on wilderness areas and destructive environmental pollution. 'These dreams', she says, 'reflect deep lacerations in the collective unconscious regarding the loss of the instinctual life.'

If clients have such dreams they may refer to a sense of personal injury and/or a lament for the environment, something that is useful to bear in mind as a therapist.

> I dreamt I went outside, it was raining and I was depressed but then I noticed a blossom appearing on the branches of a bare tree. The other night I dreamt I went outside to be surrounded by colourful spring flowers?

Old modes of thinking and behaviour are threatening to destroy our planet and we need to re-appraise the way we define ourselves and what it means to be a human being. Bertrand Russell, was once asked by some critics why he bothered to study philosophy. He replied that such remarks might be expected from: 'a historian or a scientist, but not from a soul facing the prospect of cosmic loneliness'. He was implying that the metaphysical must matter, because it is part of our perennial quest to find meaning above and beyond the automatic physical responses of daily existence. In the next chapter we will see how dreams relate to these fundamental issues.

CHAPTER 6

RITES OF PASSAGE

Down through the centuries, civilisations have used the energy and power of rituals to signify important events in individual lives and to draw communities together, honouring life and all its mysteries. We can still see them in public ceremonies, Courts of Justice, state openings of parliament, memorial days and so on. Even sitting together at table at Thanksgiving or Christmas is a ritual to mark a special time.

A rite of passage is a special point in life when there is a change in a person's status. Sometimes this is marked by a special ceremony, such as a baptism for the Christian child or the bar mitzvah of the Jewish young person at adolescence. These changes are not only signified by outward ceremony but also appear symbolically in dreams. Going to school for the first time, leaving home, getting married, having a child, the menopause and the mid-life passage are all significant transitions which are reflected in dreams.

Rites involve prayer, offerings, sacrifices, declaration and intent, the will to change and the desire to encompass something different, something more. In counselling, it is this movement to a deeper awareness of what is central to our existence which gives more than material comfort. Each client, with their unique history, has a personal journey to undertake and, whatever the external circumstances, the need to bond with others, to connect, to be a 'member', to remember, is stitched into the thread of being human. In our journeys as counsellors and clients, therapists and patients, helpers and helped, we weave all these single strands together, form an interlinking web of the sheerest strength and discover our mutual humanity. Kate Duff writes:

My dreams have repeatedly suggested that prayers and ritual offerings can help me to heal and retrieve lost parts of myself, and I know I am not alone in that, for Russell Lockhart (Jungian analyst) has observed that the dreams of sick people often involve what he terms a 'call to ritual'.

PATHS OF INITIATION

Initiation is a rite in which the initiate, the person undergoing the process, experiences a transformation in either religious or social status. Traditionally, initiation involves the imparting of special knowledge or secrets, special ceremonial events, separation of males and females, special ceremonial dress, particular words or incantations and witnesses who have a designated role. There is also a *liminality* — the initiate is sent to the metaphorical borderland as he crosses from one status to another in this transitional process. Initiation rites are intended to prepare the individual for the powers, privileges and responsibilities of the new phase of life they are about to begin by developing the awareness and strength they will need in the new sphere. Generally, more industrial societies have fewer initiation rites; these having fallen away with the growth of impersonal communities where connections are more fragmentary.

Dream incubation has been used as part of initiation rituals, particularly with regard to health and shamanistic practices, to try to stimulate a dream from an oracular or a healing god, for example, Aesclepius, the god of medicine in ancient Greece. A person who wanted the answer to a question or who wanted to be healed would go to one of the many dream temples. There he or she would take part in ritualistic preparations, incantations and purification, then spend the night in the sanctuary to incubate a dream. These rites usually involved making some kind of sacrifice too. Making sacrifices helps us to realise nothing lasts forever or truly belongs to us, everything comes from an original source and returns to it, matter to matter, dust to dust.

Kat Duff believes that serious illness provides an initiation since it follows the same traditional stages of initiation ceremonies: 'separation, submergence, metamorphosis and re-emergence'. And like other initiates, those who recover from illness often divide their lives into 'before' and 'after' and are never quite the same again. Indeed, some describe the threat of death, in cancer, for instance, as a gift that transformed their life.

Cindy has 'mystical' initiation dreams occasionally which are really intense:

> I was given some occult candlesticks and I put them on the mantelpiece and went to bed. I was besieged by a sea of horrible faces which I felt would engulf me. I cried out, 'I'm not going into this, I'm going into the light.' The scene instantly changed and I was at the centre of a Wicca meeting in a wood and a group of people surrounded an altar. I was being initiated and had to swear an oath which they spoke first and I repeated. After the event they welcomed me into the group and the scene dissolved but I was left with a feeling of awe, but happy and peaceful.

★

> It was the night before I started the Women's Studies course I'm on at the moment. In the dream three different robed, tall women appeared in front of me and each explained to me the contradictions of an aspect of spiritual love. I woke feeling as I had in the previous dream — in awe, but peaceful and happy. In neither dream did I remember the main body of the dream when I woke up, i.e. the oath in the first dream and the explanation of the aspects of love in the second dream, but I also felt that I had been given the knowledge and that I would not forget it. Even if I forgot the actual wording I would not forget what they'd said — it was secret and private.

Elizabeth Wilde McCormick writes of initiations which are frequently heralded in a dream. By initiation here I mean the beginning, a start, an opening or setting something in motion, the point that marks when the client has started on a fresh path. Initiation signals the leaving of old, probably outworn, ways of being in the world and stepping across the threshold into new ways of being.

In its most general sense, in anthropological terms, initiation refers to a rite in which the person, the initiate, takes part in a transformation in religious or social status. After the initiation, the individual is changed, sometimes physically as in some circumcision rites at puberty, but is perhaps more often emotionally or spiritually transformed. As well as taking part in the rituals, the initiate is given new information which was previously restricted to the already initiated and in some instances, for example, the initiation of shamans, this knowledge is acquired partly or wholly in dreams.

Initiation dreams may include the initiatory theme of death where symbolically the old form dies in order to become the bearer of new wisdom. Other dreams include climbing a steep path, passing through a narrow valley, crossing a bridge or negotiating a maze. The sense of being on a journey is usually present and very often the terrain is unknown, though the dreamer knows it is a journey that he or she must undertake. The images in initiation dreams are often elemental: *fire*, *water*, *air* and *earth*. There may be symbolic testing or purification by fire, water may wash or submerge us in symbolic baptism, air may allow us to fly and earth may ground us, keeping us enclosed in womb-like caves or underground passages.

> I once dreamt I was in ancient Egypt undergoing an initiation ceremony. I was dressed in pure white with garlands around my head and arms. There was a voice somewhere above me which said, 'You are Isis and you are going to meet Osiris.' I lay down upon a large marble table. The next thing I knew was that I stepped off the table and I was dressed as Isis, with gold and lapis lazuli around my neck and wrists. I had upon my head the sun disc between

two wings of gold. It was heavy. I looked down at my feet and saw my golden sandals. Before me were some very steep marble steps which I began to descend. Halfway down I saw another pair of feet also in golden sandals coming up to meet me. I looked up and saw the most handsome man. He was dressed as Osiris. He held out his hand, palms upwards, his arms outstretched and I held out my hands palms down. We touched and we blended into each other. There was a sexual feeling and a oneness with the universe. It was quite an experience. I consulted an occultist who advised me that at one time I may have had a previous life in ancient Egypt in which I took this initiation. He said that in this lifetime it meant that my psyche had become one with itself. I am passionately fond of ancient Egypt and of cats in particular. On more than one occasion I have 'felt' rather than 'imagined' that I am in ceremonial robes as a high priestess of the cat goddess, Bast. Yes, most definitely, I think I once lived in a temple in Egypt.

In some societies initiation may come wholly or partly in dreams. The religious leaders in hunter–gatherer societies, shamans, priests and healers, frequently have initiatory dreams when they are ready for their rite of passage. As James R. Lewis points out: 'the dreams often include the theme of initiatory death, in which the shaman is dismembered and then reconstructed in renewed form' — one part of the person must symbolically die in order for the new to be born.

There are similar patterns of dream initiation in many societies, for example, amongst Native American Indians and Aboriginal Australians. In the Islamic Sufi tradition, mystics have dreams in which a guide appears prior to initiation — sometimes these are invited, others come unannounced — to encourage a dreamer to go further on their spiritual path. In the training of healers in the Diegueno Indians, the would-be healer has a series of initiatory dreams which culminate in a 'big' dream in which they learn their 'secret medicine name' and in the cult of the

Goddess Isis, both the initiate and the priest had to dream of the goddess at the same time in order for the initiation to begin.

Tribal people everywhere have held dreams at the centre of their spiritual world. Dreams lie at the very heart of their culture and link to spirits, ancestors, the birth of their tribe and the origin of the world and depict archetypal patterns of human behaviour, basic themes and issues that do not change with time.

Part of the power of shamanistic religions depends on the union of the female and male aspects, a symbolic marriage. The male priest often dresses in women's clothes to recreate symbolically the original, perfect state that existed before the sexes were separated. If a client dreams of wearing clothes of the opposite sex, explore the possibility that they may need more of that gender's traditional qualities to bring balance and wisdom.

SHAMANISTIC RITUALS

In the majority of human societies in the past, ritual has performed a central role in the life of the individual as well as in the society as a whole and facilitates the transition to new roles through rites of passage. Shamanism is based on the belief that the world is pervaded by good and evil spirits which can be controlled and influenced by the shamans, priests or medicine women. Through altered states of consciousness, including dreaming, the shaman travels the many layers of reality, the 'fourth dimension', which leads beyond death and time. Figures met in these dream journeys are considered every bit as real and important as those encountered in waking life and provide the wisdom needed for the survival of the community to which the shaman belongs.

Shamanic rituals of healing and divination sometimes involve the shaman or healer taking psychoactive drugs in order to be able to 'see' the causes of illness and know what kind of remedy to apply. These folk-religious therapeutic rituals act as community bonding and worship ceremonies and underlying them all is the belief and perception that there are multiple realities or worlds that can be explored in expanded states of consciousness and that 'spirits', the beings one encounters in dreams and visions, come as guides. If a shaman, priest or medicine woman appears in a dream this may indicate that inner wisdom, healing power, is active.

In traditional shamanistic wisdom, when an animal is dreamt of on three occasions, it signifies that it is a power animal, a totem to be regarded as a power guide or guardian spirit, though to Australia's Aborigines, these were assistant totems; animal guides were called on to assist in Aboriginal rituals as every animal represented a particular strength or quality helpful to the process. Where a client has recurring dreams in which a particular animal features, it is helpful to explore the essential qualities it offers.

Dreams touch unlived parts of ourselves and kick-start the awareness of inner potential. When dreams indicate a need to change, we might help clients find ways in which some form of ritual will demonstrate that change has taken place. These may be auto-suggestive rituals. 'Rituals are symbolic acts, consciously performed,' says Anthony Stevens in *Private Myths*. They turn an inner awareness into something out there in the world, they touch the transcendent and activate connections with all people through all time.

BIRTH AND BAPTISM

In baptism, there is symbolic washing away of sin, a purification rite which signifies a new life of some kind for the dreamer, often involving a new identity. It is accompanied by naming, where the dreamer is given a new name or title. The baptismal font, where water is used to mark the baby's head, is often eight-sided. As J.E. Cirlot points out, eight is the symbol of regeneration and since the Middle Ages it has been associated with the regenerative waters of baptism.

If a client dreams of baptism, at first explore if there is a waking connection to a baptism or naming ceremony and, if not, explore the possibility that it represents a new development or a fresh start. Symbolic images of baptism are found in dreams of immersion and purification where the dreamer is standing under a waterfall or shower or swimming in a river. Bathing may represent an unconscious need for some form of spiritual cleansing which is akin to baptism but not necessarily having the obvious religious connection.

> In one dream, I was in a watery world and literally shot upwards into a light-filled world. It was like a breakthrough.

FERTILITY

In reality, fire, which destroys so that new life can emerge, obliterates the decaying remnants of crops. The ground is scorched, disease is eliminated and the earth prepared for new growth. Fire may also symbolise this fertility in dreams as new life rises from the ashes. The symbolic bird, the phoenix, rises from the ashes and represents resurrection, immortal life and the indestructibility of spirit.

> I am childless and I have a recurring dream about having a child. They follow the same pattern. I am doing something and then remember that I have forgotten the baby and I always have mixed feelings towards it. I am sorry for it because it is in my inadequate care and secondly there is dread that because I have neglected it I am afraid it might be dead. In one dream I have left it on cold steps at a picket line while I was typing leaflets, I left it in a shawl and have forgotten to feed it. In another dream I stuck it in the back of a large doll whose back opened and found it dead. Then I left one in a large oven with the gas jets on — in this dream I was only the child's custodian. There is usually some mixture of feelings about how the child/baby came to be in my possession and a question about its actually belonging to me.

The ambivalence felt by Hannah towards her own fertility and her belief in her own inadequacies led to a long period of self-questioning in counselling. Here, the imagery highlights her fears and anxieties.

PERIODS OF TRANSITION

The transformation during development from one stage to another takes time, though the rite of passage, the wedding ceremony, for instance, may be over in a matter of minutes. To become a husband or wife involves learning and a period of adjustment. This transitional period is often marked by dreams involving travelling across difficult terrain, movement or negotiating an obstacle that has to be overcome. As we go through a period of transition, dreams show movement from dark to light, from the depths to the surface or beyond. This is apparent in the two dreams which follow, both dreamt by Anita at a time in her life when she was questioning her relationships with men, particularly sexual relationships.

Dream 1. I'm suspended in a dark endless area, the feeling was similar to — or I assumed that I was under water at a great depth, I could see nothing and somehow I had a great weight. I was near to panic, the darkness was impenetrable. I knew that there was a rope or line hanging near me — which I knew would lead me to safety. By moving my arms around I located the rope, it did not extend below me, it ended at me. I started to climb — it was difficult, my arms hurt and I wondered if I would have the stamina to finish the climb. I could see above me a faint light and I knew this was where I had to climb to, there was continual subdued panic. I must have made it to the top although I do not remember it. After this I talked to a woman who said she had been there. I realised that she had been in that solid darkness next to me and I hadn't realised, if I had known that then it would have been easier to bear.

Dream 2. It was part of an experiment, I was one of the experimenters. A man was shackled by his neck to a rope which was pinned to the ground. He was a muscular man, big and brown, he was the subject of the experiment. For some reason the shackle was not on right and it was my job to fix it. I had to put on a similar shackle to demonstrate the right way to put it on. Both shackles were fixed to a central point so when the rope was taut one could walk quite a large circumference. I was outside the circle of the man — but to place the shackle on myself I had to enter his sphere. The man was dumb like an animal. I was nervous of entering his area but it was my job. I placed the shackle on myself in the correct way. The man moved towards me gently, I then adjusted his so it corresponded to mine, I was still nervous although he was quite placid. One of the experiments asked me to stay there with him as he was not placid with anyone else. I had to agree as I knew that we needed to experiment with body inter-reaction. I realised that I had become a subject and had lost my status as experimenter (I had to take off my white coat). I was still nervous but strangely enough I found the man physically attractive and did not mind the thought of him touching me or of me touching him. This worried me but my excitement was overcoming my fear and I smiled at him and he smiled back ...

In the first dream, the feeling of being in a vast, empty, dark place alone with only one way out threatened to destroy the dreamer who manages to find a way to pull herself out of her pit. She finds the resources to make a strenuous escape and then realises that if only she had looked for it, the support of another woman was there. This realisation that she could allow herself to look for help from others was very healing for Anita.

The second seems to be more complex in terms of Anita's

relationship to men and she felt the way that other people around her saw her in the dream. She felt it symbolised that she was losing her 'observer' status and becoming as 'animal' as the man involved and that this meant she was losing her 'self' in the relationship. Notice how she has to enter his 'area', his territory, and take off her badge of authority, her white coat. White is also the colour associated with purity so in taking it off she is removing that protection too. Anita related these dreams to her work as a rape crisis-line counsellor and recognised that the horrific experiences of rape were disturbing her much more than she had realised before she had these dreams.

RITES OF SEXUAL PASSAGE

Games of 'doctors and nurses', mutual sexual exploration at different ages, are part of human development. There are milestones along the road to discovering our sexual identity. However, insensitive, judgemental interventions by others may cause lasting damage. Sinead's experience which is recalled below shows just how damaging it can be and many clients have similar stories to tell.

> I open a door and enter a darkened room, and have to cross to the other side of the room. There is no proper floor, only the boards that run across a floor, before the floor boards are put down. So there is a narrow board, then a large gap before the next narrow board. Somehow I quickly become aware that this is how the floor is and that it is not going to be easy to cross it. In fact it is horrendous, it takes me hours, crawling, sweating, terrified that I will fall through the black holes into nothing.

Sinead cannot now remember whether she ever reached the other side of the room, or what was there, or why she had to go there. In working on the dream she thought the room resembled an attic but she said she has always pictured this room, as the 'spare room' in the farmhouse where she lived for many years as a child. She only slept in this room as a punishment and hated it. So perhaps that accounts for the nightmare quality of the dream and the fact that it was recurring. It continued to recur into early adulthood but then it stopped once she became independent, living away from home.

The trigger for the dream was clear once we looked at the imagery and the time she first had it. She told me that at the age of ten, she was caught with three boys, of similar age, showing and feeling one another's genitals, behind the school wall, after school. This led to a very traumatic time; she was publicly caned in front of the whole school, 'a small village school, but it might have been in front of thousands' and she was told it would be reported to the police. She was interviewed by someone who told her he was a policeman and asked lots of questions and used words she didn't understand. She was also told that she now had a police record which would continue with her for ever. In addition she said: 'At home I was beaten by my dad, and sent to sleep in the "spare room", which had a very hard, uncomfortable cold bed and the room smelt of rotting apples, and I hated it. I don't remember how long I had to sleep there, but I had to be separated from my younger sister who I normally slept with, in case I contaminated her.'

Sinead thought that the nightmare started then and it continued for many years. She did not mention it to anyone at all until she met the man who became her husband and shortly after they met she poured out this story. It was very traumatic in the telling and she remembered much grief and anger and bitterness which came out and continued to come out over a period of months until she could recognise not only that such exploration between peers is a normal part of growing up, but that she had been treated in a cruel, damaging way, which caused sexual difficulties for many years.

MENSTRUATION

Prior to menstruation there are notable changes in dream

material. Many women who do not record their dreams are unaware of this pattern which is why it is helpful to encourage people to make a note of their dreams. When they do, they may find, as Tara did, that prior to the onset of bleeding, dreams are particularly disturbing.

> I have swallowed the wrong pill and I wake choking, trying to spit it out, or I have forgotten to take medicine and I wake knowing because of this I will die. Sometimes I just wake with a feeling of panic and dread but I cannot recall the actual dream — only that I have forgotten something vital. This feeling of panic and having forgotten something can make me afraid to go to bed, but I have sat and carefully tried to brainwash myself before I go to bed. I know I am not taking pills, nor have I forgotten anything so I give myself a pep talk and sometimes it works. I do occasionally have other dreams, sometimes horrid, sometimes nice, but this kind of nightmare/dream I get for about ten days up to and including part of my period.

Symbols have been used by all cultures since the earliest times. They have a power beyond words because they carry a multitude of meanings that speak to the soul, the mind and emotion. Symbols challenge us to go beyond what stares us in the face, to go beyond the obvious. Dreams use symbols to reunite the mind, body and spirit in a state of balanced harmony.

> As a survivor of sexual abuse and someone who has worked as a counsellor, particularly using Gestalt techniques, dreams have been enormously helpful in my own and others' healing processes.

Since 1992, Jo has kept a journal which includes her dreams and the ways they changed as her own process took place. They gave her the vision to understand what was going on at times when she was confused and lost and were a very important guide for her.

Her most powerful dreams have proved to come before transitional points in her life and have included a male figure who is old and wise and has the status of a guide. In some ways her active dream life has also been a source of vibrancy and life when she has been paralysed with fear in her waking life.

MARRIAGE

Union, finding a kindred spirit, joining of opposites, finding balance being united with a nurturing other — marriage is about all of these things. In dreams it can symbolise the joining together of previously disjunct, possibly conflicting, parts of the self.

If we consider a wedding as a rite of passage: there is the special knowledge of sexual intercourse which traditionally came after marriage; the separation of the sexes in the stag or hen night; special costumes of bride and groom, as well as bridesmaids and ushers, and guests, of course, who mark the ceremony by wearing 'best' clothes; the ceremony itself with 'incantations' of 'I vow to love, honour ...' and so on 'until death us do part', all of which is witnessed by the guests and those who sign the official register to confirm the wedding has taken place. We can still see initiation rites in all cultures of the world, though the details may differ dramatically.

Marriage represents the union of the male principle, the knowledge-focused aspect *logos*, with the female principle of connectedness, *eros*. This also involves some sacrifice, the giving up of certain freedoms in the negotiation of a shared state of being, where each may have to give way to the other for the sake of a jointly, mutually satisfying relationship. This, of course, is not always easy and it is dramatically symbolised in some societies where the groom ritually comes to 'carry off' his bride. There is a remnant of this in the custom of carrying the bride over the threshold. All these motifs may find their way into dream themes. At a deeper level, the symbolic union of male and female aspects of the individual, the sacred marriage, signifies the process of individuation.

DIVORCE

Rosalind Cartwright *et al.* pioneered recent investigations into major life changes and the effect on dreams. When they looked at women's dreams at a time of divorce in 'Broken Dreams: A Study of the Effects of Divorce and Depression on Dream Content', they found the dreams of those who were not depressed were longer and dealt with a wider timeframe than those who were depressed. They conclude that, when women and, probably, men are depressed, their ability to face the impact of life changes and deal with them adaptively is delayed. This has implications for those who work with depressed divorcing clients. A positive intervention at such times would look at dream imagery and encourage waking dream work so that they can be enabled to face those issues being avoided in their dreams.

> Recently I have been dreaming frequently about my partner turning away from me in some way. In my dreams he either ignores me or he falls in love with another woman. I then can't get through to him at all. He seems to turn into a different, cruel person in front of my eyes. I feel very distressed, but I act completely helpless and passive. The hurt and fear are so vivid that I carry it into wake time.

There are systematic changes in dreaming during a period of major life change. For people going through divorce without significant self-reported depression, most of the changes show adaptive dream work. The dream reports are longer, deal with negative feelings, have a wider time perspective, and include the dreamer's self in the marital role and in preferred roles. The dreams of those who are depressed, on the other hand, are less visual and story-like, more locked into a narrow past-oriented timeframe and fail to display any identification with the marital role or its loss in the dreams. Not only is the whole marital issue avoided, so too are the preferred self roles. There is a significant increase in the dream-like quality of the reports, the dream mood tone becomes more positive, the variance in timeframe increases and the role of wife again becomes a common one for the dream self to occupy.

Of the many suggested functions of dreaming perhaps the one that has been the most influential is the adaptive function proposed by Breger. This hypothesis states that dreams integrate information to do with feelings into existing memory systems that have proved satisfactory in dealing with similar material in the past. Are there, in fact, good productive dreams and less effective dreams in either reflecting or accomplishing adaptation to some emotional experience?

> I dream of my husband preferring someone else to me. He tells me so in a particularly calculated and unemotional way. Eventually I either throw him out or he leaves himself before I can tell him. I usually wake up with a feeling of relief that he is gone after causing me so much pain.

Since the break-up of her marriage ten years ago, Debbs has had many dreams of rejection though she feels she has rebuilt her life and 'is over it'.

Hauri reported a sample of women in remission following a reactive depression whose dreams were rated as significantly more unhappy than those of the control group. In fact, happy and unhappy feelings were equal in the formerly depressed but happy feelings were four times more frequent than unhappy in the dreams of controls. He also reported an emphasis on the past in the dreams of depressives in contrast to an emphasis on the present in controls.

MID-LIFE

At a mid-life point, there is often a constellation of events: parents become infirm or die, children leave the family home and physical changes such as the menopause occur. Dreams mark these rites of passage.

Rites of passage

For years I had a dream of my father. I would be waiting for large prison gates to open and my father to come out and stand in a row with other men and I would machine gun all of them. This dream horrified me as we were very close. When he died two years later after suffering great pain with cancer, the dream stopped. I have never had the same dream again.

Sometimes at these junctures there is a 'letting go' of previous, damaging habits. Candace Pert was the star of her laboratory under the guidance of Dr Sol Snyder and it was there that she made the breakthrough connection of molecules to emotion. However, Snyder and two others snatched the prestigious Lasker Prize for Science, the American equivalent of the Nobel Prize, without giving credit to Pert who had carried out the definitive research that brought the critical result: she discovered peptides. It caused an enormous split both in their relationship and the scientific world. She writes:

> The pivotal dream I had of Sol, in 1986, in which I threw water at him and he shrank up — my nemesis, the monster I myself had created — gave me the courage to write him a letter of forgiveness that allowed me to let go of the resentments that had been eating away at me for years.

HEALING RITES

In Anglo-Saxon there was a word 'hal' which meant whole, it also meant healthy and holy. Now, no one uses it, though it survives in words such as 'halo', 'hallowed' and 'hale' (and hearty). In undertaking ritual activities or rites at significant points in our lives, we move towards wholeness and connection with others. Rites are the cement that binds people together. And this cement may be love because it heals by making the loved one whole.

Energy, its presence or lack of it, is also involved in ritual healing events. It has various names: *Chi* is found in Chinese medicine, for example, in acupuncture and Qigong; and *Prana* is the name given in the Hindu Upanishads and is used in Yoga. In Christian and other teachings, light symbolises the enduring potential of energy. This appears in dreams as Vicky tells us:

> I feel dreams generally have great therapeutic qualities in helping to heal 'disease'. We are far more than just physical vehicles and I see dream as an access point to allow us to 'get in contact' with our emotional and spiritual bodies. Lucid dreaming has been a bonus for me personally, as through being aware of my dreams, and with the control and options I have, I can focus my attention on the 'disease' I find in my own life, and try to help others through my insights. On many occasions I have been able to 'send light' from my lucid dream vantage point to those who my intuition directs me to. I would point out that I have no 'innate power' as it were. I am simply redirecting what I see as positive energy; it certainly does not emanate from me. I do realise, however, that I am stronger in my lucid state (more positive, emotional, empathetic, etc.) than in my waking state, though there is no doubt that it is due to my lucid dreaming that I seem to be gaining strength in my waking state proportionately.

Many therapeutic practices focus on raising energy because of its healing dimension, for instance, the underlying principle of Reiki is to open channels so energy can flow, as Eleanor McKenzie says in *Healing Reiki*: 'Reiki is healing energy in its truest sense. When the Reiki practitioner channels this life energy through their hands to the recipient, it activates the body's natural ability to heal itself.' The process of attunement in Reiki is quite distinctive from other forms of healing. It is not giving the person something new, but unlocking, freeing up what was already there.

GREEN FOR RENEWAL

I dreamt I was on a golf course I know well. My son, who

died seven years ago, was walking towards the green, but somehow I just couldn't get to him.

Betty felt sad when she woke up because she could not reach her son. 'Yet,' she told me, 'I'd really like to believe in some kind of heaven and that he's having a good time.' The longing is all too apparent, as is the frustration of being unable to get to him. In the dimension of time in dreams, past and future co-exist at the same moment, and space encompasses near and far, and in this shared space dead and living meet.

Green is worthy of further consideration because it crops up in a number of dreams in which death is involved:

My mother died and I went to sleep in a beautiful place where the grass is unlike any I've ever seen, it was so green.

In the Egyptian *Book of the Dead*, the elaborate rites surrounding death are described, including the ritual preparation of the dead for their journey to the next world. One part of the ritual involved a scarab made of green stone which symbolically gave the power of speech in the next life, emphasising the regenerative aspect of green. We see this connection in the custom of making wreathes of holly and ivy to decorate doors and homes at Christmas, a legacy from our pagan ancestors who brought in branches of evergreen trees to signify that, even at the darkest point of the year, life continues and light will return. From the cycle of growth in vegetation we see the pattern of renewal — what dies in the winter miraculously grows again in the spring.

Even in the most horrific of battles, the battle for Stalingrad where men reached levels of brutality and despair hardly ever equalled, there was still room for ritual. Malnutrition, the freezing cold and little hope of getting out alive did not prevent preparation for Christmas: 'Advent crowns were fashioned from tawny steppe grass instead of evergreen and little Christmas trees were carved out of wood in desperate attempts to make it "just like home".' In his bunker in the steppe in the north-west of

Stalingrad, Kurt Reuber, a doctor, amateur artist and friend of Albert Schweitzer, drew on the only paper available to him, the back of a captured Russian map. He drew 'an embracing, protective, almost womb-like mother and child, joined with the words of John the Evangelist: "Light, Life, Love". When the drawing was finished, Reuber pinned it up in the bunker. Everyone who entered halted and stared. Many began to cry. To Reuber's slight embarassment. his bunker became something of a shrine.' The need for connection is part of what it is to be human and where no rituals exist we make our own.

LAST RITES

Funerals are endings, they mark the end of physical life. Novelist Jim Crace, speaking about the events following the death of his father, said that his father had been a staunch atheist and had forbidden any funeral fuss. No guests, no readings, no drinks just get rid of the body. These wishes were followed but, as Jim said: 'It was probably the worst decision of my life.' He was left with a sense of emptiness and hollowness as if his father's life had not been marked in a fitting way. Rites of passage at death are for the living. They draw a line under a life and allow new beginnings. Without some marker, a longing rests in our hearts, a need to say in a public way even if it is only to a small group of intimates, this was a life and here it ended.

Dreams of death may be preparation for death or they may signal the end of one period of life as a new age begins. We will investigate this in depth in the next chapter but it is worth noting that last rites do influence dreams and have a part to play in the healing process. The connection with what has gone before is central to the existence of people who see beyond the physical reality of life, to the spiritual realm which permeates everything. In *Of Spirit and Water*, Patrice notes:

> Among the Dagara, the older you get the more you begin to notice spirits and ancestors everywhere. When you hear a

person speaking out loud, alone, you don't talk to them because he or she may be discussing an important issue with a spirit or ancestor. This rule applies more to holy elders than to adults in general.

Archetypal dreams are linked to the core issues — death and rebirth — as described earlier.

> If I dream of the dead I always say a prayer for the repose of that person's soul, which is something I was taught to do as a child.

Sometimes, depression feels like the self has died and death rituals are included in the dream. Theresa, for example, had dreams of being buried and shouting out 'I am not dead' but she said nobody could hear her as they stood around the grave into which the coffin was lowered.

When one twin dies, whether in the womb or at some point afterwards, the impact on the surviving twin is profound. The Yoruba make an image of a dead twin to prevent the surviving sibling from missing their other half too much. This recognition of the special impact of the loss of a twin makes such rites healing.

Our early ancestors prepared their dead for journeys beyond the burial plot or the funeral pyre. As well as ornaments, the Egyptians placed food for the dead in the coffin. Today, family and friends may place mementoes, flowers, poems or other significant objects in the coffin in much the same way as their ancient ancestors did. It maintains a symbolic link with the dead person.

'Sitting Shiva' is a Jewish tradition that marks the rite of passage for seven days following a death and *Jahrzeit* is the annual ceremony of remembrance. In other cultures there are festivals held at the burial places of the dead as well as specific ceremonies for ancestor worship and re-membering. Many believe that the dead come back to participate in these events. We see a consistent belief in some form of reincarnation after death.

Many traditions of the past that marked death in the past have now disappeared: kissing the dead; taking the body back to the home or having it rest there; the wake; stopping the clocks; closing curtains; covering mirrors; dressing in black or wearing black arm bands to inform the world at large that you have been bereaved. There are others — following the cortege (rather than preceding it) as it goes to the burial; lifting your hat or standing still when a hearse passes by and so on — all rituals which stop time in some way or cause us to reflect because an overt change has taken place: one of our kind has died. In Western societies, more often than not, these rituals are no longer observed. Instead we hurry on oblivious to the loss of one of our members.

However, the dead person remains in hearts and minds, in dreams and memories. We can't bury these hurriedly and tidy them away neatly like parcels of papers. For centuries, rituals and traditions have been built up precisely to focus on psychological and spiritual needs at times such as these. They have been developed around the needs both of the dying and the bereaved for their own good and the good of the community. In forgetting these rituals, we miss the opportunity for healing; we might find that retrospective counselling which comes months or years later might not be quite so necessary if such rituals were still followed. To our detriment we deny our frailty, our weakness and our inevitable mortality and when we do that we also forget our human need for ritual.

MEMORY BOXES

Creative, innovative rituals, appropriate to our times, can be based on creation myths, poetry, literature and all kinds of imagery. Our inherited characteristics, our pre-programmed instincts, biological drives and survival mechanisms carried in the body's memory all call out to us to engage in rituals because they are healing for individuals and for the world.

When Ruth Picardie knew she was dying she wrote wittily in her 'evolved, post-feminist chick' style of her deep sense of loss, particularly in relation to her twin children who were not yet two years of age:

Rites of passage

What hurts most is losing the future. I won't be there to clap when my beloved babies learn to write their names or kiss their innocent knees when they fall off their bikes.

Eventually she made memory boxes for her Lola and Joe and included letters to read when they are older. Perhaps other generations left such things in the form of physical legacies but where people die at a young age now, memory boxes are more consciously assembled to include objects of significance that the dying parent or the parent who is giving up a child for adoption, for instance, wishes to pass on to their child.

The ritual of marking death by the use of symbols is found throughout the world and springs from a deep need to connect with the dead person. Giving money to favoured charities instead of placing wreaths on the coffin and at the graveside or memorial spot is, of course, logical and laudable, yet it misses the symbolic significance of these acts. The glorious colours of the flowers, their celebratory, bright blooming that will wither and die, symbolises life. This age-old custom of marking death with flowers is a visual pointer to the transient cycle of life, a marker to signify the passage. Lanterns floated out onto water, a lake or a sea, are part of a Japanese ceremonial rite to mark the passing from life to death and is yet one more way to mark this rite of passage. I took part in this ritual once, on the anniversary of Hiroshima. To see the lighted candles floating out in tiny paper boats onto Lake Ullwater in the Lake District, just as dusk fell was profoundly moving. The flickering lights below the moon seemed universal, no language barriers separated us, there was only connection: 'Light, Life, Love.'

Spontaneous acts that arise in response to loss come from the very deepest part of our beings. Witness the flowers placed outside Kensington Palace and throughout the United Kingdom at the time of Princess Diana's death and the placing of candles at the site of a road death in some countries. One young boy with Down's syndrome told me how he had left seeds in the little shoe box in which his rabbit was buried because the pet could eat them on his way to heaven. No one suggested he do it, it rose from an instinctual need which we all share whether we are conscious of it or not. In working with clients, it is essential that we respect the need for the rituals they wish to perform in order to mark rites of passage and, indeed, where they have no awareness of rituals, we may actively raise this as part of their healing process.

Plato defined philosophy as the practice and preparation for death; when on his deathbed he was asked to state his philosophy in a single sentence, he replied: 'Practise to die'. We will return in Chapter 9 to this theme of dreams as part of the individual's preparation for, and initiation into, death.

CHAPTER 7

CREATIVE SOLUTIONS

> Dreams teach us how to live an enchanted life: how to glimpse underworld themes and characters in daily life, how to look at and listen to the arts, how to reflect deeply on relationships, and how to see the soul in our work.
>
> (Moore)

THE CREATIVE PROCESS

There is a certain genius in dreams that emerges from time to time and spontaneously touches the highest forms of creativity. They yield new and original ways of looking at the world. Throughout history people have used dreams creatively to inspire artistic and scientific endeavours. One reason for this lies in the fact that spontaneity and creativity are closely linked, often as spontaneity dries up so does creativity. Dreaming is a spontaneous activity which comes unbidden and in service of wholeness. There are many sources of creativity, one of which is the wound, physical or emotional, which has forced the individual to look inwards. The symptoms, so to speak, are used as a stimulus for expression, and dreams frequently direct the dreamer to the path that might lead to ease of suffering.

Montague Ullman MD, whose inspirational work spoke to my belief that dream work is not only the province of the professional analyst but can be used by anyone with a mind to do so, said: 'The dream as an accessible and ever available source for self-healing is reason enough to generate more interest in them. Most people are unaware of the remarkable power of their own creative imagination to select and shape images that have so much to say of immediate relevance to their lives.' His influence has changed the way in which dreams are used in group therapy in particular and in popular dream groups more generally.

Sybille Bedford, novelist and author of the definitive biography of Aldous Huxley, revisits early childhood losses as part of her creative journey, which is also one of healing past pain. Of her father she said in an interview with Patrick O'Connor for the British Sunday newspaper, *Observer*: 'I wish I'd known him more. I was ten when he died. I sometimes dream of him. I dream that he's alive and that I have not written to him for thirty years and it's absolutely appalling, because he's completely forgiving but very, very lonely, still sitting in the chateau. It still haunts me.' In her writing these re-connections find a voice.

The roots, as revealed in dreams, add creative force:

> I had a dream about therapy just after I'd stopped training, I was in a yard, all stone and concrete, the kind of thing you find a lot in the Potteries in place of a garden, and this woman was washing off blood from a chopped up carcass with a hose, and then hanging the pieces of meat on the line to dry, I was horrified and screaming don't wash all my blood away ... Not long after this dream I actually had a haemorrhage and lost a lot of blood ... I had to stay in bed flat on my back for a few days; I read Nor Hall's book, *The Moon and the Virgin*, which is very much about processes of creativity and the unconscious, lots of poetry ... one in particular ...

> what ever you have to say, leave
> the roots on, let them
> dangle
> And the dirt
> just to make clear
> where they came from
> Charles Olson

Sonia, who has worked with dreams in therapy wrote: 'I think most of our dreaming is a form of healing. They ask us to look at ourselves, difficulties in our lives, aspects of self which require change in order to grow and develop.'

CREATIVE LANGUAGE

The process of dream creation has its own title, Oneiropoiesis, which derives from the Greek *Oneiros* meaning 'dream' and *poiesis* meaning 'to create' (you can see the derivation of the word 'poetry' here too). Where creativity is blocked, dreams bring new clarity to old issues and offer solutions in a language full of symbols and metaphors that trigger the outpouring of transformative energy.

The language of dreams is deliciously inventive and dreamers each have their own 'vocabulary' that comes from personal experience. Ailsa, who had a brain tumour, had a dream in which she was lying on an operating table as a slug went into her mouth. Ailsa commented that the most distressing aspect of her illness for her was the progressive 'sluggishness' that she felt in body, mind and spirit.

Words are spun together in innovative combinations and images are juxtaposed so that completely new meanings come into being. In his book, *The Meaning of Dreams* which was based on a great deal of reseach into universal aspects of dreams, Calvin Hall sums up why symbols in dreams are not there to disguise meaning: 'There are symbols in dreams for the same reason there are figures of speech in poetry and slang in everyday life. Man wants to express his thoughts as clearly as possible in objective terms ... He wants to clothe his conceptions in the most appropriate garments ... For these reasons, the language of sleep uses symbols.'

Puns are a wonderful example and can be important in dreams:

I'm in a shop trying on hats, I know it's *'if the cap fits ...'*

> I'm working in a restaurant. The man I serve says, 'I don't like this trifle.' I say, 'There's nothing wrong with it.' Then he shot me with a silver gun. There was no blood but I was wounded. In my shocked mind I could hardly believe that I'd been *shot over a trifle*!

This second dream wittily mirrored the dreamer's irritation after a minor argument that she had had with her boss. She had to back down because it was a 'trifling' matter and she resented the power he had to impose his opinion.

> I was in a school classroom attending an evening class in Italian. It was the first lesson and the female teacher said she hoped we didn't mind working without a text book. She seemed to prefer that method but I wasn't very pleased. She then produced a story in Italian that was typed on a sheet of paper which we were to translate, just then all the lights went out and we continued translating *in the dark*.

Ignoring our most basic inner, creative self can lead to all sorts of frustrations and despair.

> I am in a garage which is dusty and cluttered. I begin clearing it out and remove paper waste. There are five dirty knives. A man has a key but he is holding it tightly. As I kiss him, he releases it easily.

Gina was practised at interpreting her own dreams: 'This is the garage in which the vehicle that takes us through time could be kept. I am trying to clean out the clutter in my subconscious, and I feel the knives represent my suppressed anger. With love, symbolised by the kiss, the key to understanding is released.'

ART OF THE INNER WORLD

> In dreams as in art, the unconscious seems to work toward insight in the language of pictures, a language of symbols.
>
> (Meyerhoff)

Dreams are multi-layered expressions of colour, narratives, symbols and 'formless', abstract representations of light and depth. As such, they are not only beautiful in themselves but express the landscape of our inner life. The philosopher, Emanuel Kant, warned us not to underestimate dreams because: 'in doing so we might well be carelessly overlooking one of nature's great mysteries'. He even suggested that ideas in dreams were 'clearer and broader than even the clearest in waking life'.

In *Myths to Live By*, Joseph Campbell talks about the inspiration for Oriental art:

> There are legends of ... some saintly monarch who will have had a dream in which he will have seen, as in a revelation, the whole form of the temple or city to be built. And I wonder if that may not be the reason why, in certain Oriental cities one can feel, even today, that one is moving in a dream; the city is dreamlike because in its inception it was actually suggested by a dream, which then was rendered in stone.

Tapping into this inner world enables clients to access personal resources previously undreamt of and knowledge of the success of others who have harnessed the creative power of dreams can be a distinct advantage. The artist, William Blake, for example, had been struggling to develop a new engraving technique and one night he dreamt that his dead brother demonstrated a new technique to him. When, on waking, he tried that method, he found it was exactly what he wanted to achieve. The previous thought that had gone into the problem was consolidated in the dream solution, a common feature of many problem-solving dreams, whether they are to do with science, the arts or personal relationships.

In his book, *The Dreaming Brain*, J. Allan Hobson concluded that while we sleep we engage in a process of 'fantastic creation. The brain of one and all is fundamentally artistic'. When our creativity is not recognised, I believe it causes us a sense of loss, a half-recognised grief that part of our lives is missing, which in turn manifests itself in feelings of an unsettled lack of meaning or direction. Like an unknown lost twin, we seek the other half, even when we have no conscious knowledge that an 'other half' ever existed. Part of the therapeutic work with clients is the introduction to such wholeness. 'Each of us', Hobson said, 'is a surrealist at night during his or her dreams: each is a Picasso, a Dali, a Felini — the delightful and macabre mixed in full measure.'

DREAMS AND THE ARTS

Many musicians, from Mozart and Beethoven to Sir Paul McCartney, have credited dreams for their compositions. Perhaps one of the most interesting examples of such inspiration is 'The Devil's Trill' by Tartini. In his memorable dream he sold his soul to the devil and gave him his violin to see how he could play it. 'But,' he said, as de Becker records, 'what was my astonishment when I heard him play with consummate skill a sonata of such exquisite beauty that it surpassed the most audacious dreams of my imagination. I was delighted, transported, enchanted ... and I woke up. Seizing my violin, I tried to reproduce the sounds I had heard. But in vain. The piece I composed, "The Devil's Trill", was the best I had ever written, but how remote it was from the one I had heard in my dream!'

LITERATURE

We live in and through stories. They conjure up worlds. We do not know the world other than the story world. Stories inform life. They hold us together and keep us apart.

(Mair)

People make meaning of their lives by organising their experiences, the pivotal events in their lives, into a narrative, a story that has a thread. Like the legend of Ariadne's thread which led Theseus safely out of the labyrinth, we can use dream strands and threads to guide us out of danger. We can weave their wonder into wisdom. In fact, one creative and revelatory technique to use when working with dreams, which I haven't mentioned so far, is to write the dream as if it were a fairy story. Begin 'Once upon a time ...' and cast yourself or ask the client to cast him or herself as the king or queen, a wicked step-mother or prince or princess and then relate the tale. The results are often startling and give great insight.

The contemporary novelist, Lesley Glaister, described the creative process as she knows it: 'I think it's very close to what happens when you dream. I dream all the time. I love it.' She came up with the title *Sheer Blue Bliss* after she dreamt she saw a book with that title on a library shelf.

In numinous dreams there is often a sense of profound healing. Emily Brontë referred to these when she wrote of dreams 'that have stayed with me ever after, and changed my ideas; they've gone through me and through me, like wine through water and altered the colour of my mind.' She felt creativity to be divinely inspired by the 'numen', the sacred.

Dreams and poetry have a number of characteristics in common, the main one being that they are more than the sum of just the words or images that are portrayed; it is the unique juxtapositions to reveal and evoke feeling in a novel way which make them so affective. They both 'create webs of associative meaning' as Anthony Stevens explains in his excellent book, *Private Myths: Dreams and Dreaming*. Poetry and dreams both call on archetypal images and knit them into the world of here and now. It is easy to see why Stevens concludes: 'dreams are poetry; consciousness is prose.'

There is the spark of the divine in dreams, in their creative potential to transform and transcend life. There is a freedom in the dream state and before visions melt away, we can capture them and dwell in them. For Linda Pastan, a Washington poet, they are the heartbeat of creativity:

Waking

In the first light,
in the first slippery light
we are born again,
and with the same struggle
every time. Thrown from the hammock of sleep on
hard ground
we lie there half amphibious,
watching our dreams move
helplessly away like fading
lantern fish.

And dreams are symbolic lanterns in their illumination of essential matter. Poets, from William Wordsworth to Ted Hughes, have believed in the power of dreams to enlighten and enhance creativity and we frequently see dream imagery included in their poetry.

Dreams play a part, not only in bringing inspiration for poetry, drama and novels, they are used within these as a device to put across the writer's views. Aeschylus, in verses 104 and 1–5 of the Eumenides, goes so far as to make Clytemnestra say that in her sleep, thanks to the visions of her dream, man's essence reveals itself with great clarity, whereas during the day the fate of mortals is hidden from them.

DREAM INCUBATION TO ENHANCE CREATIVITY

As we saw in Chapter 1, dream incubation was extensively practised in Ancient Greece and in many any other cultures and we have clear evidence that there is a close association between dream incubation and artistic inspiration. As with all dreams, they are influenced by cultural factors and suggestion and the dream wisdom, the 'inner oracle', reflects this.

This technique can be used successfully in therapeutic work with clients whether individually or in groups. It involves asking the dreaming self for creative inspiration, as in problem–solving to which we will turn our attention later in this chapter. The process is quite straightforward. In the following examples you can see different approaches to dream incubation: visualisation, in which the person or situation is pictured before sleep; a verbalised request for assistance, which may be simply stated or repeated like a mantra or ritual; or merely bringing the issue to mind and sleeping on it.

> I work with people in conflict situations; quite often I find I can't see any way of resolving either some personality difficulty that I'm having or some practical difficulty. I have two methods of asking for help from my dreams, depending on how I see the conflict; then as I am falling asleep at night I will picture the person or the difficulty and I will ask my dreaming self for a dream to help explain or resolve my difficulties. I look at my dreams the next morning with the problem in mind, and usually I will find a dream that makes some general if not specific comment on the problem.

> Sometimes I simply feel out of sorts or out of touch with myself, then as I am falling asleep at night I ask for a dream to harmonise my being. The dreams I've remembered from this have always been very therapeutic — in one of them I took a train back to about five years old, and I found myself in a pottery playing with clay and feeling blissfully happy and at peace, totally absorbed in what I was doing ... it was also a pointer in the sense that I need to have some kind of practical creative expression, otherwise I begin to feel very out of touch with myself.

★

> If I have a problem I need an answer to, I go to bed with the problem on my mind and repeat it over and over before falling asleep and then a few days later I'll dream about it.

When I wake I write it all down, sort the symbolism out and then I seem to have a solution or warning.

★

At night when I go to bed, I simply concentrate on whatever subject I wish to dream about and then relax into sleep. I do sometimes miss that night as if my brain had already chosen subjects for that night but I usually cover the subject the following night. I can shuffle through the problems in my head and choose to dream of something in particular and not leave dreams to chance.

One other technique I use for dream incubation is the Calling Card. I ask clients to get a piece of card, postcard size, and to make a drawing that represents what they wish to receive guidance about, and to write their request below the drawing. The card is then placed under the pillow before the client goes to sleep and in the morning the nature of the dream(s) that they have had can be considered; frequently the dreams do respond to the Calling Card request.

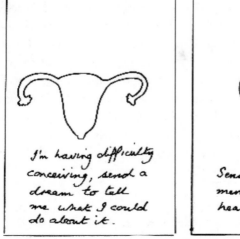

Examples of Calling Cards

Dreams, in their compensatory role, also provide an honest picture of the dreamer's inner world, revealing aspects that he or she needs to own and integrate. Dreams which arise from incubation direct towards balance and wholeness and it empowers clients to reach their higher, creative, problem-solving selves.

PROBLEM-SOLVING

> Whatever you can do or dream you can, begin it a genius has boldness, power and magic in it.
>
> (Goethe)

As we saw in Chapter 1, the problem-solving nature of dreams has been recognised throughout history in the everyday saying 'sleep on it.' This restorative function involves the dream drawing on memories of similar situations which might offer a resolution. The process of sleep and dreaming allows the mind to continue working on whatever issue is problematic and via dreams we call on earlier solutions to help with the present difficulty. In some way dreams scan our experience and draw on that knowledge base to bring forward new answers. As Deepak Chopra says: 'Memory is more permanent than matter,' and our bodies, like everything else on earth, contain atoms from the beginning of time and the origins of the universe. Kat Duff sums this up beautifully: 'Past and future time inhabit the present like threads so tangled the ends cannot be found.'

Many involved in the development of dream therapy have commented on their problem-solving nature. Alfred Adler saw that the dream 'indicated an attempt to face an actual difficulty in the life of the dreamer' and was 'a tentative feeler towards the future.' William Stekel saw the dream as seeking resolutions to the conflicts of the patient and as a 'guide to the life conflict of the patient.' Maeder, who saw the dream as communicating from the unconscious to the conscious for purposes of exerting 'suggestive and quiet influences' on the conscious ego, said in 1912: 'They seek and reach attempts at solutions of current conflicts.'

Research carried out by Bruce McNaughton and colleagues at the University of Arizona shows that during deep sleep the brain lays down memories but it needs regular bursts of REM sleep to clean up or strengthen the 'playback' equipment. This is likened to cleaning the head of a video tape recorder. The brain uses sleep to turn the day's fleeting patterns of nerve activity into more permanent memory traces. Scientists know that research volunteers deprived of REM sleep develop learning defects, which confirms that dreams have a vital role in day-to-day learning.

> ... Asking for a dream, when I was in my early teens and pre-puberty if I had a problem, I used to sleep on it, and sleep walk; often I would wake up either with the problem solved or at least with some peace of mind. My cousin, who is a year older than me, used to solve mathematical problems in her sleep ... my aunt recounts how she would walk around muttering to herself, having gone to sleep with some problem in her maths homework unresolved and would wake in the morning with a resolution.

*

> Dreams are the most helpful things I have found in my life. They explain how my childhood is affecting my adult life and they indicate what I can do about it. They help me face things I could not otherwise face and help me sort out problems.

OVERCOMING DIFFICULTIES

Dreams often provide clues as to how an individual is coping with an issue. For Helen, this dream indicates how successfully the problem has been dealt with:

> In my dream I am trying to cross a wooden bridge over a river. I see the water lapping over the bridge, in the middle.

I am afraid that if I continue and cross that part I will fall into the water but a stronger feeling forces me onward. I get to the other side OK without sinking in.

'Getting to the other side' symbolises overcoming the difficulty. Her other dreams help in different ways. In some she hears a voice telling her something, she is told to go ahead, everything will be OK. In others, she is shown a number of choices, then directed to the best one. When she dreams in very good colour, where all things and people are in bright colours, it signifies that problems will soon clear up as in life. Tara shows how, by working on her own dreams over a period of time, it is possible to build up a personal interpretive guide.

THE HEALING LANGUAGE OF DREAMS
The mind offers dreams at different levels, depending on the type of problem involved. Some deal with short-term problems and yield to simple, straighforward interpretations; others refer to deeper, more persistent anxieties and these often contain Jungian symbolism.

Food can have particular significance in the creative language of dreams. 'For me,' said Lucy, 'food always refers to current difficulties.' She told me of the dream that follows — it demonstates what she means. 'I had fallen asleep after asking my dream-mind for help to sort out a particularly difficult letter which refused to go into acceptable draft form; I woke and had this dream at the second attempt:

I was in the canteen where Arthur, my husband, works. It was under new management. Only two meals were on offer; I asked for the roast chicken, but had to make do with fried fish. There was a very large quantity on the plate, including chips, and the vegetable was served on a separate plate. The fish was broken up as if it was over-cooked, and there was some danger from bones. The vegetable was a small whole cauliflower au gratin. I ate what I could, but there was far more than I could manage. Arthur came in for his meal, took the first mouthful of fish and stood up — there seemed to be a fishbone in his throat.

This encouraged exploration of the type so wonderfully described by Ann Faraday in *The Dream Game*. In this you play with the language, allow images and connections to surface and see where they lead. What Lucy thought of, in relation to this dream was: 'food for thought'; 'fishy' meaning there was something was suspicious about the situation; 'more than I could chew', too much to take in; 'bone of contention', source of conflict; 'more than meets the eye', echoing the idea that some subterfuge was involved. The fish and cauliflower were coated/covered in breadcrumbs and this would make them harder for anyone 'to swallow'. This hardly told her anything new, but it did seem to clarify issues, bringing them into sharper focus and she managed to write the letter later that day. The whole issue no longer 'stuck in her throat', communication was as complete as it needed to be for her to get on with her task.

After working on a dream, not everything will be completely understood and neatly compartmentalised. Instead, there may be a feeling of loosening, an appreciation of mood that enables the dreamer to move forward. This is a form of lateral thinking, a mad idea with a grain of usefulness in it so that, having dreamt about them, problems do not appear as bad.

REHEARSAL

As we have seen, dreams prepare people for situations they have to face. Unlike waking visualisation, motivational imagery used by sports coaches amongst others or interview role-playing, for instance, these rehearsals arise spontaneously whilst we sleep. They increase confidence and self-esteem as well as enhancing performance. This dream occurred a couple of days before an interview for Zoe's first teaching appointment in a nursery:

I recall myself being escorted to an important and exciting

interview place. It was full of differing levels and opportunities which overawed me. I was receiving rather privileged treatment as I moved about these futuristic premises.

Then I am sitting facing an interview panel and looking how I would like to have looked. My face looked pretty and my normally unruly hair was styled to absolute perfection. I looked relaxed and answered the questions in a particularly confident and informed manner.

Looking back I may well have been confident deep down. I was well-informed on nursery education, had distinctions in academic teaching practice at the very same school *but* on a conscious level I was a bag of nerves, dreading it enormously. At the interview, I am grateful, even now, that the *dream feelings triumphed*. I got the job and the head said, more than once, that she had never known anyone interview so well. The feelings from that dream have continued, strong and enduring, and return at interview times.

Thank goodness I had this dream and, moreover, that I was in favour of myself since it is not exactly typical of me to treat myself this way in waking.

My dreams are helpful because they let me experiment on things I wouldn't have the courage to do in normal daily life. They are useful for carrying out socially unacceptable patterns of behaviour and fantasies ... Basically, dreaming is a road to freedom, you can do what you want when you want while dreaming. It's free time for you to use as you desire ... I can take chances I wouldn't normally take in day-to-day situations, and make decisions I could not make in everyday situations.

This spontaneous rehearsal in dreams may not always provide such positive imagery as Zoe's. In my research with pregnant women, many report distressing dreams of labour and delivery and fear that giving birth will be traumatic. However easy or difficult it may be, research by Carolyn Winget and Frederick Kapp into the relationship between dreams and childbirth found that the things a woman had dreamed about while pregnant were directly related to the length of her labour. Women who had delivered in less than average time, in less than ten hours, had anxiety in more than 80 per cent of their dream reports. The more the woman had anxious dreams of labour, the more likely she was to efficiently deliver her first child. The dreams express realistic anxiety prior to the big event and, in so doing, clear the way, so to speak, for a positive experience of childbirth.

Patricia Garfield, the celebrated American dream researcher, writes in *Creative Dreaming* of her own dreams about breast-feeding about which she felt anxious. She had dreams of starving kittens and worried about how she would feed them. She felt that her anxious dreams about nursing helped to prepare her to cope successfully with the situation in real life.

DREAMS AND SCIENTIFIC INVENTIONS

Part of the process of dreaming involves the scanning of all our stored memories in order to file information and experiences with those we have previously encountered. The completion of the dream message sometimes wakes the dreamer. This is a view shared by many of those who took part in Morton Schatzman's research into problem-solving and dreams. In many cases, once the solution to the problem had been found, the dreamers awoke. Many inventors have brilliant flashes of inspiration or make world-changing scientific discoveries via their dreams which complete their waking work.

Kelkule concluded his report to the Benzole Convention (1890) with these words: 'Let us learn to dream, gentlemen, and then we may perhaps find the truth.' F.A. Kelkule had for years been investigating the problem of the molecular structure of the benzene molecule. Driven to distraction and at a loss as to how to progress, he had a waking dream, a hypnogogic experience. In it, he 'saw' a snake swallowing its own tail, the archetypal symbol of the *urobos*. This snake, though, was a chain of atoms of carbon and hydrogen turning itself into a circle. He says he was awake in a flash, 'as if struck by lightning', as he realised that this ring pattern of atoms depicted the structure that had so far eluded him and all previous researchers. From his dream problem-solving, he discovered the foundation of modern chemical structural theory.

Danish physicist, Niels Bohr, was awarded the Nobel Prize for his formulation of quantum theory which has revolutionised our understanding of science. Like Kelkule, he had grappled for years with the problem. In Bohr's case, he was wanted to know how basic elements existed and how they maintained stability. One night he dreamt that he was at the races. The horses ran in clearly marked lanes, which they could change if they maintained a precise distance from each other. On waking, he knew with complete certainty that the 'rule of track' applied to electrons as they orbited their atom. Once again, the dream solution completed his waking work and made a vital contribution to our understanding of the universe.

Albert Einstein said that a dream he had as a young man inspired his scientific research. In the dream he was sleighing down a mountainside at the speed of light. He noticed that the stars refracted light curved into a spectrum of colours and he was so deeply moved by this that he puzzled over it and thought about it for days on end. In fact, he said that his complete scientific achievement had been the result of meditation on this dream which eventually led him to the theory of relativity.

There are many other examples of scientists whose dreams have extended the sum of knowledge that has benefited humankind: Dimitri Mendeleyev, a Russian chemist, fell asleep listening to chamber music and dreamt that the basic elements were linked to each other as melodies are; thus, the solution to the construction of the periodic table of elements was discovered. Elias Howe, inventor of the sewing machine, as we saw earlier, at one point was stuck with the final design problem of how to introduce a needle that would work with the series of mechanical 'teeth'. He dreamt of spears and at the tip of the spears were oval holes. He had the solution and knew where to put the eye of the needle so that his invention was finally completed.

These inventions do not come out of the blue but are the culmination of long, waking hours of dedicated research. When the focused mind is switched off, the creative side can come into play and release the solution. This is akin to the way in which, when we forget a name, instead of struggling to recall it, we say to 'Oh, it will come to me,' and — lo and behold! — it pops into our mind later when we are giving no thought to it. Sometimes, letting go means letting in.

DREAMS, ILLNESS AND CREATIVITY

> No one has ever written, painted, sculpted, modelled, built or invented except, literally, to get out of hell.
>
> (Artaud)

Dr Anthony Storr in, *The Dynamics of Creation*, supports the idea that writers and artists have created works to save their souls as well as their minds. The poet, Antonin Artaud, who suffered recurring bouts of mental illness, shared the view, held since earliest times, that art first heals the artist and then helps to heal others. 'Poetry led me by the hand out of madness' wrote the poet Anne Sexton, who, like Artaud, was hospitalised for psychosis. Lowell, a twentieth-century poet, captured the duality of health and creativity when he asked: 'Is getting well ever an art, or art a way of getting well?'

This obviously has implications for our work with troubled clients because the therapeutic value of creativity which springs from dreams is healing. Creativity has many functions:

~ it provides a means of escape from pain by giving another focus

~ it allows order to come from chaos

~ it acts as a cathartic outlet

~ it gives distance from anguish

~ it allows inner feeling to become visible in some form

~ it provides relief

~ it is a form of communication to others.

In *The Alchemy of Illness*, Kat Duff wrote of a healing gift she recieved:

> One of the most valuable gifts I received during my illness was a painting a friend made of a dream I had, and told him, about being sick. I hung it over the door to my bedroom, so that I could see it when I was lying in bed, and that painting, with its image of fingers of sunlight reaching into the dark folds of a lush landscape, has nourished me ever since, because it reflects my dream back to me magnified through the eyes and heart of my friend.

Inside each of us there is a creative soul trying to communicate. It may be through words, in painting, in dance or through music but, whatever the form, that spirit of creation has all too often been beaten down by insensitivity and ridicule. Yet like a plant covered by harsh tarmac, it struggles once more to seek the light and forces its way through to our consciousness, often through our dreams.

Fiona's dreams of being naked in public and being observed when she was on the toilet relate to her creativity. Afraid that her poetry would be judged harshly, she avoided showing her work to anyone and finally stopped writing. Eventually, though, her dreams forced her attention to the consequences of this suppression of her talent; she dreamt she was being chased by a female vampire through a series of tunnels. 'When I woke up,' she said, 'I knew I had to get back to writing poetry because all those tunnels were about me trying different ways to please other people, but they were leading nowhere. And the vampire was that part of myself that wanted to suck my life's blood, because I know now that without expressing that creative part of me I might as well be a zombie, which is what happens to you after a vampire gets you.

THE SIGNIFICANCE OF COLOUR

In my book, *Creative Visualization with Colour*, the significance of colour in relation to vibrational energy, the chakras and symbolic associations, are described at length, as is their relationship to healing visualisations. There is not the space here to explore colour in dreams other than to say briefly that colours give information about the mood and emotional health of the dreamer. This is apparent in art therapy as well as dreams.

Kay Redfield Jamison, in *Touched with Fire*, a book about manic-depressive illness and the artistic temperament, cites the evidence that manic patients tend to use vivid and highly contrasting colours, whilst depressed patients primarily use black and colder, darker colours. My experience is that depressed clients also have many dreams in which grey is prevalent and, as mood lightens, the dream palette brightens. Look at colour as an information code For instance, if someone is driving a red car in a dream, it is helpful to know that red is the colour of power and energy and the car often represents the physical self. Red also relates to the first chakra which is the life energy centre; if the car had been grey or gold there would be different connections to be made.

Colour is associated with healing as well as creativity. When working with clients it is important to note the dream colours, their range, the psychological connections the dreamer makes to them and how colour changes during the therapeutic process, as demonstrated in Yvette's dream series:

> I just know that in times of emotional pain, working my way through 'baggage' I saw a lot of green and turquoise or blues. Peace and calm, throat and heart chakra, power and self-expression and love and understanding. So when I have been given these particular colours, (a) I feel a sense of peace and

calm, (b) I place it within the context of my present emotional well-being. This is healing to me because it tells me I am making changes, opening myself to other forms of being, which I had probably closed myself to before.

My psychic visions always come/evolve out of a white/blue light. I would suppose this is so that one is not frightened as white is pure and protecting and blue is calm. Blue is also of spirituality and green of healing growth. More recently I see a lot of pink, in various ways. Once it was the outside lights of a house, the other day it was just this haze in front of me. To be honest, I was just too lazy to waken myself fully to write down the dream, so all that stayed with me was the colours.

I have also had dreams where people in the dream direct this forceful beam of green light through their eyes. I, at this stage, can only take this to mean healing. I know that after I see a colour, I feel marvellous.

There is often discussion about whether people dream in colour or experience other senses in dreams. I have found that all the senses are recalled in dreams, though not by all dreamers. Tim spoke of his own experience:

I dream in technicolour, with sound, smell, taste, everything. Some people have told me they dream in black and white, or silently. This has amazed me. My dreams are like being there.

Black and white dreams may indicate a tendency to see things in 'black and white', with little gradation or room for manoeuvre. Margaux had dreams of cameo silhouette cut outs: 'They seem to have been about the trouble between my husband and I. They showed conflict, negotiation, legal documents, lawyers, to me these are all black and white issues.'

THE CREATIVE POTENTIAL OF 'HOUSE' DREAMS

> I can see cracks and damp patches in the ceiling gradually getting larger so I know the roof is falling in.

'It is a rare thing for a house not to represent the body of a woman,' wrote Nor Hall, the Jungian therapist, and my research into women's dreams certainly confirms her view. Not only do houses signify the body, but rooms, the state of repair, the cellars, dark and hidden, in fact, almost everything to do with our dream house may reflect our uniquely personal, physical or psychological state. As clients often bring dreams in which houses or related buildings feature, it is worth giving them particular attention.

Charlotte explained how her dreams changed during a particularly traumatic time in her mid–twenties:

> The house is a good indicator of my psychological state. It has developed from being decayed to being burnt down, to being just the wooden framework and now the top rooms are beautifully decorated. The lower floors are still waiting.

She has been seeing a therapist for two years and has gained great insight into both the causes of her poor physical health and the depression that haunted her from adolescence. As she has improved, so her dream house has risen from the ashes and has been transformed. She still has work to do though — the cellar awaits. In Jungian terms, the cellar is the foundation of our emotions where our deepest, earliest experiences which lay down the foundation of our life are hidden.

Brain tumours are greatly feared and often hard to diagnose, as we saw earlier. Alice, in 1991, was diagnosed as having a benign brain tumour after she had sought orthodox and alternative remedies to cure a variety of symptoms. Her symptoms were getting worse but no one could tell her why or what was wrong. 'During that time,' she told me, 'I had a recurring dream. It always took place in an unknown building. In it, I would enter the front door, and start searching every floor for the "ghost". As I got to the top floor there was always a closed door and I knew the ghost was on the other side.' Somehow, this illusive phantasm symbolised the unidentified mystery of her illness; just as she couldn't find the ghost, her doctors couldn't find the cause of her illness. She explored the landscape, she went from the bottom to the top of her dream building and came to a locked door at the top where she finally located the problem. Similarly, she was checked out from toe to head and finally the 'head man', the senior consultant, discovered her brain tumour.

Since the operations to remove the tumour, Alice has never had the dream again. In so many instances, once there has been a correct diagnosis and treatment for a condition dreams alter or stop. Their work of communication has been completed. The top of the house or building frequently represents the head or brain of a dreamer, either on a physical or intellectual, cognitive level.

Rooms often signify particular aspects of our character and can reveal much about how aware clients are of themselves and their motivations. Are the rooms open and accessible, or closed off? Many people see the doors to rooms in their dreams but cannot get into them. However, as their situation changes, these previously out-of-bounds rooms become open, as was the case for Alice. In working with clients it is helpful to be aware of access to rooms, for instance, do doors have handles? can they be opened?

FANTASY WORK

Lucid dreaming is the awareness, while dreaming, that we are dreaming. The brain and body are in the same physiological state during lucid dreaming as during most ordinary non-lucid dreaming, that is, REM sleep. Dreaming is a result of the brain being active at the same time as the sense organs of the body are turned off to the outside world. In this condition, typically during REM sleep, the mind creates experiences out of currently active thoughts, concerns, memories and fantasies. Knowing that you are dreaming simply allows you to direct the dream along constructive or positive lines, much as we would direct our thoughts when awake. In addition, lucid dreams can be highly informative because a dreamer can observe the development of their dream, which arises from the their own feelings and actions, while being aware that they are dreaming. Some clients may find that waking visualisations, day dreaming or meditation may help them to develop lucid dreams. One simple way to do this is to dream the dream onwards, in other words imagine what might have happened next if the dream hadn't finished where it did. What if another character had come along? Any aspect of the dream can be developed in this way and it can be useful since it puts control back with the client.

Active imagination is a useful approach for clients who are plagued by nightmares. In 1973, Luthe and Schultz formulated the therapeutic imagery techniques of **autogenic training**. Their research confirmed that the systematic practice of Jung's active imagination techniques are associated with a decrease of disturbing nightmares, presumably because the anticipation of the material desensitises the client. Also, they noted a remarkable thematic continuity between autogenic imagery and subsequent nocturnal dream imagery. The systematic and repeated induction of a waking fantasy state also brought an increase in archetypal dreams.

Meditation, active imagination and visualisation all involve the same regression process, drowsiness and a meditative state where attention is removed from the usual attention-demanding activities of everyday life. Also, the three processes may have bizarre elements and some interchangeability of function. Many people who meditate or who practise active imagination find that their dream life becomes less intense since areas common to both are being accessed during waking hours. It is as if the need to dream has been satisfied. Jung found that when fantasies are made conscious in waking life, then the nature of dreams changes. They become weaker in impact and less frequent because the waking images anticipate the dreams.

When people begin meditating, their dreams often begin to include more highly symbolic material. Experienced yoga meditation practitioners have been found to have more archetypal dreams, higher dream recall and richer dream content than non-meditators. Clients who practice meditation, particularly if they have done so over a long period, will find active imagination easier.

THE FUNCTION OF LUCID DREAMING

In one of my lucid dreams I was shot in my arm which immediately started pouring with blood and made me fall to the floor. I suddenly thought what is all this fuss about, I can do as I please, this is only a dream and on this reflection, I stand up although my arm's still bleeding and I observe myself walking off into the distance pleased as punch ... Sometimes I have the same dream over again and in my dream I always find myself saying, 'I've had this dream before!' and I know exactly what is going to happen.

The laws of physics and society are repealed in dreams. The only limits are the reaches of imagination. Some argue that much of the potential of dreams is wasted because people do not recognise that they are dreaming. Anxiety dreams and nightmares can be overcome through lucid dreaming because if the dreamer knows he or she is dreaming, they have nothing to fear; dream images cannot hurt and the dreamer can control the action. In addition to helping the dreamer lead dreams in satisfying directions, lucid dreaming brings fantastic adventures and can be a valuable tool for success in waking life. However, it is important not to use lucid dreaming as yet another way to deny access of the unconscious to the waking mind by attempting to control every dream.

To my continued amazement I enjoy the thrill and satisfaction of the creative aspect of my dreams, particularly my lucid ones. I have painted, written poetry and re-arranged countryside views to my specifications. Many such creations have filled me with such joy that I have woken in tears of happiness, yet in my waking life I am generally a down-to-earth type of person. Perhaps it is no coincidence that I am having some success in the arts in my day-to-day living. Quite a few of my ideas have their origin in my lucid experiences.

Daniel found that his awareness of wider spectrums of colours, emotions and possibilities grew in lucid dreaming. These are all attributed to his lucid experiences. He also feels he has more confidence, energy, understanding and insight into past experiences than he ever believed possible because of his lucid dreams: 'I have learned that life itself is relative and certainly not absolute. Dreams are also types of reality and these too have many sub divisions. I strongly feel that one does one's self a great injustice to put all one's life's efforts into one aspect/reality. Integration and growth needs to be made on all levels and that of course means our "dream lives". Dreams have the advantage of letting us access our subconscious more easily — and that cannot be a bad thing, especially if we can act on our self knowledge.'

OUT OF BODY EXPERIENCES

Out of body experiences (OOBEs) are sensations in which the dreamer feels he or she is separated from their physical body and looking at it from a distance.

> Twice I have had an 'out of body' experience. Where I dream or do I? This is so strange, that I float out of my body around the bedroom only and I can see myself asleep and dreaming looking very snug and comfortable. This is a weird experience but very nice and gives a feeling of satisfaction.

OOBEs have been reported throughout history and all over the world and are given as arguments by those who believe that consciousness goes beyond the body. Astral travel, an older term for OOBEs, is often described by dreamers in terms of spiritual dimension and this is the area to which we turn now as we explore healing, 'soul journeys' and related phenomena.

CHAPTER 8

HEALING THE SOUL

> The dream is a little hidden door to the inner most recesses of the soul.
>
> (Jung, 1990)

In the therapeutic relationship, some clients have a deeply rooted need to explore the spiritual dimension of their existence. Whatever the nature of a person's spiritual path, it will probably feature in the dreams brought to therapy. Whether it is in the sense of a universal interconnectedness, the Gaia view or related to a spiritual practice such as Zen, mindfulness meditation or Christianity, it touches the core of the client's life.

THE TRANSPERSONAL DIMENSION

The spiritual approach to counselling and psychotherapy call upon the integration of two aspects of what it is that makes us human. A consideration of the origin of the word 'human' helps: *hu* comes from divine; man comes from *mana*, which means mind. When divinity and thought are joined, our full potential may be realised. 'Transpersonal' means 'beyond the ego'. When working with clients in a transpersonal framework, personal crises or breakdowns are seen as purposeful; they act as warnings and indicate a need to change, grow, break through and renew. The aim is to build on people's strengths, balance inner and outer life, to integrate creativity with receptivity and to find expression for a spiritual perspective on personal development and interaction.

In Britain, **transpersonal psychology** is regarded as a branch of humanistic psychology, following the work of Carl Rogers. In the USA, humanistic psychology and the transpersonal are more differentiated and the latter has a more spiritual base. Jung was the first to use the term 'transpersonal' to refer to the 'collective unconscious' which we have discussed in earlier chapters. The transpersonal centre of each individual has different names — the soul, the spirit, the transcendent self which is distinct from the personal ego.

Transpersonal psychology focuses on the assumption that human beings have higher needs, such as the need for love, close friendships, dignity, individuality, self-fulfilment and so on, needs that go beyond biological requirements. Where these transpersonal needs are not met then distress and pathology may result. Many of us don't hear the voice that calls us to redress this loss, because the frenetic whirlwind of our lives smothers the sound. We get to the end of the day and can't explain where it went or why there was not even half an hour just for ourselves. Insidiously, dis-ease sneaks up in the form of headaches or listlessness or an inexplicable feeling that something is wrong. We can't describe it adequately, words fail to capture its essence: depression? mid-life crisis? relationship breakdown? loss of hope? is it physical or is it something else?

In particular, Abraham Maslow saw a direct relationship between 'peak experiences' and self-actualisation. Peak experiences can occur in dreams where the higher or inner self becomes apparent. In meditation, reverie and prayer, the 'still small voice within' has room to speak. Personal growth experienced in counselling ultimately leads to an increasing self-realisation, knowing one's own spiritual nature.

Throughout history the spirit has spoken through dreams, particularly in the language of imagery which communicates where words are inadequate. Transpersonal therapists use symbolism and techniques involving images extensively and anyone wishing to work with the variety of esoteric images that come in dreams, especially those of a spiritual nature, is well advised to become well-acquainted with the traditional symbolism of the culture to which the client belongs. In addition, some awareness of legends, myths, astrology, Tarot, Celtic and shamanistic tales and alchemy are helpful since images related to these frequently crop up, as we have already discovered.

THE TRANSCENDENT FUNCTION OF DREAMS

Sacred means 'set apart' — set apart from our mundane daily activities, set apart from our typical space and perhaps set apart from our habitual ways of thinking and being. Often it is related to someone or something other than ourselves, be that God, or Gaia, the universal other or whatever else is held to be transcendent by the individual. These sacred activities are not necessarily associated with religious organisations — though they may be — but they may equally be personal, spiritual paths.

Opposites such as good and evil, love and hate, life and death can according to Jung be reconciled. Indeed, it might be a life's work to reconcile this duality; 'awareness of the shadow means suffering the tension between good and evil in full consciousness, and through that suffering they can be transcended' (Stevens). Jung argued the transcendent function can only become manifest through symbols. In attending to dreams, symbols spontaneously arise as if our unconscious answers our conscious concerns. The unconscious mind keeps working as we sleep.

> It is with the soul that we grasp the essence of another human being, not with the mind, nor even with the heart.
>
> (Henry Miller)

THE WEB OF CONNECTION

Our dreamscapes provide maps of pathways that can advise us in a host of different ways. In some instances, there is a direct physical correlation between the dream image and physical condition, as we saw in Chapter 3; in others, the mapping relates to the emotional or spiritual dimension of our existence. Many people find it hard to go to a doctor and say: 'I've lost my path, I don't know what I'm doing with my life.' That seems too nebulous, too self-indulgent, though many of us are afflicted with great doubts, depressions and free-floating anxiety at some point in life. Somehow it is more acceptable to go along with a physical disorder that can be seen or felt by the doctor than it is to go with complaints about feeling distressed. To overcome this, we may unconsciously develop physical symptoms which 'legitimately' gain access to the attention we need. Psychosomatic illness is every bit as real and painful as organic illness though it is still viewed as suspect in some quarters. Holistic healing includes the whole mind, body and spirit in taking care of the totality of our being and can start anywhere. But often the signpost comes in a dream and points to a spiritual vacuum, a soul loss which longs for connection.

Kelly Bulkeley, who has focused his research on dreams and spirituality, describes how dreaming connects, integrating psychological and religious aspects of life. Originally the word 'religion' meant 'to tie' or 'bind'; religion, in essence, is the binding, the connecting, of humans with the divine. Spiritual dreaming, in cultures all over the world, served to connect people more closely to the powers of the sacred.

We find powerful evidence of spiritual forces at work in many people's dreams, forces that stimulate the emergence of a more complex, creative and developed self-consciousness and a closer relationship with whatever it is that the individual recognises as the ultimate power and reality of the cosmos. Dreams also spur us to new and vigorous growth, often by stirring up our emotions, confusing us, challenging our habitual assumptions and mischieviously disturbing our waking conventional responses. The creative power of dreaming depends on making, breaking, connecting and disconnecting and, ultimately, re-connecting in a way that re-inspires life.

Quantum physics has shown there are no building blocks of nature — instead there is only the interconnecting web of energy relationships, as described by James Redfield in *The Celestine Vision: Living the New Spiritual Awareness*. And this interconnecting web goes beyond the individual to reach out to our planet and to the universe. At the Spirituality and Health Conference I attended at Durham Castle, the lack of the sacred in everyday life and the spiritual vacuum that is left was described as being at the heart of many physical and emotional maladies. Moreover, as Dr David Bellamy, the famous environmentalist, said:

> A lost spirituality means a lost ecology. When the spirit is crushed, we do not protect the earth. When the earth is in crisis, everything suffers.

UNMAPPED TERRITORY

The Jungian analyst, Arnold Mindell, worked with comatose patients. It led him to believe that they are not in an unreachable, unconscious state, but are going through 'inner experiences' that carry powerful meaning. These travellers in an unknown territory, he argues, experience ecstasy, terror and personal transformation which prepares them for death, or for re-entry into life. Its lesson may be that we have to be prepared to die in order to live.

Serious, possibly life-threatening, illness can push the patient into deep contemplation, where their priorities are re-assessed and the meaning of their existence dwelled upon. Dreams as active communication provide relevant data. On recovery, where this was not expected, the 'survivor syndrome' may emerge with its close companion, depression, which we have already seen. Nightmares are experienced in Intensive Treatment Unit (ITU) syndrome while patients are recovering from surgery, coma or other potentially life-threatening treatment. They have initial dream horror, waking up from sleep terrified without any obvious external cause. These dreams may be so disturbing that the patient tries to avoid sleeping at night, which hinders the recuperative process. Of particular interest in terms of healing the soul is the fact that ITU syndrome is accompanied by intense feelings of spirituality, whether or not this had been of interest to the patient previously. In their dreams, walking with the dead, visiting other worlds, out of body experiences and shamanistic rites all play a part, to the astonishment of the patient who has never had such dream experiences before. This rarely investigated phenomenon has been graphically described by Professor Joel Richardson of Manchester Metropolitan University, who experienced ITU syndrome first hand and survived to tell the tale.

Quite by chance, psychotherapist, Helen Deutsch, noticed something different in the dream narratives she was hearing. It was one of those random coincidences in which a number of her new patients were reporting similar dreams; what they had in common, she discovered, was that they had all recently had surgery. She found that post-operative dreams were full of angels, death and the patients' own funerals. As with many of the ITU patients, being opened, literally through surgery and metaphorically too, triggered a different emphasis in their dreams ranging from the worldly to the more spiritual.

TOUCHING THE VOID

In autobiography, biography, literature and poetry, the sharing of experiences can be of immense therapeutic value in healing the soul. *My Year Off* by Robert McCrum tells of his brush with death after suffering a stroke at the age of forty-two. His 'brush' in fact, led to a sweeping away of previous preoccupations, a clearing out of old habitual responses and a re-assessment of life and the importance of love. The crisis, as so often happens, brought about a transformation.

After his book was published, hundreds of people from all over the world wrote to him to share their experiences, to meet with a fellow sufferer who knew the 'stroke' territory, who knew what it was like to have 'an insult to the brain', as it is also termed. In his article 'The Suffering of Strangers' (*Observer*, 7 February 1999), he wrote:

> ... This especially distressing letter, in the spidery writing of the dying, arrived just before Christmas from a London hospice:

'I am a terminal cancer patient of 72 with tumours on the right side of my brain who has undergone an experience of collapse somewhat similar to yours. I am extremely grateful to you for using your expertise in reporting back from post-stroke country so as to make it plain to my family and friends what I am going through.'

McCrum's wife, Sarah, was also affected by his stroke, as is the case for many friends and partners of victims of illness who may seek counselling because of their own loss. In her diary for 16 August 1995, Sarah recorded:

I dreamed last night that I had polio (her father had suffered polio as a child) and couldn't walk. For a bit — but when I started to recover Robert still had it far more seriously. I felt pathetic and weak and sorry for myself, while my side was paralysed. I keep wondering what it is like for him. I feel very alone and scared.

McCrum wrote: '... there's the pain of despair, loneliness and loss — the aching void in the lives of the bereaved ... In Anglo-Saxon times life was characterised by the poets as a sparrow fluttering out of the howling storm into the brightly lit mead hall, circling through the laughter and smoke for a moment, before disappearing once more into the dark ... Sometimes when I read these letters, I sense that dark just beyond the window.' We and many of our clients may share that sense.

Robert McCrum's illness initiated him into another world:

At times, my year off was one of all-pervading slowness, of weeks lived one day, even one hour, at a time, and of life circumscribed by exasperating new restrictions and limitations. The poet Coleridge observed that it is the convalescent who sees the world in its true colours, and, as a convalescent, I have been forced into a renewed acquaintanceship with my body and into the painful realization that I am, like it or not, imprisoned in it. I have learned, in short, that I am not immortal (the fantasy of youth) and yet strangely, in the process I have been renewed in my understanding of family and finally, of the only thing that really matters: love.

As the Quakers have suggested, the gates of the soul can be opened by great pain and also by great joy. For Robert and Sarah McCrum, their great pain was followed by a joyous event: On Candlemas, 2 February 1997, their daughter, Alice, was born.

In his extraordinary novel *Quarantine*, Jim Crace touches on the heart of healing, the spiritual healing of physical barrenness of Marta, who had come to the desert for forty days to fast and seek a cure for her infertility. Gally, the young man from Galilee who came to seek his god, has died after thirty days of complete fasting and Marta dreams of him after being violently raped by Miri's malevolent husband. She speaks to Miri:

> 'I watched somebody walking up. I hid. I thought it was your ... Don't even make me say his name. You know. Then I saw him. I knew it had to be the Gally. The same dead face. Just skin and bones. He was as near to me as you are now. I could have touched him. But he touched me. He touched my cuts and bruises. And then he kissed my feet.' Miri laughed. 'That only happens in women's dreams.' 'He touched my stomach afterwards, like a priest. He said, "This is a son for Thaniel." How could he know my husband's name? He said he's given me a child, just with his fingertips. That's something else that only happens in a woman's dreams.'

Marta had never seen the young man except in her dreams, a hundred times she dreamt of the face that she only saw in the flesh when she and Miri were preparing him for burial. A face as familiar as her own, yet known only through dreaming. Though this is, of course, a work of fiction, Crace explores what people experience in their dreams, a sense of intimate knowledge of another person, a guide or a healer and an overwhelming belief that they have been healed, cured, renewed.

STUCK: PARALYSIS

> Things do not change; we change.
>
> (Henry Thoreau)

Clients bring dreams of being stuck, unable to progress through what feels like muddy treacle or glue which sticks to their feet and hinders progress. This is a motif repeated throughout diverse cultures: 'The essential archetypal motif in "Everywoman ..." is simply getting stuck — turning to stone, falling asleep, being given impossible tasks to perform. This extreme stage of development generally occurs — but not always — prior to enantiodromia, to the creative freeing of bound-up psychic energy' (Nor Hall, *The Moon and the Virgin*).

Thus, being held back or in one place may signal the point of germination which is about the burst through to visibility, the activity is there but it is happening at an unconscious level. Knowing this can be reassuring to both client and counsellor since this can be a 'sticky' phase in the therapeutic process and it is useful to explore this concept together. Also, the feeling may not always be unpleasant, as Annie's experience reveals:

> In this dream I was waiting for some potential/promise to be fulfilled. I felt treasured, warm and happy. I was surrounded by soft white light.

THE DIVINE CHILD

In the Western world, the most familiar Divine Child story is the birth of Jesus Christ. It is a fraught time and, immediately after the birth of Jesus, King Herod attempts to kill all male babies in order to preserve the inheritance for his son rather than the baby his seers have told him will become 'King of Israel'. Joseph's dream angel warns him of the oncoming onslaught and so the family escape. In this we have the typical sense of threat which is so characteristic of Divine Child motifs. Although beset by danger, the baby survives and, with it, inextricably woven into the motif, is the sense of hope and a sense of future.

Creative new potential is at the heart of many 'baby' dreams, though the destructive shadow aspect is usually present too. This symbolises the conservative aspect of human nature which wants to fight any change and prevent growth to maintain the status quo. Yet the journey of individuation battles on. It symbolises the eternal conflict of status quo versus growth, safety in the known and fear of the new, no matter how self-limiting this may be. In work with clients, baby or Divine Child dreams often come at a time when they are 'stuck', when they feel unable to move out of the familiar though uncomfortable rut and are holding on to outworn, sometimes self-destructive, patterns of behaviour and thinking. There is a need to throw off the old order.

The Divine Child has many unusual attributes which may include the ability to speak another language or to utter poetry; to carry out unusual actions; and to offer startling insights. A Divine Child is aided by nature, animals or magic creatures and has the task of bringing light to the world to dispel the 'darkness' that causes sorrow to body and spirit.

The presence of a baby is an archetypal motif in dreams and myth, typically, the unexpected nature of the baby's birth or presence or the baby may be abandoned, lost, forgotten, not fed and so on. In the archetypal neglect dream, baby rarely has a name. This is a significant factor since most who have this dream have busy, full lives with 'named' activities that fill diaries, leaving little, if any, space for that unnamed creative potential, or spiritual side, that has been crowded out of life. One way to move forward with clients who have this dream is to discover what aspect of themselves it represents and to name it. 'My creative self', 'the artist' and 'the writer inside me' are some my clients have chosen.

In this act of owning and naming the 'baby', it is accepted and recognised as being in need of nurturing.

In *The Living Labyrinth*, Jeremy Taylor wisely says that all dreams come 'in the service of health and wholeness'; no matter at what point in life the dreamer has this dream, it is an affirmation that he or she has the potential to transform their life, to grow by harnessing the creative spark within, for: 'The Divine Child is the patron of all such changes in consciousness and creative possibility.'

> In this dream my husband and I are in a large room. There are lots of children in cots and beds. My husband and I cover the children with blankets and tuck them in. I know we are helping them to keep warm and safe. Somewhere in the room is a child who belongs to us but we are caring for all of them.

THE COMFORT OF DREAM COMPANIONS

We have seen many examples of threat and anxiety in dreams. However, we also find companions, guides, advisors and healers in dreams who aid the dreamer and recover lost souls. Physicality is often much less important than the spritual dimensions:

> In this dream I do not have a body but it seems as if I am linked with another presence that is very calm, kind and loving. This being seems to be guiding me through a clear space and helping me to identify other gaps and spaces.

It is there, between night and day, as we sleep, that deeper messages whisper in dreams and light radiates to reveal new pathways that can answer those very questions. Gina recalled what happened to her:

> One time, when I was going through a period of spiritual changes after I felt I was going to die, I travelled from my

dream, all the way to the edge of the Sea of Galilee. I met a being who to me felt like the one we know as Christ. He was very, very brilliant and there was a tremendous feeling of knowledge but I did not tell anyone because I did not want to end up in a psychiatric ward. Besides which, it didn't have the same religious connotations for me as it might for some people. I was suspicious about what someone like that was doing with me and why I had been drawn to that being when I was in such a vulnerable state.

The dream opened the locked door of awakening. It was unexpected because, as she said, she was not religious in the conventional sense, images of Christ were not part of her everyday life. And yet, such images are commonly present if the spiritual side of a person is developing — which is understandable when you think of them as shorthand symbols. For Gina, brought up in a Christian tradition, there are dimensions that give solace and insight, as the dream shows. Where these may lead who can say, we only know that Gina herself, surprised as she was, felt enriched and empowered by her dream.

Whatever a person's culture there will be certain icons that are linked with specific aspects of spiritual life or physical life. We are all influenced by the images of the culture in which we live and, if you live in the West, you can easily see many Christian icons — the cross at Easter; the star and crib at Christmas; and images of Mary, Jesus and angels. Angels in particular are to be found everywhere, on wrapping paper, in food advertising, and this mirrors the upsurge in interest in 'Angelology'.

Swans and angels may not immediately impress you as being anything to do with healing but for Dina they were a godsend. Having had heart trouble for some time she was particularly upset when she had a fall. The pain was excruciating and she was rushed to hospital. There had been a huge football match in the city and a bloody brawl, so, as she was quiet and undemanding, she'd been put on a trolley in the Emergency Department and left in a cubicle. She was in considerable pain and drifted into unconsciousness.

> I dreamt of swans which turned into angels. At one stage these angels definitely tended me and comforted me assuring me I would soon be well.

The nurses and doctor who eventually treated her, were amazed at how 'good' their patient was in view of the fact that she had a broken hip. They said they couldn't understand why she hadn't been screaming in agony. 'I didn't tell them about the angels though, I thought if I did, they'd take me to the mental ward instead of theatre! ... Whatever the truth of it,' she said, 'I awoke out of pain to feel healed and comforted.' In fact, apart from the operation wound she had no further pain whatsoever. Since then she has had other dreams of angels when she has been unwell. When the pain has gone, the 'angels' change to swans and, though she has tried to reach out and touch them, they elusively swim away as swans. Dina's protectors are a sustaining source of comfort and hope.

Comfort may come from a variety of sources. When she woke from this dream, this young woman found that the feeling of being cared for remained with her for some time:

> I enter a room, I am crying (I was very upset on this occasion, when I went to sleep). At the end of the room is a dais with flowers arranged around it — mainly white in colour. Three women are sitting on this dais. As I approach, one woman, a slim woman dressed in black with black hair, holds out her arms to me. I cry in her arms and she comforts me. I feel much better.

RADIANT, HEALING LIGHT

I had a dream which I thought was a spiritual dream, I was

being held in my father's arms in a most beautiful radiant brilliant light.

The 'dark', as in Teri's dream, symbolises unconsciousness whilst light symbolises consciousness. This archetypal motif appears in myths worldwide. In the North American myth, the Raven steals the sun in order to bring life-giving light to the world. Without his intervention all living creatures would exist in both physical and spiritual impoverished loss so he saves the world by rescuing it from darkness. On a symbolic level, we can see this in dreams. When John was contemplating suicide, he had a dream in which 'it felt like there was divine intervention. Somebody or something was providing a very bright light to guide me.'

Margaret went through a series of horrendous life crises which culminated in an acrimonious divorce. When she thought nothing more could go wrong, she was diagnosed as having osteoarthritis at the base of her spine. At thirty years of age this felt like the proverbial 'last straw'. Conventional treatment hardly alleviated the pain and one night, in desperation, she prayed. 'Oh God,' she said, 'I can't cope with this as well, please help.' Shortly after this she was in the local library when a book fell — 'jumped' is how she described it — from a shelf. It was called *Your Healing is Within You* written by Jim Glennon, an Australian. Margaret read the book, followed the 'instructions' for prayer and asked for healing. She went to sleep and dreamt or awoke in the small hours. She described what happened:

> I was aware, though I couldn't actually see them, that there were people to the left of the bed. Suddenly a beam of light appeared from their direction and it seemed to fuse the coccyx area of my spine. I was conscious of intense, though not unpleasant, heat and I knew that the welding sensation had healed the problem area. I thanked them and fell back asleep.

Margaret never had the pain again and her doctor was astounded at the remission. Was this a healing dream, a miracle wrought by the power of prayer or spontaneous remission?

> Prayer is not asking. It is a longing of the soul.
>
> (Mohandas Gandhi)

If in a dream such as Margaret's there is a spiritual response to a physical problem, then perhaps meditation, reflection or prayer is the most useful starting point to develop self-induced healing. The difference between prayer and meditation, according to an old saying, is that prayer is where you talk to God and meditation is where God talks to you!

As counsellors or therapists, whatever we believe, whether we think of God as someone or something out there who is responsible for the world or whether we see ourselves as completely self-sufficient, the important thing is that we are sensitive to the spiritual dimension in our clients' lives. We need to provide the space and time to look inward.

Jack Angelo, a spiritual healer, says in his book, *Your Healing Power:* 'One of the important functions of the dream is to heal. Material may be processed in a dream and this brings about the healing. Very often people receive healing in the dream state when they are more accessible to the energies ... patients' dreams are a valuable part of the healing process.' He cites the experience of Gordon who had direct healing while in the dream state:

> He initially came for spiritual healing because of a temporary loss of hearing. On his second visit Gordon spoke about a dream which had occurred the same night as his first healing session. In the dream he saw himself standing quite calmly and relaxed. He watched in amazement as his head was tipped first towards his right shoulder then to his left shoulder, as if his neck was made from rubber. What he described as 'gunge' seemed to pour from each ear. This action was repeated until the flow from his ears had ceased.

Gordon was having a powerful healing dream, for the next morning he was awakened by birdsong, his hearing had returned.

Amy experienced guidance in dreams:

Since 1982 I have kept a journal which includes my dreams and the ways they changed as my own process took place. They gave me the vision to understand what was going on at times when I was confused and lost and were a very important guide to me. My most powerful dreams have proved to come before transitional points in my life and have included a male figure who is old and wise and has the status of a guide for me. In some ways my active dream life has also been a source of vibrancy and life when I have been paralysed with fear in my waking life.

Meditation and reflection are powerful ways to quieten the mind so that the inner voice, the one that speaks in dreams, has a chance to be heard above the clamour of waking life. When we turn inwards out of choice rather than fear, our consciousness has the chance to expand, to gain insight into realities beyond the waking three-dimensional world. Then it is possible to become aware of spiritual potential, that which has been called the 'divine spark' which is in each of us. We'll return to meditation later after hearing other experiences of dream-inspired healing.

In 1993, Jill began to experience numbness in her right hand, especially on waking in the morning. After a week or so, it was affecting her whole hand and wrist, which also began to hurt throughout the day. She went to see her doctor who diagnosed carpal tunnel syndrome. He advised her that if steroid injections and physiotherapy failed then she would have to have an operation on her wrist. He prescribed painkillers initially and asked her to return in a month, unless the symptoms became unbearable, in which case immediate surgery would be necessary.

As the pain and numbness worsened, Jill felt certain that she would have to have an operation and was worried sick at the prospect. She remembered seeing a programme about the power of positive thinking to conquer pain and decided to try it out. In effect, she was applying the principle of **intentionality**, the idea that we can alter invents by believing they will change — prayer is one form of intentionality. She tried to visualise being symptom-free but there was no dramatic change. However, one night just before she went to sleep, when the pain was particularly intense, Jill offered up a mental prayer that it would ease. During the night she had a dream:

> I dreamed of my grandmother, who had been dead for ten years. She was bathed in a golden light and told me she would make my hand better. She asked me to take her hand, which I did with my affected hand, and as I did I felt a warm glow spread up my arm.

In the morning Jill awoke with no pain or numbness for the first time in months. Not only did she escape the dreaded surgery, painkillers too were thrown out as she relaxed into feeling pain-free once more. As she said: 'I have occasional twinges in my fingers on waking, but these soon pass and I know if the pain ever did recur, I would find relief in my dreams.'

Jill's dream has a number of features which are common in healing dreams; intense light, the presence of a relative who has died, a sense of being looked after or comforted and, on waking, a definite feeling that the dream was not an ordinary dream. The special quality of the numinous dream shines through.

Light is traditionally associated with the spirit. Without light we are in perpetual darkness and the sun, since Egyptian times, has been a symbol of the source of awareness. Jill said that the luminous intensity of the golden light in this dream was immediately recognisable as different from any light she'd noticed in other dreams. She felt the healing warmth as it touched her hand. Light is the creative force, the cosmic energy that gives life. Psychologically speaking, to become illuminated is to become aware of the source of light and consequently to be spiritually strengthened. From our earliest beginnings we have tried to move away from primal darkness. Jung equated our need for light as being a symbolic longing for consciousness and we long for that light which gives insight and heals us.

JOURNEYS OF LIGHT

> The Buddha when dying was asked by his followers what they should do to maintain their practice after he was gone. He said, 'Be a lamp unto yourself.'
>
> (Stephen Levine)

It is worth returning to the light which we have already explored, since this links closely to the feeling of spiritual illumination that is so crucial to the whole process of birth, death and renewal. It is interesting to see how so much research into near death experiences (NDE) cites the transformative nature of the light that comes. For example, Raymond Moody who has written extensively on this subject, quotes a woman who was briefly 'dead' and 'brought back to life through heart massage':

> I floated right up to a crystal clear light, an illuminated white light. It was beautiful and so bright, so radiant. It's not any kind of light you can describe on earth. I didn't actually see a person in this light, and yet it has a special identity ... It is the light of perfect understanding and perfect love.

Jung would call this light a visual form of self, the highest form of our being and that which we share with the collective unconscious, with all who have gone before and who are part of the universe. This melding with the universal extinguishes normal body parameters, enabling us to become part of the infinite.

George Fox, the founder of The Society of Friends, also known as the Quakers, recorded a dream in his journal of 1647, in which he said, 'I saw also that there was an ocean of darkness and death, but an infinite ocean of light and love, which flowed over the ocean of darkness.' Lightness ultimately triumphs over the forces of darkness.

In paintings and icons of spiritual leaders — saints, holy figures, gurus and enlightened men and women — brilliant, redeeming light is a repeated feature. This transcendent spiritual development, symbolised by surrounding light, halos and the like, is a sign that they can help others in their spiritual journey, just as Jill's grandmother helped her in the dream. That glorious light is not reserved for famous deities, it is there in everyone and shows itself in dreams such as Isabelle's:

> I was again surrounded by bright light and I felt enfolded and infused by joy. I also felt that I had been given an important message.

At critical points in life, we frequently question the whole basis of our existence. What are we actually doing with our lives? Why are we here? Is this body all I am about? When I die, will that be it, will everything about me just end? Somehow, having looked loss in the face whether it is through illness, divorce, failure or bereavement, we turn to face ourselves. The questions come. This is a very salutary experience for in the cold light of appraisal we often do not like what we see. The painful questions slow us down. The frantic, blind activity that fills our days comes under a searchlight and, if we are open to the power of the crisis, we create a space to listen, an opportunity to grow to our full potential. By way of an example of this communication, engagement without physical contact in the spirit world, Hazel described a dream she had had:

> I was in a room with two other girls, and I was thinking 'Oh, there are people in this room, I can feel it. They're amazed and smiling at the same time. I can feel it but I can't see them and they're looking at one another. Well, it's a bit late now

Hazel, I think we'll be going.' So I walk up the hall and say 'Bye, see you again.' They've gone and I turn round saying, 'Well. I wish you'd appear to me, one of you at least. Please make yourself known ...' One did appear and it was a man. Small stature for a man, wearing a dark suit and tie. Very handsome. He introduced himself and said, 'I'm David and I'm going to make it all up to you when you come over here.' Vaguely I could recall him but not quite. And he just threw his arms around me and said 'We've no need for sexual interaction here.'

... It was a beautiful euphoric feeling as he put his arms round me in the dream. So euphoric that it lasted for a day or so. But I get these feelings consciously but I don't actually see. The only things I see are like displaced spots of light, like lead crystal, shiny and sparkling. Little bits of lead crystal just in the air. Very strongly and they can be maintained there for some time. Or else, I feel that someone is very, very close to me, physically. I can feel the body heat etc... spirits can make themselves known in the natural world through dreams ... it's a nice bonus.

HEARING VOICES

Clarissa Pinkola Estes, in *Women Who Run With The Wolves*, tells of ancient physicians who studied the structure of the body and who dissected cadavers to increase their anatomical knowledge. They thought that the auditory nerve was divided into three pathways into the brain. Because of this they formed the view that we were meant to, and could hear at, three different levels. One level was for everyday hearing, one was for learning and art, whilst the third 'existed so the soul itself might hear guidance and gain knowledge while here on earth'.

Whilst some people have visionary dreams, others hear voices. Not voices in everyday conversation but more a disembodied voice that speaks with particular authority or insight. Such a voice may come completely out of the blue, apparently unrelated to what is happening in the rest of the dream yet, it has such clarity that it cannot be ignored. Clara knows of the third pathway, because in some of her dreams a voice actually spoke to her, not in a strange ethereal tone, but in an undistinguished male voice. But is it a dream or is it something else? Clara isn't sure, all she 'knows' is at that time she'd been worrying and was very uncertain about her life:

> I woke up in my front room once to a voice telling me that everything was going to be all right. There was a voice coming from the corner, I felt as though there was someone present. After this I felt such a wonderful peace that I have never had in my life before. I felt complete contentment, free of worry. It sounds silly but it was as if God had spoken to me.

Like so many people I meet as clients or at dream workshops, Clara had never spoken to anyone of her dream before, believing, as she did, that people would think she was crazy and lock her up! So many people from all parts of our world have similar experiences as well as sharing the fear that they'll be seen as raving mad if they speak of it. These inner voices and guides who offer direction when we are lost are released from the unconscious through dreams or meditation. The well of wisdom and compassion is there deep within us all, it gives us the courage to continue when it feels as if every avenue is closed. Sometimes, the voice heard in dreams prepares us. Before the death of his wife, Sam had two striking dreams:

> In the first I was visiting the hospital when a coffin was brought in. In the second the coffin was brought into my wife's ward and a voice said 'You've brought the coffin in two days early.' Then this was repeated.

Sam's wife died two days later.

Dr Gordon Claridge, Fellow of Psychology, Magdalen College, Oxford, wrote *Echoes From The Bell Jar* and explored the link between creativity and psychosis. He believes voice hearers have a 'highly attuned nervous system which enables them to pick up stuff that the rest of us miss', a 'leaky' barrier between conscious and unconscious, between fantasy and reality. Sometimes such phenomena can be afflicting, the antennae too attuned to the world so that there is no respite which can cause intense stress for some people.

Rosie summed up her feelings about sound in her dreams:

> I'm glad we can dream. Some of my dreams have been like gifts. For instance, one night I went to bed very unhappy and dreamt that I heard the most beautiful song I ever heard. With it there was such light and an experience of joy that I thought I could never be unhappy again.

I had a dream when I was struggling with my book *Women Dreaming*. I was trying to come to grips with the reason why directly opposing feelings or actions are so often part of dreams. The conflict and confusion seemed to obscure dream meanings, as I knew from my clients, and I was trying to clarify my thoughts so I could express them in the book. In my dream I was doing a jig-saw — a symbol for the puzzle I was faced with — and trying to fit in the last piece, but it just wouldn't go. Suddenly, a voice said: 'Turn it upside down. Everything fits together. The wild and the tame, the kitten and the lion, they are all part of the same. That's the paradox.'

I woke up surprised and yet quite clear that all the opposing parts of ourselves, the loving and hating, the free and imprisoned, the kind and the vicious, are all part of our one nature. We need to embrace all in order to be whole. There was no other person in the dream, just the jig-saw, myself and the voice, and for me it was a turning point. I was able to develop the idea. It was a powerful dream which has coloured my view of the world ever since.

Our inner wisdom lets us see and hear ways of healing our lives, both physically and spiritually, if we tune in to that level of awareness. This can happen spontaneously in dreaming or consciously in meditation. Whilst I am primarily concerned with dreams, the work of such people as Dr Bernie Siegel, author of the best-selling *Love, Medicine and Miracles* and Jon Kabat-Zin, who wrote *Full Catastrophe Living*, show that even in the most high-tech medical settings in America, there is an important role for meditation as an adjunct to conventional treatment. Both provide authentic evidence of the increased recovery rates of people suffering from such diverse conditions as psoriasis, cancer, heart disease and infertility when they practice mindfulness meditation. When we meditate we go to that same level of mental activity that we engage in REM sleep or dream sleep and so we release our self-healing power.

DREAM GUIDANCE

Trudy was brought up by her grandmother and felt as close to her as she did to her mother, if not closer. When her gran eventually died twenty years later, Trudy was devastated: 'I took her death very badly,' she told me. 'I cried every day and cried myself to sleep at night. For about four months, I was very low in spirit and just was not interested in anything even though my husband and children were there caring for me. I didn't really have time for them, I was so miserable.' One night she went to bed and dreamt that she was in a tunnel. At her end it was dark and gloomy but the other end was very light. Her dream progressed:

> I got a little way down this tunnel and then I was in a room which felt warm and cosy but, joy of joys, there was my Gran sitting in a chair. I just went on my knees and cuddled her, I said 'Thank God, Gran, you're here,' she never spoke. Standing at the other side of her was this tall man who said in a strong voice 'What do you want here?' I thought it was none of his business but I said I wanted my Gran. His reply

was 'Well, she doesn't need you so go back where you came from.'

The next thing I knew it was daylight and I felt so calm, I felt as if a weight had been taken from my shoulders. I didn't cry anymore after that.

Trudy, still shocked by the dream, immediately rang her mother and told her about it, including a description of the tall, no-nonsense man with the strong voice and curly hair. Her mother asked: 'Do you know who he is?' Trudy said she had no idea, she'd never seen him before, besides it was a dream, why should she know? 'She told me it was her father who had died about eight years before I was born,' said Trudy. The description fitted Trudy's grandfather exactly.

Since that time Trudy has never worried about her grandmother. The dream was all she needed to stop grieving and pick up the pieces of her life because she felt her grandmother was cared for and safe and that she had been given permission to stop mourning. Her whole family was helped by that single dream. Many people who dream that someone they love is safely taken care of beyond this life are helped in this way.

THE WORDS OF THE WISE WOMAN

Some dreams are like a blow that stuns, forcing us to stop and take notice. Kathleen, from Hampshire, gave an instance that prompted a life-long belief in dream diagnosis.

When her son, Tom, was a baby he became ill and he coughed hoarsely throughout the night. There was no immediate cause for alarm and Kathleen took care of him expecting the worst to pass. In the days before easily obtainable antibiotics, letting the illness take its course was the usual practice and, besides, getting a doctor's opinion was expensive then and she was poor. But one night, when Tom was very weak, she had a vivid dream.

An old lady stood by the fireplace, lighting a coal fire. She was unfamiliar to me though I thought she bore a family likeness. As she watched the flames burn brighter, the old woman said in a forceful voice, 'Pneumonia, pneumonia! Hospital!

The next morning Tom's condition had worsened so Kathleen called out Dr Sellis. He examined the boy, wrote a prescription and told her he would call in after the weekend, four days later. Kathleen was so moved by the impression of the dream that she said: 'I believe my son has pneumonia. Please get him to hospital or else he'll die!' She was so unusually insistent that Dr Sellis went to phone from the house next door and arranged for Tom to be admitted to hospital. He stayed in intensive care for six weeks! At one point, the pneumonia took such a strong hold that he was christened in case he died. He did pull through and Kathleen is sure that without the powerful message of her dream, she would never have dared insist on a different course of treatment — a life and death difference, as it turned out. As Kathleen said: 'I shall always be grateful for that dream and to the mysterious old lady lighting the fire.'

But who was the 'mysterious old lady'? There was the family resemblance which Kathleen noted but that wasn't enough to explain the irresistible impact it made on her. In dreams, as in folklore, old women often symbolise the 'wise woman', the 'witch' whose knowledge of herbs and medicinal poultices and the like were used in earliest times to treat disease. In times of distress our minds may tune in to earlier knowledge and wisdom to guide us through the difficulties we cannot navigate alone. Whether it is a primitive part of our own problem-solving brain which is activated or whether we tune in to a collective unconscious wisdom of healing, such dreams are part of the healing world.

SOUL TRAVEL

Since classical antiquity and probably before, 'soul journeys' have been regarded as a special way of dreaming in which the 'soul' leaves the body in search of otherwise unattainable knowledge.

This is also known as astral travel, and whilst there is not enough space to deal with it here in any depth, it deserves some regard since clients do bring such dreams for exploration.

Carol has had numerous such dreams in which she feels as if she is leaving her body and goes out, light and free, to meet people in places she has never travelled to before. These places and people, though, often seem familiar and it is in this type of dream that she sees future or past events that she has no knowledge of. She told me:

> I believe that our consciousness or soul travels in dreams and merges with other souls. I believe that despite the fact that most people are unaware of it, many of us lead 'double' lives. While the physical body sleeps, the inside body continues to experience, learn, travel and develop. One travels in one's astral body every night.'

In our dreams, we can perhaps even travel in time. This is open to conjecture but there are large areas of the brain, as yet uncharted, and we have a lot more to learn about the power to practice mental projection and astral projection.

Ella has had numerous dreams over the past ten years which have left her in no doubt to the veracity of astral travel.

> After a dream about teaching someone to fly and flying myself, over a prison ironically enough, I realised I was having an astral type of dream. I was awake, that is, I could hear my husband breathing next to me, and yet I knew I was dreaming.
>
> I was very interested and flew on and on ... I saw a fire across the road with lots of smoke. I knew I had to go through the fire and felt I had been protected, which I was. I came to a bank of sand and was told I could not fly over it. I flew straight at it and was surprised to find I went into the sand quite easily, travelled through it with ease and felt the sand trickling past my face.

In another dream I slipped out of my body feet first, conscious of my breathing being louder than usual and wondered if it would disturb my husband. I went upwards as usual but at one stage felt rain on my face. I thought I was going up through a rain strata.

The sensations of this type of dream are very positive for Fiona too: 'I feel they are like mystical experiences. Numerous times I feel I am leaving my body and feel very free and light. I meet people and find myself in places I have never seen, although they frequently feel familiar. It is in this sort of dream that I see future or past events.' Fiona explained at length about the various types of dreams which have helped in her own spiritual development. Dreams in which she has visited dead relatives, explored other realms and helped to free earth-bound spirits. Her descriptions of the process may prove useful if you or your clients experience this out of body experience:

When leaving the physical body people often experience different sensations; perhaps feeling a build up of power or vibration before feelings of whirring or rolling over backwards very fast; sound of rushing wind and sometimes feelings of terror which jet one awake.

I have sometimes experienced difficulty in realigning the astral and physical and felt myself literally manhandled into position — perhaps an astral shove on my feet to get the two bodies to fit.

The first time I remember clearly returning to my physical body, I stood at my own bedside looking down on my sleeping self and felt a deep reluctance to get back in the body on the bed. I remember thinking how heavy that physical body felt compared with the glorious freedom and lightness of my spiritual body, like a stone, like being imprisoned in a statue, I thought. Then when I began slowly to fit into my body I found myself waking up. I remember feeling that my arms, in particular from the elbows to the wrists, felt huge and clumsy; it was as if my wrist was about eighteen inches or so in circumference and most unpleasantly heavy.

The next time I was again looking down at myself prior to returning to the physical, and I turned to a friend who had come with me — a friend who passed on some years ago, and said to him, 'Oh, I do wish I did not have to go back, it is just dreadful having to walk around in that heavy, clumsy body after being here like this.' My friend smiled understandingly and helped me in, then I awoke. I would like to add that I am quite slim and weight about eight and a half stone, which at five feet four is not heavy and clumsy. At least I don't think so.

The idea that the soul separates off in the dreaming state has often been associated to the idea of a soul as distinct from the body. In dreams we enter a different realm, a spiritual realm, where the physical falls away, where we can meet friends and family who have died, where we can fly or find ourselves transported to different places, even different worlds. If we accept that the conscious self separates from the physical self, it is not too great a leap to conclude that the 'soul' that leaves the body in sleep may also be able to survive the death of the physical body.

AN AWFULLY BIG ADVENTURE ...

Unless we have been bereaved, death is, as Auden put it, 'like the rumble of distant thunder at a picnic' it has no immediate impact and so it is not dwelt on. We live our lives in blithe innocence of that most permanent rite of passage. Yet facing death — exploring the transformative dreams that prepare for that 'awfully big adventure' — is part of therapeutic work, as we will see in Chapter 9.

CHAPTER 9

HEALING INTO LIFE, HEALING INTO DEATH

Knock
And He'll open the door.
Vanish, And He'll make you shine like the sun. Fall,
And he'll raise you to the heavens.
Become nothing,
And He'll turn you into everything.

Rumi

At critical points when we are faced with serious illness or loss of physical power, or radical change or death, dreams often take on a numinous quality. They prepare the dreamer for transition and transformation. Those who work with Aids patients, the terminally ill and in intensive care accompany their patients on a profound journey where dreams may be used as the compass to point the way. This is a very tender spiritual process which requires the greatest sensitivity and compassion on the part of the companion — the counsellor, care staff, the chaplain or family members — who may be privileged to share this part of the person's life journey.

For so many of us, it is only when all hope has gone that we call out for help, even though we may have no idea to whom, or what it is that we call for. At points of crisis we also feel great fear, though this often only becomes uppermost in our dreams and nightmares. When we are awake we spend a great deal of emotional energy on putting a brave face on things, pretending to ourselves and others that everything is under control.

DREAMS OF DEATH

> When the way comes to an end, then change —
> having changed, you pass through.
>
> (The *I Ching*)

Michel Foucault, the French dream philosopher, considers dreams of death to be the most important dreams available to the dreamer. He says they are about the completion of existence when life reaches its fulfilment and as such they have powerful information to communicate.

Dreaming of death often prepares us for a beginning where old, outworn patterns and habits are being abandoned. We have to let go of the past — the past must die to us — and dreams of death speak to us of these matters. They allow the opportunity to prepare for loss, which is what Helga experienced:

Some time ago I had some dreams about my father and grandmother dying, which really upset me. Both my dad and my grandmother are quite ill, so it is not a completely unrealistic dream. At the same time, I have never really been confronted with death before, so I feel extremely vulnerable in that respect. It sounds stupid, but until recently I could not imagine anybody around me could die, or rather, I did not *want* to face it, although all my relatives are quite old. I feel these death dreams that I had made me experience death for the first time and made me face up to reality. It was like an advice to prepare myself mentally/emotionally for the possible event of death of a person close to me. By dreaming about the death of my father and the extreme pain and grief I felt, I became aware for the first time of how much I feel for him (although we have never ever been close to each other at all) and how much it makes me sad that we never had a proper relationship.

It is important to communicate to clients who dream of death that the dreams come when a new process of maturing is taking place and do not appear as a certain portent that someone will die. One client who regularly dreamt of death, her own or other people's, was working with her own sense of alienation and abandonment. In this dream you can see how 'invisible' she feels she has become:

> The dominant theme overall has been isolation. Either everyone is dead except me, or I am the dead person and they are all alive and can't see me, but shiver and turn up their collars when I come near as if I brought an icy chill. I shout to them to look at me and speak, but they look through me and shiver.

When dreams such as this are brought to counselling, we need to look at self-image, self-esteem and the nature of the client's relationships. For instance, in this example, what is this 'icy chill' the dreamer brings? Is she emotionally cold or is that the way she presents herself, or feels she presents herself, or feels she presents herself? Has she been given 'the cold shoulder' by others? Getting to understand the social dynamics of her world are part of the process of development towards healing.

Another client brought a dream at a point of breakthrough. In it, she dreamt that she died and was very disturbed and cried for some time when she woke up. What she realised, she said, was that this was the breaking down of an old self so that she could begin a new cycle of existence. There is both mourning for the old self and a sense of renewal and liberation.

In this disturbing dream, the dreamer faces mortality:

> I have three times dreamt of being in total darkness, where there are no visual images or sounds, yet I am aware that I am there, but I believe I am dead. In one of these dreams I am curled up, sideways on just like a baby and everything is black around me and nothing is happening.

In the dream the image of the foetal position indicates renewal. We will consider this in greater detail later in this chapter.

Acceptance is a sign of healthy mourning, though the journey to get to that point is often very painful. Donna, after the death of a very close friend, had terrible nightmares in which she 'saw his shooting and the scenes afterwards as his father and medical staff tried to revive him; his operation, his death and his funeral.' Though these nightmares were disturbing Donna recognised that they helped her express pent up feelings held back during the day and they 'helped me accept he was gone and nothing would bring him back'.

Healing is the title we give to the phenomenon of the mind and heart coming back into balance.

(Stephen Levine)

DEATH IS PART OF THE PROCESS

Elizabeth Kubler-Ross, a Swiss-born physician and psychiatrist, in her celebrated book *On Death and Dying*, helped American society to view death in the same way that most of the world always has — as an inevitable part of the process of life itself. Now, in America, thousands of courses on death and dying are taught in medical and nursing schools, and the hospice movement, where the ill can end their lives in a loving, non-hospital environment, has flourished. In many hospitals, although receiving medical care, a dying patient is often socially isolated and avoided because professional staff and students find contact painful and embarrassing. What can they say? Do they sensitively tell the truth about approaching death or fudge issues with euphemisms? If this happens, particularly where family and friends have been advised against telling the truth about the patient's condition, the dying person may be denied the opportunity of sharing his or her feelings and of discussing their needs with those on whom they depend.

On analysis of her many experiences of dying patients, Elizabeth Kubler-Ross believes that there are five stages that nearly always accompany adjustment to dying:

1 A period of **denial** — the person does not believe that they have a terminal illness, often seeking a second opinion.

2 The patient experiences a feeling of **anger**: 'Why me? I have so much to live for, it's not fair,' is a common reaction. The patient often blames the doctor or their spouse for not paying attention to their complaints earlier, or they may blame God. People often get furious with God.

3 The **bargaining** stage — the patient tries to bargain for a longer period of time before death. They may, for example, ask God if they can live just long enough in order to complete a certain task or finish some business they have to attend to.

4 A stage of **depression** — the patent realises that they are about to die and they see the world in a blanket of depression.

5 If allowed to grieve, eventually the stage of **acceptance** may be reached. The dying person can finally accept their fate and they are able to die peacefully. This is not a happy stage, in fact it can be almost without feeling, a void. The patient wishes to be alone or silent much of the time and communication is mostly non-verbal as the patient prepares to die.

The stages are by no means linear and progressive, some may be missed out altogether and others remain for much longer. It is not uncommon for the period of acceptance never to arrive with the result that the patient dies in fear and anger. Clients may come for counselling because they are the partner of a dying man or woman and need to express their own loss. But they may also need to gain support to talk openly about feelings, to become a better travelling companion in this journey which will lead to a separation, to the crossroads where one continues to an unknown destination whilst the other turns back to their previously shared world.

DEATH, TRANSFORMATION AND RESURRECTION

Denial at times can be healthy. It can give a breathing space, a time to gather the strength needed to face the crisis fully, whatever form it might take. Some people have to live for a long time with the knowledge that they are dying and denial helps them to go on with their daily lives. It allows them to mobilise their defences. And what of the role of hope? Is ultimate hope that which stretches beyond death? Is hope against hope what saves us from despair? What hope sustains our clients and patients as they face death, their own or someone they love?

Ruth Picardie, an English journalist, was thirty-two when she developed breast cancer. The chronicle of her illness, *Before I Say Goodbye*, captured in letters, emails and articles written for the *Observer*, expresses the see-saw of emotions on that journey. She mailed her friend Carrie:

> The latest spread is bad news only in the sense that it is evidence of the disease's inexorable spread, as yet unchecked by Tamoxifen/acupuncture etc. and it means more bloody treatment. But I knew I had secondary bone cancer anyway, so it's not a huge disaster. I still can't quite believe I'm going to die and, deep down, assume there will be some miracle. You're right about pain relief, though I still have a lingering dislike of medication — my body is a temple and all that. But let's face it, the temple has been completely desecrated already.

Shock, denial, despair and always, somewhere the sustaining hope that a miracle will come and death will be thwarted. Where that does not happen, healing can still take place, a healing into death and a letting go of life.

> All who live must die. Passing through nature to eternity.
>
> (Shakespeare, *Hamlet* 1, 2)

Healing into life, healing into death

Freud argued that there is a compulsion towards death — it is a drive as powerful as the sex drive. He saw it as an instinct that is in every living organism, hard-wired as it were, into the very essence of being: 'If we are to take it as a truth that knows no exception that every living thing dies for *internal* reasons — beomes inorganic once again — then we shall be compelled to say that '*the aim of life is death*'.(1984) In 1932, in a letter to Einstein he re-iterated this idea saying: '... this instinct is striving.to reduce life to its original condition of inanimate matter.' (1991). This was a view Jung shared (1990):

> Like the sun, the libido also wills its own descent, its own involution. During the first half of life, it strives for growth; during the second half, softly at first and then ever more perceptibly, it points towards an altered goal. And just as in youth the urge for limitless expression often lies hidden under veiling layers of resistance to life, so that 'other urge' often lies behind an obstinate and purposeless cleaving to life in its old form.

In Greek mythology, death was envisaged as the daughter of the night and the sister of sleep. Plato taught that the human soul continued after death as if it slept and awoke in a different realm. Christianity and Buddhism also teach that there is life beyond the grave and, like many, Chelsea felt her dream confirmed this:

> When my son was born, I saw what I thought was my father. My father died before he knew the baby was on the way. On my second night home from hospital I slept downstairs with my son in his pram. I woke up in the early hours of the morning to something white coming into the room. It went up to the pram, looked in and walked out. I just knew it was Dad. I was not afraid. Up till then I had not cried when Dad died because it was a merciful release. But after this I just burst into tears. And nothing happened again after that. It was as if he had seen him.

Dreams are frequently seen as the bridge between the world of the past and present and the world of the future and so they are a powerful resource in healing at this point.

Matter can neither be created nor destroyed. To merge once more with the substance from which we came or to unite with God is what death is all about. Many clients have dreams which intimate that there is life beyond death. Jung, in *Memories, Dreams and Reflections*, said: 'Although there is no way to marshal valid proof for continuance of the soul after death, there are nevertheless experiences to make me thoughtful. I take them as hints.' Marie Louise von Franz, student of Jung and later his colleague and accomplished Jungian analyst, writes in *On Dreams of Death* of many dreams of death and states that many: '... symbolically indicate the end of bodily life and the explicit continuation of psychic life after death. The unconscious "believes" quite obviously in a life after death.'

> In the midst of winter
> I finally learned there was in me
> invincible summer
>
> Albert Camus

COMPANIONS

Elisabeth Kubler-Ross, in the foreword to Kalweit's *Dreamtime and Inner Space*, wrote of her experience of 'companions' who may come in waking as well as dreaming time:

> Only a few of us who live in modern Western civilisation understand that benevolent, 'helping spirits' and 'imaginary friends' are by no means projections of an imagination gone riot. The critically ill children in my care refer to these spirits as their 'playmates'. They are very real companions to them — guides and helpers at a time of isolation, loneliness and suffering. Such companions are known by children everywhere. Only when children grow up in an unbelieving

world, that tends to laugh at such follies, do they as a rule lose their ability to recognise these helpers.

Survivors of near death experiences (NDEs) speak of meeting 'creatures of light', friends who have died or protective beings or spiritual guides to help them on their journey. In the waking state certain extreme conditions affect the human psyche in highly unusual ways. Extreme loneliness, isolation, monotonous landscapes such as deserts or snow expanses, and lack of sensory stimulation, cause the ego structures and cultural boundaries to disintegrate. This has been recorded in wide ranging literature from Shackleton, Messner, Lindberg and Bird who all encountered phantom human companions who gave them assistance.

The famous mountaineer Reinhold Messner encountered 'companions' during his solo ascent of Nanga Parbat in 1978. He said he conversed with them in four languages, though he knew only three. In his diary for 8 August, he records:

> In this burnt-out state, this suffering, thoughts are suddenly extinguished, before I have had time to think of them. It may be that my infinitely lonely situation is bearable only because of that. I suddenly feel as if someone were sitting beside me.

He observes other men, women and children and takes immense comfort and reassurance from their presence.

Helping spirits are sought by shamans in order to enhance their healing skills and their ability to penetrate other worlds. Often these companions make their first appearance in dreams and direct the noviciate's process of becoming a shaman. Willard Park in *Shamanism in Western North America* recorded such a dream of Dick Mahwee, a Paviotso Indian:

> A man dreams that a deer, eagle, or bear comes after him. The animal tells him that he is to be a doctor. The first time

a man dreams this way he does not believe it. Then he dreams that way some more and he gets the things the spirit told him to get (eagle feathers, wild tobacco, stone pipe, rattle made from the ear of a deer or from the deer's dew claws). Then he learns to be a doctor. He learns his songs when the spirit comes and sings to him.

Sometimes, it is not the dying who dream of the companion, but someone close, such as the daughter: 'Although my father was very ill I never thought about him dying from his illness until the day before his death. I dreamt I saw my late grandmother leading him away.'

APPROACHING DEATH

Thirst is not reasoned.
There is for each own darkness.
No general compass.

Peter Viereck

Impending death is not easy to contemplate. Von Franz worked with people who were approaching death. Many were elderly and others had been diagnosed with a terminal illness. **Decathexis**, the process of letting go as death approaches, influences dreaming. Von Franz provides many examples of individuals who dream of black spots, some overhead, some as pits or holes which appear instead of the more common tunnel images in dreams of the dying. Through her work we glimpse a private world of transition and spiritual profundity. At the ending of life, a dream can offer consolation and reassurance in the form of a helping hand, though in the following instance, the dreamer was far from willing to accept that he might die and was not comforted by his dream:

In it he was going through a forest in winter. It was cold and misty. From a distance he could hear the moan of a chainsaw and from time to time the crack of falling trees. Suddenly the dreamer was once again in a forest, but on a higher level, as it were. It was summer. His father — who in reality had died long before — walked towards him and said, 'You see, here is the forest again. Do not concern yourself anymore with what is happening down there.'

His father was telling him not to focus on the hewing down of the trees but to let go, to move on to a higher plane where the cold of winter was left behind to reveal a new spring. There is a resurrection motif in these dreams, the forest is renewed. In dreams, we have a voice from our higher selves, a wiser part, which comes to help at times of major transition. For this man, the 'cutting down' refers not only to traumatic surgery he had to undergo, but also symbolically refers to the 'cutting down' associated with the grim reaper, death, who carries a scythe.

DREAM SYMBOLISM

> In my experience the image of the journey in dreams is also the most frequently occurring symbol of impending death.
>
> (Von Franz, 1985)

When my sister died of a brain aneurysm at the age of forty three I was stunned. I had a series of dreams over three nights which featured a bear prowling around a house in the wilderness. Initially it was trying to break into the room where I seemed to be trapped and I was terrified, tormented by its power and ferocity, as it scratched at the door and pounded against the walls. In the subsequent dreams its anger abated and the bear appeared to lose interest in getting to me. It switched its attention to its natural pursuits in the wooded mountains in which the dream was set. When I explored the primal strength and ferocity of the bear and the sense of threat I felt, I realised how devastated I felt about the unexpected death of Rona, who I loved dearly. As well as feeling vulnerable to the awesome power of the bear, I also recognised its beauty and its right to be in its place, the environment in which I, a city dweller, was the stranger. Metaphorically, I was in a strange land and in the grip of a tremendous natural force. In facing death where personal control is relinquished, I was humbled and captive until the moment passed and the rhythm of life continued. Most people who have been bereaved feel a sense of inadequacy. We wonder why everyone else can carry on as normal when life as we knew it has just been irrevocably changed. 'Don't they know what has happened?' screams the animal instinct inside and though, on the surface, calmness may prevail, our dreams reveal a different world. And our psyche seems to contain archetypal images of death being something other than annihilation.

The bear is the symbol of resurrection. In alchemy it corresponds to the *nigredo*, the prime material, and is related to all initial stages and to basic instincts. It is also linked to the perilous aspect of the unconscious, which fits in with the notion of being 'bare' — when we are stripped of all pretence, right down to the essentials, as I was at that time.

Maria Louise von Franz and Elisabeth Kubler-Ross are renowned for their excellent knowledge of the imagery of dying people, whether young or old. Traditional symbols, such as travelling to the west, towards the setting sun or being in a boat are all common death images and light is prevalent, as are the images of rebirth. Archetypal images such as butterflies symbolise the transformation of one life form to another and these are frequently found both in the dreams and the artwork of children approaching death. In the Van Gogh museum in Amsterdam I noted that in paintings completed in the days before his death Vincent Van Gogh has included butterflies in his work, an unusual motif for him since they are not apparent in other paintings prior to this time, as far as I am aware.

Rainbows also feature widely. They connect heaven and earth, above and below, as they arc between earth and sky, bridging two worlds. In China, the rainbow denotes the union of heaven and earth. Its radiance has a supernatural quality standing out as it does in the sky for all to see. For the Israelites, it was the sign of the covenant between the Creator and his people. Bridges, like rainbows, figure in dreams at points of transition. In many cultures they symbolise the link between what is perceived and what lies beyond perception.

Like the rainbow, the mandala has no end or beginning. Mandalas represent the map of the cosmos in Eastern traditions and symbolise the cycle of life and its unending renewal. These can appear in dreams as flowers, parts of the landscape, gardens, or in an object. To Jung, when a mandala appeared in a dream, it heralded wholeness and self-integration because it is a completion where the start and the end are no longer separate; instead there is a continuous, never-ending eternity.

DARKNESS INTO LIGHT

> Think then, my soul, that death is but a groom,
> Which brings a taper to the outward room.
>
> John Dunne

Light, coming into the light, being surrounded by light or variations on these themes are associated with release from darkness. Light figures in many dreams of physical or spiritual renewal. For example, towards the end of a highly involved dream about the threatened annihilation of herself and her children, a woman dreamt:

> I closed my eyes and prayed with all my might that they, my daughters, would feel nothing. A bright, white light came through my eyelids to the left and pushed the darkness away to the right and I died. I cannot describe how it was when I woke up. All I can say is that I felt as if I had come through something and that time was temporarily different from usual — much as I felt when my father died. I just wanted

to sit and savour this sensation and not have to deal with the trivia of the day ahead.

Von Franz related the following:

> A woman woke up one morning in her hospital bed and told the nurse that she had had the following dream: she saw a candle on the window sill that was burning down, and it began to flicker, and she became terribly anxious and felt the great darkness coming. Then there was a moment of blackout, and again she saw a light; this time, however, the candle was outside the window, the wick burning quietly. She didn't comment on it, but four hours later she died. The reality, you see, was that the light went out, but in another medium it burnt on.

The patient died completely at peace.

John Sanford, in *Dreams, God's Forgotten Language*, amplifies the Jungian idea of light phenomena accompanying death. He gives the example of a Protestant clergyman, who had had the following dream just a few days before his death:

> ... he sees the clock on the mantelpiece; the hands have been moving, but now they stop; as they stop a window opens behind the mantelpiece clock and a bright light shines through. The opening widens into a door and the light becomes a brilliant path. He walks out onto the path of light and disappears.

Notice how the 'door' of light is behind the clock, the marker of time, a symbol that time had run its course. Beyond time, beyond the passing of minutes registered by the clock in its prominent position on the mantelpiece, a path waits for him. A clock stops in the material world whilst a path of light appears so he may journey on.

> Death surrenders us completely to God; it makes us pass into God.
>
> (Telihard de Chardin)

Research with people who have had NDEs reveal that they are connected with a sort of psychic rebirth, transformation, and an affirmation of continued existence. Through their survival of clinical death, most people develop a new attitude towards dying and they lose their fear of death. One of the most characteristic features of NDEs is the intense bright light after darkness. In this light, the person feels absolute love and acceptance and often leads to profound spiritual transformation in the survivor. Early alchemists regarded this light as the window of eternity which looked towards infinite life beyond the mortal coil.

PRECOGNITIVE DREAMS

Precognitive dreams are dreams that precede an event which takes place in the everyday, waking world. Somehow, the dream tells what will happen in the future. Dreams as premonitions are not unusual. For thousands of years there have been examples of extra-sensory experience (ESP) in dreams, particularly in relation to personal tragedies. This should come as no surprise really, since dreams have been regarded as vehicles of ESP since records have been kept.

Dream telepathy — the giving or receiving of information in the dream state — works most frequently with a member of one's own family or with someone to whom we feel especially close. When Tania's husband was in hospital she had this dream:

> I dreamt that my husband sat up in the intensive care unit and indicated that he had had enough — he no longer wanted to live. I was wakened from this dream by the phone. It was the hospital to tell me that my husband was dying. Ten minutes later they phoned to tell me he was dead.

Tania may well have inferred from her husband's demeanour that he felt he had come to the end of his struggle; he had never said that he wanted to die. This dream, though, brings the knowledge into consciousness at the point at which he is approaching death.

> The dreams I use in my life are the very vivid ones of powerful experiences which are like certainties: A man takes me by the hands, looks into my eyes and shows me what courage is; I experience myself in another lifetime working with colour; a healer takes me to the woman's garden at night and tells me to eat the fruit of the pineapple; I go through death and survive. To me there is no difference between these experiences and the ones I have when I am awake.

It is probable that some dreams about messages from the 'other side' are reflections of the important position that certain people hold for us. The importance of their views and the strong impression they left is revealed in dreams and the intimacy and guidance continue.

PROPHETIC DREAMS AND FAMILY LINKS

Dreams which appear to be, or turn out to be, prophetic in that they inform us of an event that will happen in the future can be both disturbing and difficult to deal with. Disturbing because the dreamer often feels some anxiety about them and may fear they will be ridiculed by others if they talk about them. Then there are questions: are they really precognitive? will they be proved untrue? if the events don't come to pass, has the dreamer worried needlessly? One way to approach this dilemma, for those who want to find out if they have such dreams or as a counsellor working with a client, is for records to be kept of the dreams. That way we can look back and confirm whether the dreams did foretell or forearm the dreamer. Also, people who do have these dreams find that the quality of the dream is significantly different from their 'ordinary' dreams, so marking them in the dream record could help to pinpoint them for reference later.

Precognitive dreams can be very frightening, particularly if a dream concerns a member of the immediate family, and especially when it comes 'true'. Lorraine has been recording her dreams long enough to recognise those which are of a prospective nature, looking into the future:

> Three in particular were spiritual in context. When my first baby was expected I just felt he wouldn't live and he was stillborn. My mother's death three months before was shown in a dream and when a neighbour died, he came to me in a dream to say goodbye. I knew when I awoke that he was gone. I got this all-over feeling of peace. I felt no sorrow.

Whilst Lorraine's experience was comforting, it was not the same for Anna. This dream left an indelible scar on the dreamer's psyche:

> This was a terrible nightmare. About twelve years ago in late August I awoke absolutely horrified because something ghastly had happened to our two grandchildren. It was so dreadful that I could not even tell my husband and I repressed it, so except for the feeling I do not know what I dreamt. In September the police came and told us that our daughter-in-law had killed the children and had tried to commit suicide. This happened four to six weeks after the dream. She had post-natal depression but we knew nothing about this, six months after the second child was born. I often wonder why such a dream should occur and if I had taken notice of it could I have prevented such a thing. (We now have two other grandchildren, by our other son, who was a twin of the other father.)

Now she sometimes dreams of her dead grandchildren and finds great comfort in meeting them again on the dreaming plane.

For most of us hotels are places of transition where we stay for a short time before coming home again or going on to a new location. In dreams, they often symbolise this impermanence where the normal everyday world is held in abeyance. It is significant that it was in a small hotel that Freda's dream took place:

> I appeared to be in charge and was preparing for guests. A friendly Alsation dog kept me company. Everything was clean but I felt worried because I needed some help to bring up a barrel from the cellar. Suddenly, there was a loud knock on the back door, and when I opened it my mother's youngest brother and his youngest daughter, Amy, were there. My uncle told me sadly that they had come to see me because they were going away. When I asked how long for he said, 'We won't be back,' and they faded out of the picture. I went on with my work and the dog lay watching me. There was another knock on the door and standing on the doorstep were my late mother and father. I welcomed them and asked if they had come to help me. They said very gently, 'No dear, we can't stay, we have a job to do.' At that moment I awoke.

Freda had not seen her uncle or cousin for at least twenty years, yet on waking, felt sure she would have some family news. At 10.30 a.m. her mother's sister rang to say that the uncle in her dream had passed away at 6.00 a.m. and his youngest daughter, Amy, was with him at the time. Although she was surprised and upset at the news, Frieda was soon to be even more shocked. 'At 1.00 p.m.,' she said, 'that same aunt phoned again to tell me that my mother's eldest brother had also died that day. I could scarcely believe my ears. My parents had been dead for four years and my mother had always been close to her brothers and sisters.'

There are many examples which indicate that caring carries on in another realm beyond death and, at times of death or great distress, a helping hand is extended to those who must pass over. But what of this Alsation in Freda's dream? She didn't have a dog and could make no easy connection to it, other than that its protective presence felt comforting. A dog is a symbol of faithfulness and often appears at the feet of women in the engravings on medieval tombs. In Christian symbolism, the dog, deriving from its role as sheep-dog, is seen guarding and guiding the flock, and in certain parts of Europe, Alsations are still the chosen dogs for this function because of their loyalty, strength and reliability. However, in a more profound way, the dog in myths is traditionally the companion of the dead on their 'night sea crossing', which is associated with life after death.

A BEACON OF HOPE

Elly's mother was diagnosed with cancer and within the space of a week she was in hospital undergoing surgery. The morning of the operation, Elly found herself in her dream, on the roof of the terraced house opposite to her mother's home looking down:

> There were two funeral cars, I watched as my sister and I came out crying, dressed in black. We got into the cars and then I woke up. I felt so upset, so weak as though I had cried for a week.

After a few minutes the feeling lifted and a deep sense of peace and acceptance descended. Her mother died eight months later but Elly said: 'I felt all my sorrow was taken in that healing dream. It gave me inner strength knowing the outcome of my mother's illness. The dream was so very vivid, emotional and prophetic.' In a sense it does not matter whether such a dream is 'prophetic' or a rational response to a diagnosis of cancer where the prognosis is poor and death the likely outcome. The important point for Elly, and others who have healing dreams, is that they do give a sense of peace and acceptance, a beacon of hope in the mist of sadness. Where a client presents such a dream, it is important to stay with the authentic tone the dreamer feels and to explore the implications of such experiences.

Elly knows her 'special' dreams because they are in colour, vividly emotional and intense. The feeling stays with her for a very long time afterwards. There is a special impact with these dreams which is unforgettable, as most people who have them testify.

To lose someone we love is a transforming experience. However much we prepare ourselves and rationalise, when death comes it strikes hard. However, for someone like Triona, though the grief is still acute, certainty of a life beyond death, amplified in the following dream, gives enormous comfort and reassurance. She told me that when she was a student her father had been ill on and off with epilepsy, but it gave the family no real cause for concern because he was generally hale and hearty and medication effectively controlled his *petit mals*. Her dream indicated something different:

> In the dream my mother and I were standing on the pavement near the local railway station. My mother said, 'Your father's dead.' I replied, 'He'll be alright, he's with Jesus now.'

A few weeks later Triona had an urgent phone call at the hotel where she was working in her summer vacation from university. 'I was summoned home because my father had taken ill,' she said. 'And as I put the receiver down I immediately recalled the dream.' Her father did die as she knew he would from the dream and the local railway station, the dreamscape setting, was the last place she saw him alive. Now, several years after it happened, Triona still draws comfort from her belief that her father is safe and at peace in heaven.

What are true dreams? Are they only those which come at a particular point in the dream cycle that continues throughout the night, following the rhythms from lighter to deeper REM sleep? Or are they also visions that come as we doze in reverie in moments of pure peace? Moments when we switch off the outer world and switch on the inner world and tune in to another dimension. Whatever the answer — or answers — the essential point is that we harness dreams and value their power to inform and heal life.

Viv, who took part in my research for my book *Women Dreaming*, expressed a view many other women spoke of:

> I think as much research as possible should be done on the question of prophetic dreams, particularly those experienced by women. Prophecy, clairvoyancy and dream interpretation are traditionally associated with women and it seems likely that such power would be heightened during menstruation and pregnancy. I cannot remember if I was menstruating when I had terrifyingly precognitive dreams about the death of my father, but I do know that I stopped bleeding for about four or five months after his death. I remember confiding my experience to a well-meaning Freudian who informed me that I had not, in fact, foreseen the death of my father but, quite simply, had wished him dead. Had my father not died I would have been comforted by the good doctor's view, feeling that the dream was the result of some repressed antagonism on my part and, quite simply, relieved that my father was not going to die in the near future. However, it is another matter when the person you have 'wished dead' actually dies two days after you have the dream.
>
> Freud's attempt to rationalise the hitherto unexplained, succeeded only in bringing about in me some irrational, primitive idea that I may be some sort of witch.

Jung and Maeder developed the 'Finalist dream doctrine of the Zurich School' and after much research concluded: 'The prospective function is an unconscious anticipation of future achievements, like a preliminary exercise or a preliminary sketching of a preconceived plan.' This approach was taken up by Jung after Maeder 'discovered' it because he became convinced that 'every living being strives for wholeness, or at least for the creation of a spiritual equilibrium.'

> For a seventy-five-year-old man it does not come amiss to reflect now and then upon death. The thought of death does not in the least disturb me, because I am firmly convinced that our spirit is altogether indestructible and thus continues from eternity to eternity. It is like the sun, which to our eyes seems to disappear beyond the horizon, while in actual fact it goes on shining continuously.
>
> (Goethe, letter to Eckermann, 2 May 1824)

J.W. Dunne in his book *An Experiment in Time* developed the theory that time does not pass in a linear way, going from past, through present to future. Rather, his experiments led him to believe that time is held in a kind of fourth dimension where past and future are held in the same place as the present moment. This is why, he argued, people could have memories of experiences their living body could have not have been privy to, and why others could foresee future events as yet unknown in our waking reality. It is a reality beyond our empirical reasoning.

Gerald shared his experience of such a dream, which he had during the closing months of World War II:

My brother, who was in the Royal Engineers, had been taken prisoner in Crete and shipped to Stalag 18A, at Klagenfurt, Austria. Because my parents were still in India, I was registered with the Red Cross as his official next of kin in the UK. We corresponded at frequent intervals and I sent him the permitted quota of parcels but during the second half of 1944 his letters no longer arrived, and I assumed this was due to disorganisation behind enemy lines. Towards the end of 1944 my mother came over from India and was staying at my lodgings in Southampton. Then one night during the winter, I had my dream.

I dreamed that my brother was sitting on the floor of the dining room, in his Army uniform, with his legs stretched out in front of him. His left trouser leg was pulled up to above the knee, to expose a flesh wound about the size of a sixpence at the top of the shin bone and about three inches below the kneecap. The wound looked like raw meat and there was no bleeding. Within a minute or so, an ambulance arrived at the front gate, two men in white coats got out with a stretcher, entered the house, picked him up in the sitting position, placed him on the stretcher and took him away. I woke up immediately after that. At breakfast, I told my mother of my dream, and then cycled off to work. When I returned for lunch, my mother was in tears, and handed me an Air letter which had arrived that morning. It was from my father, who was still in India.

My father had addressed the letter to me, and said that a friend of his had heard over the German radio that my brother had lost a leg. The announcer gave my brother's full name, his Army number and my father's name and full address in India. These details were recorded by my father's friend, and were accurate. So my father believed the report to be correct, and asked why I had not kept him informed. My mother said to me, 'that was your dream.'

I telephoned the Red Cross for information but they had none. The next day I went to the Royal Engineers Records Office in Brighton. Because the clerk could not help, I asked to speak to the Commanding Officer but was told that the CO would not see me unless I had an appointment. After about four hours the CO agreed to see me, and I was ushered in. I showed him my father's letter, but did not tell him about my dream. He said sternly that my father should not be listening to the enemy radio, and that he had no information about my brother. However, he undertook to have a thorough search made, and promised to send me a telegram to report the results. The very next day, I received a telegram which stated simply: 'Left leg amputated. Regret no further details.'

A month or so after VE Day my brother was repatriated

from Italy on a hospital ship, and my mother and I went to see him at Wolverhampton hospital. When I asked him how it had happened, he described how the USAF Super Fortresses would fly over at 30,000 feet, in attempts to bomb the marshalling yards about a mile from the camp. My brother remembered hitting the earth only a few yards from the entrance to an underground shelter. He was aware of a lot of pine cones falling on him, and thought that one had hit his leg. When he came to, he was in the shelter, having been rescued by his comrades. Then he said to me, 'A piece of shrapnel must have hit me. All I had was a small flesh wound just below the knee,' (indicating the precise spot which I had seen in my dream). 'I remember it hardly bled at all. But it turned gangrenous and the German doctor said he had no means of treating gangrene. So he took my leg off.'

There are so many examples of this type of dream communication that I could write a book dealing only with them. However, in terms of the therapeutic process, as counsellors and therapists we need to be open to the hidden potential of the mind and ensure our clients trust us enough to share them. Also, to recognise, as it was for Gerald, that such dreams can utterly change a person's sense of the world, his understanding of how it operates and can transform his perception of life and death.

Many of the patients with whom Dr Bernie Siegel has worked have spoken about precognitive dreams once they realised it was permissible to talk about such things. He recalled a patient who dreamt of seeing a picture of her son under water; the next day he drowned. Another patient who had breast cancer dreamt that her head was shaved and on it was the word 'cancer'. She awoke certain of the fact that she had metastases in her brain even though she had no symptoms, three weeks later the diagnosis was confirmed. There was a college student who dreamt of two stones being dropped from a bridge and rising up out of the water as spirits. He wrote a poem about it. Shortly after, while he was on vacation, he sent home a postcard of Californian surf, the next day he and a friend drowned at the exact spot on the postcard. The poem he wrote was read out at his funeral service.

DREAMS FOLLOWING BEREAVEMENT

> The world is not only that which we can see. It is enormous and also has room for people when they die and no more walk about down here on earth.
>
> Mankind does not end its existence because sickness or some other accident kills its animal spirit down here on earth. We live on, and there are those who say that it is what we call the soul that prevents us from dying.
>
> This is not simply what the shamans tell us, those who understand the hidden things; ordinary people who know how to dream have many times seen that the dead appeared to them, just as they were in life. Therefore we believe that life does not end here on earth. (Nalungiaq, Netsilik Eskimo quoted in Ramussen)

The sorrow of loss is a deep hurt that changes us. Whenever someone to whom we have been bonded, whether through blood or love, leaves us, we have to adjust. No matter how easy or difficult the relationship, the opportunity to make good the wrongs or tell the person how much they meant to us is gone. At least it is gone on the corporal, the bodily, level. The death of another person also makes us more aware of our own limitations, especially our own mortality, and the quest for the meaning of life often intensifies.

Dreams following bereavement can be a source of solace or torment. In dreams, we may still meet and communicate and this can be a truly healing experience. However, some people who have been bereaved long to meet the person who has died, they yearn to dream of him or her. Others fear sleep in case they dream that the deceased is on the point of death once again, repeating the actual events leading up to their death. Some people cherish the dream encounters yet dread the prospect of facing the great ache of longing that arises once they wake up to the stark reality that it was 'only a dream'. As Kyle said: 'My dreams of my wife are sometimes healing but its painful when they raise again feelings of being utterly bereft because she has gone and cannot be touched or kissed, and her warmth that I long for has gone forever.'

The process of grieving may be mapped in dreams:

> After my father died I had a series of dreams about him. First I dreamed he really wasn't dead. Then that he wouldn't accept that he was dead. Finally I dreamed that he was getting better in 'the other world'. Then a lovely dream where I met him. He was wearing a light blue shirt and looked years younger than when he was dying of cancer. He put his arms around me, told me he was fine now, that he loved me and told me not to worry about him anymore. I felt good when I woke and have felt good about him ever since.

Following this dream, there was a real sense of healing and letting go. The dreams reflect the process of disbelief leading to final acceptance that Faith's father is dead, and renewal, in that she is released to enjoy her life and to live it without focusing on her loss.

Clients who are stuck in their grief, may become aware of this through their dreams. Sadie, had a recurring dream that her mother, who had died, was at home with the rest of the family. She dreamt that she would say to her: 'They thought you would die, didn't they, Mum, but you didn't. You fooled them all.' 'In my dream,' she said, 'I really believed that she had just been very ill and that somehow she had pulled through after her operation,' which is, of course, what Sadie wished had happened. After working through her grief, she had a dream about her family once more and this time her mother was not present and she was delighted. 'I really felt, emotionally, that I've passed a milestone,' she said, 'and I've finally come to terms with her death.'

Over the door to his home in Switzerland Carl Gustav Jung carved the words:

> Called or not, the god will be there.

Death is not only the spiritual renewal of life in terms of resurrection or reincarnation, but also materially in the regeneration of matter. The stuff of compost heaps is the food for new healthy plant life. The darkness of death finds rebirth in light, night becomes day, form may be destroyed, but not essence. Death is the ultimate liberation because it brings this possibility of transformation.

As we age, it is normal to be concerned about failing strength or diminished capabilities. However, life can still have direction and meaning. It is at this stage that our most important opportunity presents itself, a time for self-reflection and completion. Dreams at this time often reflect these issues. Where feelings of purposelessness prevail there may be dreams of being lost or being unable to see through fog or mist. These can be helpful in persuading the dreamer to take some direction rather than to continue wandering around lost without companions. Indeed it may be the central theme of therapeutic work at this stage. Once again we find dreams reflecting waking attitudes and preoccupations.

Helen Keller, who was blind and deaf, found her dream life a source of pleasure, despite enormous handicap:

> I like to think that in dreams we catch glimpses of a life larger than our own. Thoughts are imparted to us far above our ordinary thinking. Feelings nobler and wiser than any we have known thrill us between heartbeats. For one fleeting night a princelier nature captures us and we become as great as our aspirations.

Marie Louise von Franz recounts the dream of a man who was diagnosed as having terminal cancer, a diagnosis he could not accept. That night he had a dream:

239

He saw a green, half-high, not yet ripe wheatfield. A herd of cattle had broken into the field and trampled down and destroyed everything in it. Then a voice from above called out, 'Everything seems to be destroyed but from the roots under the earth the wheat will grow again.'

He understood that what might be outwardly destroyed, left behind the seed for the future. His death on earth was one part of a continual cycle of death and rebirth. In many dreams, there are variations on this theme of a world beyond the one in which we live. In dreams and in accounts of near death experiences, people are told that it is not yet their time to go on to this other place, that they have other matters to complete on earth.

> Dreaming itself is the workshop of evolution.
>
> (Sandor Ferenczi)

Like a rainbow, a tree connects sky and ground, heaven and earth and is an image of continuing life. A dying seventy-five-year-old man, fearful of the irrevocable end his death signalled, dreamt:

I see an old, gnarled tree high up on a steep bluff. It is only half rooted in the earth, the remainder of the roots reaching into empty air. Then it becomes separated from the earth altogether, loses its support and falls. My heart misses a beat. But then something wonderful happens, the tree floats, it does not fall, it floats. Where to? Into the sea? I do not know.

The sense of awe and glory in the image of the floating tree is so reassuring, so uplifting that it is hardly surprising that dying did not seem so terrible after all. The dreamer is symbolically detaching himself from all that 'roots' him so that he can continue his journey, his 'awfully big adventure'. Though there is no certainty about what will happen next, his dream brings renewing energy to sustain him. Pinkola Estes describes the renewal that can come from the darkest of our experiences: 'At bottom is where the living roots of the psyche are. At bottom is the best soil to sow and grow something new again. In that sense, hitting bottom, while extremely painful, is also the sowing ground.'

In the summary of *On Dreams and Death* von Franz says: 'All the dreams of people who are facing death indicate that the unconscious, that is, our instinct world, prepares consciousness not for a definite end but for a profound transformation and for a kind of continuation of the life process which, however, is unimaginable to everyday consciousness.' A re-connection can come from the darkest experiences of our lives. In the deepest sadness, the depths where we feel so desperately alone and vulnerable, we may find the very meaning of life.

Before she died, fourteen-year-old Tracey Wollington kept a journal and in it she wrote:

> I have accepted death, after all everyone dies. I am no different in that respect. In a sense we are all born to die, the only difference is I realise this and want to do something with my space between. I am ready, it is those who are not that I feel sympathy for. Everyone thinks they will be here tomorrow. Each day is precious and I know death will come. Perhaps this is something we all should realise, death exists for everyone.

The borders, where life and death meet, are hazardous places and it takes courage to stop and merely 'be' there. Not to rush through, not to escape, but to stand, simply, in the borderland. As Bani Shorter says: 'Not all who attempt to do so will cross and for some they may arrive by turning back.' Whatever the cause of the journey to this place, it is in that very space that we can focus on our hearts and souls without the distractions of all that takes us away from this most profound of experiences. There we can heal into life or heal into death, and both are equally numinous.

REFERENCES

Adler, A., *The Individual Psychology of Alfred Adler*, eds, Heinz L. Ansbacher and Rowena R. Ansbacher, New York: Harper Torchbooks 1956.

Acheterberg, Jeanne, *Imagery in Healing*, Boston: Shambhala New Science Library 1985.

Angelo, J., *Your Healing Power*, London: Piatkus 1994.

Aristotle, 'On Dreams', tr. R. McKeon in *The Collected Works of Aristotle*, New York: Random House 1941.

Artaud, A., *Selected Writings*, Berkeley & Los Angeles: University of California Press 1988.

Aserinsky, E. and N. Kleitman, 'Regularly Occurring Periods of Eye Motility and Concomitant Phenomena during Sleep', *Science*, 118.

Bach, S., *Life Paints Its Own Span*, New York: Daimon Books 1991.

Bakan, P., 'The Right Brain is the Dreamer' in *Psychology Today*, 10/6 (1976), 66–8.

Beck, H.W., 'Dream Analysis in Family Therapy', *Clinical Social Work Journal* 5 (1977).

Beevor, A., *Stalingrad*, London: Penguin 1999.

Bertoia, J., *Drawings from a Dying Child*, London: Routledge 1993.

Boss, M., *The Analysis of Dreams*, New York: Philosophical Library 1958.

Bossard, R., *Psychologie des Traumbewusstseins*, Zurich: 1951.

Breger, L., Hunter, I. and R. Lane, *The Effect of Stress on Dreams*, New York: International Universities Press 1969.

Bulkeley, K., *The Wilderness of Dreams*, New York: State University of New York Press 1994.

Campbell, J., *Primitive Mythology: The Masks of God*, New York: Penguin 1959.

References

— *The Hero With a Thousand Faces*, London: Fontana Press 1993.

— *Myths to Live By*, New York: Bantam 1988.

— *The Power of the Myth*, New York: Doubleday, 1988.

Capra, F., *The Tao of Physics*, New York: Bantam 1977.

Cartwright, R.D., 'Night Pilot', interview in *Psychology Today*, July/August 1988.

Cartwright, R.D., Lloyd, S., Knight, S. and I. Trenholme, 'Broken Dreams: A Study of the Effects of Divorce and Depression on Dream Content', *Psychiatry*, 47 (1984), 251–9.

de Chardin, T., *Divine Milieu*, London: HarperCollins 1966.

Chopra, D., MD, *Creating Health: How to Wake Up the Body's Intelligence*, London: Thorsons 1990.

Cirincione, D., 'The Functional Approach to Using Dreams in Marital and Family Therapy', *Journal of Marital and Family Therapy*, 6 (1980).

Claridge Dr G., *Echoes From The Bell Jar*, London: Macmillan 1990.

Clark, R.W., *Freud, The Man and The Cause*, New York: Random House 1980.

Coalson, B., 'Post Traumatic Stress Disorder', *Journal of Psychotherapy*, Utica, New York, 32/3 (1995).

Coghill, A., 'On Depression' *Self and Society*, XVI/6 (1988).

Cousins, N., *The Healing Heart*, New York: Avon 1984.

Crace, J., *Quarantine*, London: Penguin 1998.

de Becker, R., *The Understanding of Dreams*, London: Allen & Unwin 1951.

Delayney, G., *Living Your Dreams*, New York: Harper & Rowe 1979.

Dement, W., 'Dream Recall and Eye Movements During Sleep in Schizophrenics and Normals', *Journal of Nervous and Mental Disease*, 122 (1955).

Deutsch, H., 'Some Psycholanalytic Observations in Surgery', *Psychosomatic Medicine*, 4 (1942), 105–15.

Duff, K., *The Alchemy of Illness*, London: Virago 1995.

Dunne J.W., *An Experiment in Time*, London: Faber & Faber 1934.

Evans, G., reported in 'The Truth Dawns', *Guardian*, 13 May 1997.

Faber, P.A., Saayman, G.S. and R.K. Papadopoulos, 'Induced Waking Fantasy: Its effects upon the archetypal content of nocturnal dreams', *Journal of Analytical Psychology*, 28 (1983).

Faraday, A., *The Dream Game*, New York: Harper & Rowe 1974.

Fenwick, E. and P. Fenwick, *The Hidden Door*, London: Headline 1997.

Ferenczi, S., *Further Contributions to the Theory and Technique of Psychoanalysis*, London: Hogarth Press 1934.

Flannery, R.B., *Post-Traumatic Stress Disorder: The Victim's Guide to Healing and Recovery*, New York: Crossroad 1992.

Flowers, Dr L.K., 'The Use of Pre-sleep Instructions and Dreams in Psychosomatic Disorders', *Psychotherapy and Psychosomatics* (1995) 64.

Freud, S., *On Metapsychology*, vol. iv, Harmondsworth: Penguin 1984.

—— *Civilisation, Society & Religion*, vol. xxi, Harmondsworth: Penguin 1991.

Fromm, Erich, *The Forgotten Language*, New York: Grove Press 1951.

Gardner, J., and J. Maier (trs) 'The Epic of Gilgamesh', New York: Vintage Books 1984.

Garfield, P., *The Healing Power of Dreams*, New York: Simon & Schuster 1992.

—— *Creative Dreaming*, London: Futura 1976.

Gersham, H., 'Current Application of Horney Theory to Dream Interpretation', *American Journal of Psychoanalysis* 43/3 (1983), 219–29.

References

Glaister, L., *Sheer Blue Bliss*, London: Bloomsbury 1999.

Glennon, J., *Your Healing is Within You*, London: Hodder & Stoughton 1996.

Green, C.E., *Lucid Dreams*, Oxford: Institute of Psychophysical Research 1968.

Greenleaf, E., 'Senoi Dream Groups', *Psychotherapy: Theory, Research and Practice* 10 (1973) 218–22.

Guest, H., 'The Origins of Transpersonal Psychotherapy', *British Journal of Psychotherapy*, 6/1 (1989).

Hall, C.S., *The Meaning of Dreams*, revised edition, New York: McGraw-Hill 1966.

Hall, J.A., *Patterns of Dreaming: Jungian Technique in Theory and Practice*, Boston, London: Shambhala 1991

Hall, N., *The Moon and the Virgin*, London: The Women's Press 1980.

Halliday, G., 'Direct Psychological Therapies for Nightmares: A Review', *Clinical Psychology Review*, 7 (1987), 501–23.

Hannah, B., *Jung: His Life and Work*, London: Chiron Publications 1998.

Hart, J., 'Dreams in the Classroom', *Experiment and Innovation: New Directions in Education at the University of California*, 4 (1971) 51–66.

Hartmann, E., MD, *Dreams and Nightmares: A New Theory on the Origin and Meaning of Dreams*, New York: Plenum 1998.

— Symposium: 'A Contemporary Theory on the Nature and Functions of Dreaming'; response by Kelly Bulkeley, 'The Interplay of Connecting and Disconnecting', *Dreaming, Summer* 1999.

Harvant, G., 'The Life Context of the Dreamer and the Setting of Dreaming', *International Journal Of Psychoanalysis*, 63/4 (1982) 475–82.

Hauri, Dr P.J., *Case Studies in Insomia*, New York: Plenum Publishing 1976.

Heather-Greener, G., Cornstock, D. and J. Roby, 'An Investigation of the Manifest Dream Content Associated with Migraine Headaches: A study of dreams that precede nocturnal migraines', *Psychotherapy and Psychosomatics*, 65 (1996) 216–21.

Hillman, J., *The Dream and the Underworld*, New York: Harper & Rowe 1979.

Hobson, J.A., *The Dreaming Brain*, New York: Basic Books 1988.

Hodgkinson, L., *Spiritual Healing*, London: Piatkus 1990.

Hodgkinson, P.E. and M. Stewart, *Coping with Catastrophe: A Handbook of Disaster Management*, London: Routledge 1991.

Horowitz, P., reported in R.B. Flannery, *Post-Traumatic Stress Disorder*, New York: Crossroad 1992.

Horney, K., *Self-Analysis*, London: Kegan Paul, Trench, Trubner & Co. Ltd 1942.

James, W., *The Varieties of Religious Experience*, New York: Mentor Books 1900.

Jamison, K.R., *Touched with Fire*, New York: Free Press Paperbacks, Simon & Shuster, 1993.

Janov, A., *The Primal Scream*, London: Abacus 1973.

Jayne, W.A., MD, *The Healing Gods of Ancient Civilisations*, Yale: Yale University Press 1925.

Jenks, K., *Journey of a Dream Animal: A Human Search for Personal Identity*, New York: The Julian Press Inc. 1975.

Jung, C.G., *The Concept of Collective Unconscious, Collected Works 9*, Princeton USA: Bollingen series 1936.

— (ed.), *Man and His Symbols*, New York: Doubleday 1964.

— *Dreams*, Princeton: Bollingern series.

— *Dreams, Memories and Reflections*, New York: Vintage 1990.

Kabat-Zin, J., *Full Catastrophe Living*, London: Piatkus 1990.

Kaplan-Williams, S., *The Jungian–Senoi Dreamwork Manual*, Wellington, Northamptonshire: The Aquarian Press 1984.

References

Keller, H., *The World I Live In*, London: Hodder Stoughton, 1908

Kellerman, J., 'Behaviour Treatment of Night Terrors in a Child with Acute Leukemia', *Journal of Nervous and Mental Disease.* 167/3 (1979).

Koestler, A. and J.R. Smythies (eds), *Beyond Reductionism*, London: Macmillan 1970.

Kovel, J., *A Complete Guide to Therapy*, London: Penguin 1978.

Krakow, B. and J. Neidtardt, *Conquering Bad Dreams and Nightmares: A Guide to Understanding, Interpretations, and Cure*, New York: Berkley 1992.

Kubler-Ross, E., *On Death and Dying*, London: Tavistock Publications 1970.

La Berge, S.P., 'Lucid Dreaming as a Learnable Skill: A Case Study', *Perceptual and Motor Skills* 51 (1981) 1039–42.

Lao-Tzu, Tao *Te Ching*, Twelve, translated by Gia-Fu Feng and Jane English, New York: Random House 1972.

Lerner, A., 'Guided Affective Imagery: A Method of Intensive Psychotherapy', *American Journal of Psychotherapy*, 23 (1969).

Lerner, B., 'Dream Function Reconsidered', *Journal of Abnormal Psychology*, 72 (1967).

Levine, S., *Who Dies?*, Bath: Gateway 1988.

Levitan, H., MD, 'Dreams Which Culminate in Migraine Headaches', *Psychotherapy and Psychosomatics* 41 (1984) 161–6.

Lewis, J.R., *The Dream Encyclopedia*, Detroit: Visible Ink 1995.

Lincoln, J.S., *The Dream in Primitive Cultures*, London: University of London 1935.

Lloyd, G.E. (ed.), *The Medical Works of Hippocrates in Hippocratic Writings*, Oxford: Blackwell 1950.

Luthe, W. and J.S. Schultz, *Autogenic Therapy Volume VI: Treatment with Autogenic Neutralisation*. New York: Grune & Stratton 1973.

Maeder, A., *The Dream Problem*, New York: New York Publishing Co. 1916.

Mair, M., 'Psychology of Story-Telling Psychology', *International Journal of Personal Construct Psychology*, 2 (1988) 1–14.

Malone, C., Farthing, L. and L. Marce, *The Memory Bird*, London: Virago 1996.

Mallon, B., *Women Dreaming*, London: Fontana Paperbacks 1987.

— *Children Dreaming: The Meaning and Significance of Children's Dreams*, London: Penguin Books 1989.

— *Helping Children to Manage Loss: Positive Strategies for Renewal and Growth*. London & Philadelphia: Jessica Kingsley 1998.

— *Creative Visualization with Colour: Healing Your Life with the Power of Colour*, Boston: Element Books Inc.; Shaftesbury: Element Books Ltd 1999.

Manley, F., *The Effect of Intentional Dreaming on Depression*, The Fielding Institute, USA, 1982.

Martin, P., *The Sickening Mind*, London: HarperCollins 1977.

Maslow, A., *Religious Values and Peak Experiences*, London: Penguin 1994.

Mattoon, M.A., *Applied Dream Analysis: A Jungian Approach*, Washington DC: V.H. Winston & Sons 1978.

McCrum, R., *My Year Off*, London: Picador 1998.

McKenzie, E., *Healing Reiki*, London: Hamlyn 1996.

McNaughton, B., reported in 'You Must Remember ZZZ', *New Scientist*, 30 November 1996, 19.

McNiff, S., *Art as Medicine: Creating a Therapy of the Imagination*, London: Piatkus 1992

Meier, C.A., *Ancient Incubation and Modern Psychotherapy*, tr. M. Curtis, Evanston, Illinois: North Western University Press 1967.

Messner, R., *All 14 Eight-Thousanders*, Marlborough: The Crowood Press 1999.

Meyerhoff, H., 'Art as Therapy in a Group Setting: The Stories of Batja and Rina', *American Journal of Art Therapy*, 16, 1977.

Mindell, Arnold, *Dreambody*, London: Routledge & Kegan Paul 1984.

References

Moody, R., *Life After Life*, New York: Bantam 1976.

Moore T., *The Re-Enchantment of Everyday Life*, London: Hodder & Stoughton 1997.

Myss, C., *Anatomy of Spirit*, New York: Bantam Books 1997.

— *Why People Don't Heal and How they Can*, New York: Bantam Books 1998.

Natterson, J.M. (ed.), *The Dream in Clinical Practice*, New York: Jason Avonson Inc. 1993.

Nuland, S.B., *How We Die*. London: Chatto & Windus 1994.

O'Connor, P., 'The Daily Why', *Observer*, 30 April 1989.

O'Keefe, M., 'Aspects of the Listening Process', *Journal of the British Association of Counselling*, Summer 1986.

Orbach, A., *Life, Psychotherapy and Death*, London & Philadephia: Jessica Kingsley 1999.

Palambo, S.R., *Dreaming and Memory*, New York: Basic Books 1978.

Park, W., *Shamanism in Western North America*, Chicago: Evanston 1938.

Patrice, Some, Malidoma, *Of Spirit and Water*, London: Arkana 1995.

Penfield, W., *The Mystery of the Mind: A Critical Study of Consciousness and the Human Brain*, Princeton NJ: Princeton University Press 1975.

Pert C., *Molecules of Emotion*, London: Simon & Schuster UK 1997.

Picardie, R., *Before I Say Goodbye*, London: Penguin 1998.

Pietroni, Dr P.C., 'The Penny Edwards Memorial Lecture in Counselling', November 1992, 239–41.

Pinkola Estes, C., *Women Who Run with the Wolves*, London: Ballantine Rider Press 1992.

Rachman, S.J., and G.T. Wilson, *The Effects of Psychological Therapy*, New York: Pergamon Press 1980.

Rasmussen, K., *The Netsilik Eskimos: Social Life and Spiritual Culture* 1921–1924,. *Report of the Fifth Thule Expedition*, (Copenhagen) 8 (1931) 315.

Redfield, J., *The Celestine Vision: Living the New Spiritual Awareness*, London: Bantam Press 1990.

Richman, J., 'Coming Out of ITU Crazy: Dreams of Affliction' (personal communication) 1999.

Ross, J.S., *Siegfried Sassoon*, London: Richard Cohen Books 1999.

Ross, S., 'Psychological Trauma: An historical perspective' *Counselling*, May 1999 139–42.

Rossi, E.L., *Dreams and the Growth of Personality*, New York: Permagamon Press Inc. 1972.

Rubenstein, H. (ed.), *The Complete Drugs* (especially Scarf, M., 'The Sleep Clinic'), London: Jonathan Cape 1974.

Sachs, O., *Awakenings*, London: Picador 1982.

Sanford, J., *Dreams, God's Forgotten Language*, San Francisco: HarperCollins 1989.

Schatzman, M., 'Solve Your Problems In Your Sleep', *New Society*, 9 June 1983.

Seigel, A., 'Dreams of Firestorm Survivors' in *Trauma and Dreams*, Barrett, D. (ed.), Cambridge: Harvard University Press 1996.

Sexton, L.G., and L. Ames, *Anne Sexton*, New York: Houghton Mifflin Co. 1992.

Shealy, N. and C. Myss, *The Creation of Health: The Emotional Psychological and Spiritual Responses that Promote Health and Healing*, London: Bantam Books 1999.

Shorter, B., *Border People*, London: Colmore Press Ltd, Guild of Pastoral Psychology, 1982.

Siegel, Dr B., *Love, Medicine and Miracles*, London: Arrow Books 1988.

Singer, J.L., *Imagery and Daydream Methods in Psychotherapy and Behaviour Modification*, New York: Academic Press 1974.

References

Sontag, S., quoted in Antonin Artaud: *Selected Writings*, Berkeley & Los Angeles: University of California Press 1988.

Stekel, W., MD, *The Interpretation of Dreams*, New York: Liveright Pub. Co. Lowell 'Unwanted', lines 116–17, Day by Day, (1943) 24.

Stevens, A., *Private Myths: Dreams and Dreaming*, London: Penguin, 1982.

Stolorow, R.D. and G.E. Atwood, *Psychoanalytic Phenomenology of the Dream*, New York: Analytic Press.

Storr, Dr A., *The Dynamics of Creation*, London: Secker & Warburg 1972.

Sylvia, Claire with Novak, William, *A Change of Heart*, London: Piatkus, 1994.

Tart C., *Altered States of Consciousness*, New York: John Wiley & Son 1969.

Taylor, Rev. J., *Where People Fly and Water Runs Uphill*, New York: Warner Books 1993.

—*The Living Labyrinth*, New York: Paulist Press 1998.

Tihansky, T., 'Case Report: Mixed Arthritis', *Journal of Medical Hypnoanalysis*, 3/3 (1982) 118–20.

Ullman, M., MD, 'Learning the Forgotten Language. Deprofessionalising the Dream', *Contemporary Psychoanalysis*, 18/1 (1982).

van der Post, Laurens, *Jung and the Story of Our Time*, London: The Hogarth Press 1976.

von Franz, M.L., *Shadow and Evil in Fairy Stories*, Zurich: Spring Publications 1987.

— *On Dreams and Death*, London: Shambhala 1986.

Wallin, D.J., 'Intentional Dreaming: An active approach to the imagery of sleep', Diss. Abs. Int. 38/6B (1977) 2893.

Wilde McCormick, E., *Living on the Edge: Breaking Through Instead of Breaking Down*, Shaftesbury: Element 1997.

Winget, C. and F. Kapp, 'The Relationship of the Manifest Contents of Dreams to the Duration of Childbirth in Prima Gravidae', *Psychosomatic Medicine*, 34/2 (July 1972).

Witkin, H. A., and H. B. Lewis, 'The Relation of Experimentally Induced Pre-sleep Experiences to Dreams', *Journal of the American Psychoanalytic Association*, October 1965.

Wolman, B.B. (ed.), *Handbook of Dreams; Research Theories and Applications*, New York: Van Nostrand Reinhold 1979.

Wolpert, Prof. L., *A Malignant Sadness*, London: Faber & Faber 1999.

— 'Sea of Troubles' *Sunday Telegraph*, 31 January 1999.